Enemy in Sight!

BY STANLEY ROGERS

NEW YORK

Thomas Y. Crowell Company

1943

Preface

The Royal Navy and the British Mercantile Marine have never in their long history failed to live up to the very highest traditions of gallantry and self-sacrifice. During those dark days of Rotterdam, Dunkirk, Narvik, and Crete they did their duty at the cost of heavy losses in men and ships. In spite of the disastrous twenty-year disarmament policy, the Royal Navy at the beginning of the war was a far more formidable sea force than that of the Axis Powers, but as the conflict swept over the world the Navy's task became an almost overwhelming burden on the thinly spread-out fleets. Ships were desperately needed to guard the convoys, to protect the British Isles, to patrol the Mediterranean and the Indian Ocean, and finally to defend Britain's Far Eastern possessions, which fell only because even the Navy could not be everywhere at once. Despite this tragic handicap, the Navy accomplished miracles in attack and defense, and in keeping open the sea lanes so vital to Britain's survival.

Much has been said, and deservedly so, of the gallantry of the Royal Air Force in saving Britain in the autumn of 1940, but perhaps not enough has been said about the debt the country owes the Royal Navy and the Merchant Marine. It is a personal sense of obligation to the men who man the ships that prompted the making of this present record of their heroism and self-sacrifice. We use the word 'heroes' with some apprehension, for it is the last thing these men of the sea would like to be called. Such praise from landsmen is perhaps better left unspoken, for sailors do not need a landsman's patronage. Hence these stories are set down with as little embroidery as possible. They need no assistance from the professional teller of tales.

STANLEY ROGERS

Contents

PART ONE

PART TWO

Three Years of War

THE TASK of the Royal Navy in the Second World War has been incomparably more difficult and more hazardous than it was in the First World War. In that war the navies of Italy and Japan were ranged with the British against the Germans. In the Second World War Italy set upon her old friend Britain after the latter had lost the incalculably valuable support of the French fleet on the collapse of France in June 1940. Then in December 1941, Japan joined the enemy and, within a few days after the opening of this new field of conflict, Japanese torpedo-carrying planes sank the 35,000-ton battleship *Prince of Wales* and the 32,000-ton battle cruiser *Repulse*. A month before, a U-boat had torpedoed and sunk the 31,000-ton battleship *Barham*. Britain lost, in the first twenty-nine months of the war, five capital ships and four aircraft-carriers, a grave blow to a nation which had been fighting alone against crushing odds since the fall of France eighteen months previously.

Nor is this tale of misfortune and disaster the worst of it. In the First World War Britain had the use of naval bases in Ireland, an immense advantage for the protection of Atlantic convoys and British defenses. But in 1938, when it was obvious that sooner or later Britain would have to fight another great war, a shortsighted government relinquished those precious bases in order to propitiate the

Irish people, and by doing so made the task of the Navy immeasurably more difficult and dangerous. The refusal of the President of the Irish Republic to permit the Navy to make use of these bases for the duration of the war cost the lives of thousands of merchant seamen and hundreds of thousands of tons of shipping. Britain's navy, hard pressed to protect the Atlantic life line which must be kept open, desperately needed the temporary use of those bases, Lough Swilly, Cobh and Berehaven. After the Irish President's flat refusal to hand them over, Winston Churchill was moved to remark: "The fact that we cannot use the south and west coast of Ireland, to refuel our flotillas and aircraft, and thus protect the trade by which Ireland, as well as Great Britain, lives, that fact is a most heavy and grievous burden which should never have been placed upon our shoulders."

After the tragic collapse of France, Germany obtained control of the entire northern coast of Europe—from the North Cape to Bordeaux on the Bay of Biscay. In 1914–18 Germany controlled only its own coast line and that of Belgium from Antwerp to Ostend. In the Second World War the enemy came into possession of hundreds of airfields along the northern European seaboard from which to strike at British shipping. He also had the use of French submarine bases from which he could send his U-boats into the convoy lanes at the western approaches to the British Isles. Focke-Wulf Condor long-range bombers, and U-boats hunting in so-called 'wolf-packs,' made life hell for British and allied seamen and took a colossal toll of merchant ships bringing planes, guns, munitions and food from America. The German government promised its people that it would starve out the English by preventing the convoys from getting through, and for a time it looked as though the enemy might succeed. However, as the convoy system was perfected and new devices were found to detect and destroy U-boats, the rate of sinkings declined, though they never ceased altogether. U-boats, dive bombers, armed raiders continued to harass and take toll of convoys.

Actually the men of the Royal Navy were only a part of the personnel engaged in the protection of convoys. In the Battle of the Atlantic only about one-fifth of the officers and ratings employed were from the Royal Navy. The other four-fifths were made up of men from the Naval Reserve (R.N.R.) and the Volunteer Reserve (R.N.V.R.). But all were welded in the crucible of war into tough and efficient fighting men, and in their record for valor there was nothing to choose between them. R.N.V.R. men, civilians from all trades and professions, proved themselves to be every bit as good in action as the regular naval personnel.

Let us glance at some of the more outstanding events of the war at sea, events which we can examine later in detail. The first naval casualty of the war was the destroyer *Blanche* and the first merchant ship casualty was the *Athenia* which was torpedoed off the coast of Ireland less than nine hours after war was declared. The first major naval loss was the aircraft carrier *Courageous* torpedoed in the English Channel when the war was only twelve days old. Then, less than a month later, the Navy received another grievous blow when the battleship *Royal Oak* was sunk by a U-boat at Scapa Flow.

The Royal Navy's first success did not come till December when the destruction of the pocket battleship *Graf Spee* in a small way redressed the balance, since Germany, with a navy a fraction the size of Britain's, could ill afford to lose a single warship. The fight between the three British cruisers *Ajax, Exeter* and *Achilles* against a superior adversary was the first important naval action of the war.

The next important sea action was, of course, the battle of the fiords when the German navy came out and met units of the Royal Navy off the Norwegian coast. During these operations the Navy lost two cruisers, six destroyers and the aircraft carrier *Glorious*. It was here that the destroyer crews distinguished themselves for selfless heroism in deeds unsurpassed in the annals of the sea.

The tragic loss of the destroyer *Glowworm* marked the beginning of the Norwegian operations. When it became obvious that Germany was using Norwegian territorial waters for warlike purposes the British Government broadcast to the world that three vast minefields would be laid in Norwegian waters, the areas being clearly stated so that neutral shipping could avoid unnecessary loss. Guarding the huge fleet of minelayers were many units of the Royal Navy from battleships to destroyers. Among the latter was the destroyer *Glowworm*, bucking and rolling in the heavy seas as she kept station on the flank of the minelaying fleet. It was while the wind was blowing its hardest that other ships read a signal from *Glowworm* informing them that she was leaving her station to pick up a seaman who had been swept overboard. Watchers from other ships saw the little destroyer turn in a wide circle to search for the man until she was lost sight of astern in the mist and rain. The minesweepers and escorts went on, leaving *Glowworm* to overtake them later, but by the time the man had been picked up and the lifeboat had been hoisted back on board precious hours had been lost and the destroyer was never again seen by the British ships.

All that night she plunged through the heavy seas under forced draught to overtake the flotilla but at dawn the squadron was still out of sight somewhere to the northward. As the sky grew lighter, *Glowworm's* company sighted two enemy destroyers approaching at full speed from ahead and the alarm was sounded for action stations. A radio message was sent to the main fleet saying that *Glowworm* was in action against two enemy destroyers: a few minutes later a second radio message laconically stated that a 10,000-ton German cruiser was approaching on the port beam and had opened fire. No more messages came and the rest of the tragic story filtered through from German sources some weeks later. The game little ship, surrounded by enemy vessels, went down with her flag flying and her guns firing to the last.

Photos of her end eventually reached England and in time appeared in British and American papers. In one, *Glowworm* is seen half hidden in billowing clouds of dense black smoke a few hundred yards from the swastika-decorated bows of a Nazi destroyer. Another and more poignant picture shows some of *Glowworm*'s crew being hauled out of the water on to the deck of one of the enemy ships. The British seamen are unrecognizable for they are covered from head to foot with viscous, black oil, their white eyes staring unnaturally in mute dejection from their oil-blackened faces. And all of this costly tragedy because one man had fallen overboard.

A few days after the *Glowworm* disaster the real battle between the British and German naval forces began. Enemy warships were speeding northward to capture the Norwegian iron port of Narvik. The first clash occurred on April 9 when the battle-cruiser *Renown* met the battleship *Scharnhorst* and the heavy cruiser *Admiral Hipper* in a violent gale off Narvik. *Renown* headed straight for the foe and opened the action with a salvo from her big guns at a range of 18,000 yards. From the unsteady platforms of the rolling, plunging ships, accurate gunnery was impossible; but eventually *Renown* scored a direct hit on *Scharn-*

horst's control tower and the latter turned away to lick her wound under a smoke-screen laid by the cruiser *Hipper*. *Renown*, putting on all speed, tried to shorten the range but the German ships had had enough and, with their superior speed, succeeded in escaping into mists to the southward.

British naval units cruising off Bergen were warned by radio and spread out to intercept the fleeing enemy but were unable to make contact owing to determined interference from German dive-bombers which kept up attacks all day and sank the destroyer *Gurkha*, as well as damaged other ships, including the giant *Rodney*, with an aerial torpedo hit on her foredeck.

Far to the north in the Narvik fiords another naval action was taking place between British and German destroyers, the most memorable and destructive of all the naval operations during the brief and bloody Norwegian campaign. Five British destroyers, *Havoc, Hardy, Hunter, Hotspur* and *Hostile* were on patrol outside territorial waters in a blinding snowstorm, when Captain R. A. Warburton-Lee of H.M.S. *Hardy* informed the Admiralty of the presence of seven enemy destroyers in Narvik fiord, and asked for orders. He was told to use his own judgment and he sent an answering radio that he was going into action immediately. Although the enemy destroyers were larger and superior in numbers, the five British destroyers entered the fiord that night and opened the attack at daybreak in a blizzard.

Warburton-Lee's plan was to steam in a circle, each ship under his command to fire her guns and torpedoes as she came opposite the enemy vessels, some of which were found to be concealed behind a whale-factory ship. When the action opened, both sides began to score hits but the enemy had the advantage of captured shore batteries which were opened fire on the British destroyers. Hell broke loose in that peaceful northern harbor. One of the British Whitehead torpedoes found its mark in the large enemy destroyer *Anton Schmitt* and blew her out of the water.

Warburton-Lee's flotilla had circled three quarters of the way round the fiord when three big German destroyers, which had been lying concealed in a narrow inlet, steamed out and began firing at almost point-blank range. The splinters from a shell bursting on the *Hardy* mortally wounded her gallant commander, and killed and wounded two other officers. All the enemy's fire was concentrated on the *Hardy,* and before long the destroyer was in flames and a wreck fore and aft.

The commander's secretary, Lieutenant Stanning, took charge of the ship and, obeying the order of her dying captain, ran her into shallow water 350 yards from the shore. The order was given to abandon ship and, while enemy shells burst round them, the crew leapt into the freezing water and swam ashore, many being killed by shell fire before they gained the beach. Commander Warburton-Lee was carried ashore but died a few minutes later. The story of how the 170 survivors, perishing with cold in their sodden uniforms, found shelter in a deserted cottage, how they were nursed back to warmth and life by two heroic Norwegian women, how they narrowly escaped capture by the enemy and were taken off days later by H.M. destroyer *Ivanhoe* and brought safely to England is another story. Meanwhile a second British destroyer, H.M.S. *Hunter* was hit by a shell and blew up. She sank within sixty seconds.

Three out of the five British destroyers escaped but *Hotspur* had been seriously hit and her sick bay was crowded with wounded and dying men. The first part of the Narvik battle was over, with two destroyers lost to the British and one destroyer and six supply ships lost to the enemy.

It was not long before the loss of the *Hardy* and *Hunter* was avenged. The second phase of the battle of Narvik, which the marooned survivors of the *Hardy* witnessed from their refuge in the hills above the fiord, opened at noon on April 10 in a heavy rain, when a British naval force led by the destroyer *Icarus* followed by eight other destroyers entered the bay and engaged the enemy. Some distance behind the destroyers the giant battleship *Warspite* steamed majestically, feeling her way through the narrow and treacherous channels into the fiord. Within half an hour the main battle was over. The enemy destroyers hiding in the mist-shrouded inlets of the fiord were hunted out and forced to give battle. While they fought desperately to give as good as they received, they were doomed from the start in spite of the aid they received from shore batteries. Again hell broke loose in the tranquil harbor of Narvik as shells and torpedoes burst amongst the enemy ships.

During the second attack four enemy destroyers slipped away in the bad visibility, hoping to escape into hiding far up the twisting Rombaks Fiord which runs into Narvik bay. When the guns ashore had been silenced and all the shipping in the harbor destroyed, four of the British destroyers went up the fiord in pursuit of the enemy, nosing their way through the ice floes and the narrowing waterway between towering cliffs of snow-covered rock. Ten miles up the fiord one of the enemy ships turned to give battle and after a short and furious exchange of fire, during which H.M.S. *Esquimo* received two hits, the enemy destroyer, *Diether von Roeder* was run ashore a blazing wreck. Leaving her to burn, the British destroyers proceeded farther up the fiord, and on rounding a point were met with a strange sight. Ahead were the remaining three enemy destroyers silent and abandoned. One had been set on fire and was blazing furiously, the other two had been scuttled and were sinking. In the Narvik battles the enemy had lost nine auxiliary merchant ships and eleven of his largest destroyers. The *Hardy* and *Hunter* had been adequately avenged.

As we have already pointed out, the first important naval action of the war occurred in December 1939 when the pocket battleship *Graf Spee* met three British cruisers off the mouth of the river Plate. The *Graf Spee*, a miniature battleship of 10,000 tons and armed with six 11-inch guns and eight 6-inch guns, had been sent out secretly as a commerce raider and her presence in the Atlantic was only suspected after a number of merchant ships, most of them British, failed to arrive at their destination. Amongst these missing ships was the big *Doric Star* homeward bound with thousands of tons of chilled meat from the Argentine. In November the Admiralty sent out in great secrecy three cruisers under Commodore H. Harwood to hunt down the mysterious raider. These ships were *Exeter*, six 8-inch guns, and *Ajax* and *Achilles* eight 6-inch guns.

Steaming down the South Atlantic they picked up radio messages which gave them the clue to the raider's whereabouts and accordingly a course was set for the coast of Brazil. A few days later, Wednesday December 13, when 200 miles from Montevideo off the mouth of the river Plate, the gray shape of the German battleship loomed against the pale light of dawn. She was erroneously thought to be the *Admiral Sheer*, another so-called pocket battleship, but, as it turned out later, the stranger was the notorious *Graf Spee*, an adversary that could throw a heavier weight of shells in one broadside than the three British cruisers together. Her captain, Hans Langsdorf, by various tricks of disguise had managed to keep her identity secret for several months. During her brief but destructive career in the Atlantic she was for a while given a dummy funnel, and for a short time masqueraded as the British battle-cruiser *Renown*.

When sighted by the British cruisers she was chasing the French passenger-cargo steamer *Formose* and the distraction caused by the fortunate arrival of the cruisers gave the *Formose* an opportunity to escape, since the *Graf Spee* had more serious matters to attend to. Captain Langsdorf was a gallant sailor, and turned to meet the three cruisers with every reason to be confident in the weight of his armament to sink the impudent adversaries one by one. His guns could outrange those of the cruisers and like the long arm of a boxer could hold off the enemy while he smashed them to pieces. His broadside of 4708 pounds was half as much again as the combined broadsides of the cruisers.

Ajax was the first to attack, closing in on the battleship and taking a fearful hammering from his 11-inch guns until she was able to bring her own 6-inch rifles within range. It seemed like suicide and would have been, without the co-operation of her two consorts which, by a prearranged plan, came in to draw part of the fire of the enemy. The British, having taken the initiative, forced the action into a running fight, with *Ajax* astern and *Exeter* and *Achilles* on the flanks. *Exeter* soon began to receive most of the enemy fire and suffered severely in her attempt to get her own guns within range. *Graf Spee* opened fire at 12½ miles, and the *Exeter* replied, but her 8-inch shells fell harmlessly in the sea 3000 yards short. The German's seventh shell hit *Exeter*'s forward turret, killing outright eight out of the gun crew of fifteen, and wrecking the captain's bridge.

Exasperated to find that his fire could not reach the enemy, Captain Bell of the *Exeter* closed in until his shells began to catch the battleship, but for his temerity the ship paid a terrible price. Within an hour all but one of her guns were silenced, numerous fires had broken out below decks, her steering gear was damaged, her hull was riddled with shell holes and she had suffered nearly 100 casualties. But in her desperate role of sitting target to draw the enemy's fire she had not made the sacrifice in vain, for it had enabled the two smaller cruisers to do great damage to the battleship without themselves being sunk for their impudence.

All four ships were now steaming towards the mouth of the Plate in a running fight. The *Graf Spee* was beginning to show signs of distress from the cumulative effect of the cruiser's fire. One of the *Exeter's* 8-inch shells had wrecked her forward turret and damaged the control tower, thus paying the enemy back for the damage she herself had received earlier in the action. But by now the British cruiser was too badly crippled to continue and was forced to drop out, leaving her consorts to continue the action.

All afternoon, the two small cruisers hung on to their dangerous adversary, cheerfully taking a battering for the privilege of hitting back, and by nightfall their tenacity was rewarded, for suddenly Captain Langsdorf broke off the action and ran for the refuge of Montevideo. Afterwards, in an interview with South American reporters he frankly admitted that the audacity of the British, and their rapidity of maneuver had completely upset his plans.

We should not overlook the Navy's part in going to the aid of the Dutch when the Nazis invaded Holland early in May 1940. When the Teutons poured over the peaceful Dutch countryside, and their dive bombers tried to lay

waste the cities and block the ports, the Hague government did not have to ask the British government for help.
It was already on the way, but no help could save Holland
and the most that could be hoped for was to hold the ports
long enough while some of the shipping, the members of
the Royal family and the national gold reserve could be
got away.

Within an hour of the Nazi attack on Holland, British
destroyers were dispatched to Rotterdam, Flushing,
Ymuiden and Antwerp to give what help they could. The
enemy was rapidly sweeping across the Lowlands towards
the coast. Accompanying the destroyers was a fleet of
minelayers to mine the harbor mouths against U-boat attacks. As the long, gray destroyers steamed into the Dutch
ports of Flushing and Ymuiden, they were immediately
attacked by wave after wave of Nazi bombers and magnetic mines dropped from the air. Exposed to this rain of
death, thousands of terrified people crowded the docks,
pleading to be taken on board the British destroyers. The
next day more ships arrived, running the gauntlet of
bombs, mines and gunfire. It was delicate and dangerous
work, navigating through the shallow channels off the
Dutch coast, exposed to U-boats and bombs, but all the
destroyers got through, scarred but still under control.

Not only did the naval units bring away to safety thousands of refugees, but they sent landing parties of sailors
and marines ashore to assist the hard-driven Dutch army
in land fighting. British tars in motor launches penetrated
the canals deep into Holland to fire oil tanks, demolish
bridges, and blow up railways and docks, all the while
subject to concentrated gunfire and bombing from the
enemy. In spite of heavy casualties, the sailors carried on
with their perilous task, blowing up power stations and
sinking barges to block the canals, until, almost surrounded

by the German army, they were forced to retire to avoid capture.

The part the Navy played in Holland was largely overshadowed by the conflagration that had broken out in northern Europe, and when, a few weeks later, the Navy's part in the lifting of the British army from France made the name Dunkirk immortal in the Navy's roll of honor, Ymuiden and Flushing were almost forgotten.

The case of the 8000-ton Canadian liner *Lady Hawkins* was a typical and a tragic example of the 'sink without warning' creed of the Nazis. In January 1941 the *Lady Hawkins* with 212 passengers and 109 crew was steaming southward in the Caribbean Sea when the conning tower of a U-boat rose to the surface less than 100 yards away on the port bow. It was a dark night and, though the ship was far from the war zone and no U-boats were expected in these waters, the ship as a precautionary measure was blacked out; no lights of any kind were showing. The U-boat's listening devices must have detected the liner's presence, for suddenly the darkness was split by the blinding white beams of two searchlights which played slowly along the length of the ship, dazzling the sleepy passengers who had been ordered on deck to their lifeboat stations. The searchlights seemed to play with the liner as a cat with a mouse while the bewildered passengers waited for the torpedo which they were warned to expect.

For a full minute the searchlights moved back and forth over the steamer but no signal came from the U-boat, which remained unseen in the darkness. Then, without any warning whatever, the first torpedo hit the ship and exploded with a shattering roar, bringing down the mainmast and blowing a number of people into the sea. The big ship immediately listed over at such a steep angle that more than 100 men, women and children were literally tipped into the sea, where they paddled about helplessly until they became exhausted and sank. Most of the 321 persons on board did not have a chance. The second torpedo crashed into No. 3 hold and exploded in the engine room, at the same time shattering several lifeboats which were being lowered over the side. To add to the horror of the night, the ship caught fire and a number of people were trapped below and burnt to death.

The *Lady Hawkins* went down in twenty-five minutes. When the U-boat commander had made sure that the liner was doomed he departed, leaving the victims to drown. The steamer went down with the British ensign flying at the masthead and her master, Captain Huntley Griffin, standing on the bridge. Only one lifeboat got away and, though it was built to carry sixty-three persons, seventy-six were crowded into her. As the boat pulled clear of the sinking ship, men and women dared not look at the white faces of those doomed to drown since there was no room for them in the overcrowded boat.

The *Lady Hawkins* was torpedoed on Monday, January 19, and the survivors were sighted and rescued after being adrift for five days. During that period five people died from wounds and exposure, so that out of the original 321 persons there were only 71 survivors. Among these were a few children, one a little girl of 2½ years. The sinking of the *Lady Hawkins* without warning was not, of course, an exceptional case, although some British and American newspapers at the time branded it as the worst U-boat crime of the war. It is the policy of U-boat commanders to sink *all* enemy merchant ships without warning and without inquiring whether there are women and children on board. As a rule he has no means of knowing whether there are women and children in the ship he attacks. The

Donaldson liner *Athenia*, sunk within a few hours of the outbreak of war, was not warned first, nor were any other attacked vessels.

During the first three years of the war the role of the naval airplane increased in importance. The battle of Matapan, which is very briefly described in Chapter VII, demonstrated the value of aircraft carriers in operations far from land. This battle was a perfect example of co-ordination between air and sea forces, and had it not been for the scouting planes of the carrier *Formidable* the presence of the enemy would have remained undiscovered. After his presence was revealed, the planes were invaluable in keeping contact with the foe.

Early in the war a Fairey Fox seaplane carried on the cruiser *Ajax* materially helped toward the defeat of the pocket battleship *Graf Spee* off the river Plate. The *Ark Royal's* planes took part in the action off Cape Spartivento in November 1940, and in the bombing of Genoa three months later. And, as we shall see in the next chapter, planes from the *Ark Royal* and *Victorious* carried out torpedo attacks on the *Bismarck* in May 1941. In November 1940, planes from the new aircraft carrier *Illustrious* and the veteran *Eagle* torpedoed capital ships of the Italian fleet in the famous attack on the harbor of Taranto. At the battle of Cape Matapan, in which three Italian cruisers and some destroyers were sunk, the aircraft from the new carrier H.M.S. *Formidable* so delayed the enemy fleet that the British squadrons were able to arrive in time to intercept it. So it is evident that despite the risk of losing these costly ships and their precious load of planes, the risk is worth the returns they bring the country. Britain, the United States and Japan were all aware of the value of these ships in modern warfare and each navy had a considerable number of such vessels whereas the Germans and Italians for various reasons began the war without a single aircraft carrier between them.

Having said so much about the Royal Navy, let us end these introductory pages with a tribute to the heroic men of the Merchant Marine. From captain down to the humblest deck-boy their quiet unassuming heroism is beyond praise. The immortal story of the ex-passenger liner *Jervis Bay* and her commander, Captain Fegen, who died with his ship in order that the convoy for which he was responsible might have a chance to disperse and escape, was an example of the spirit of Drake, Grenville and Nelson. There is also the fight of the *Rawalpindi,* armed liner, which fought two enemy warships without thought of surrender, though her position was hopeless from the start. She fired her guns until she was blazing from stem to stern and after hours of this agony went down with her flags flying. Then there was the fight of the armed liner *Scotstoun,* whose crew continued to fire the guns until the rising water covered the breech blocks, and whose grim old captain had to be forcibly pushed overboard by his officers in order to save his life because he refused to leave the ship when she was sinking.

The work of these ex-liners converted to armed merchant cruisers is particularly hazardous. Their unwieldly size, thin plating and comparatively low speed make them easy prey to enemy submarines or surface raiders. They are sent out on patrol, hundreds of miles from land and usually alone. Their duties are escorting convoys, hunting enemy raiders and general patrol work. Their lives in war are usually short but the service they perform in relieving the limited and overstrained resources of the Navy is, of course, extremely valuable.

Though this history is concerned mainly with the work

of British ships and sailors, the writer is not unaware of the magnificent part played by the United States Navy after their entry into the war. American sailors have proved themselves over and over again worthy of the great traditions of their country. Like their British cousins, they have demonstrated that the good life is an ideal to fight for, and the better one's life, the harder the fight to keep it so.

Part One

CHAPTER I

The Destruction of *Bismarck*

ON MAY 26, 1941, the people of Britain were stunned by the news that the battle-cruiser *Hood*, the largest ship in the Royal Navy, had been sunk in a naval action off Greenland. *Hood* was the pride of the Navy, and the news of her loss cast a deep gloom over the country.

Hood, reputed to be the largest warship in the world, had been completed in 1920, and was therefore a comparatively old ship. Laid down under the Emergency War Programme at John Brown's yard on the Clyde in September 1916, she was not completed until four years later. Her cost was over six million pounds, and she underwent extensive alterations to modernize her in 1930. Designed to meet the lessons of the battle of Jutland, she carried eight 15-inch guns and twelve 5.5-inch guns for a secondary armament. At her water-line was a belt of 12-inch armor-plate 562 feet long and 9½ feet deep. Of her total displacement of 42,100 tons, her armor accounted for one-third. Such a ship was believed invulnerable from a broadside torpedo attack. This, then, was the wonder ship that was believed to be almost indestructible and able to stand up to any battleship afloat. Yet a single 15-inch shell fired from an enemy battleship destroyed her.

Out of the maze of rumor and fact a clear and logical explanation gradually appeared, and, though the blow to British pride was softened in the light of the knowledge that the destruction of *Hood* was due chiefly to a lucky hit, it did nothing to lessen the grief at her loss, though when the loss was avenged by the destruction of *Bismarck* three days later it seemed as though the score had been evened, especially as the enemy had lost in this one ship one-quarter of his capital ship strength, while the Royal Navy, with fifteen capital ships, could better spare the loss.

Bismarck was the fourth vessel of that name built for the German Navy and the largest warship ever launched in a German yard. A sister-ship to the then uncompleted *Tirpitz*, with a nominal displacement of 35,000 tons (believed to be actually nearer 45,000 tons) and with a main armament of eight 15-inch guns, she was laid down at the famous Blohm and Voss yards at Hamburg in 1936 and launched in February 1939.

With a secondary armament of twelve 5.9-inch and sixteen 4.1-inch guns, she could fire a somewhat heavier weight of metal than *Hood*. The thickness of her protective armor was a well-kept secret, but it must have been considerable, since she received at least half a dozen torpedo hits without showing any indications of sinking. In appearance she was unorthodox, compared with the more conservative British design, with her 'clipper' bows, upswept fore-deck sheer line, counter stern, large single funnel, and massive superstructure. In her last and only action she carried about two thousand men, including supernumeraries on a training course for sea experience. She was under the command of Admiral Gunther Lutjens, a sailor of the old German Navy who had been converted to the Nazi creed and had become a loyal supporter of Hitler.

Early in 1941 there was much enemy raider activity in the North Atlantic. Convoys were attacked by enemy warships working at such extreme ranges that it had never been possible to identify them, but they were believed to be cruisers or the pocket-battleship *Admiral Scheer*, sister-ship to the scuttled *Graf Spee*. Some ships' captains reported that the 26,000-ton battleships *Scharnhorst* and *Gneisenau* were out in the North Atlantic preying on shipping, and a little later the battleship *Malaya* sighted at long range two enemy warships believed to be that famous pair and even fired a salvo at them, without, however, ever getting to close quarters. This was in February, and late in March R.A.F. reconnaissance planes discovered two large enemy battleships alongside the docks at Brest. Careful study of photographs brought back revealed these ships as *Scharnhorst* and *Gneisenau*. Their presence at Brest coincided with a lull in the Atlantic convoy attacks, a respite which lasted for several weeks. It was part of the work of Coastal Command planes to keep watch on the north coasts of Europe to report the movements of enemy shipping, especially those of warships. So far as was known the only other big ship in commission, *Bismarck*, was safely out of harm's way in Kiel harbor, but about the middle of May this formidable vessel was discovered to be at Bergen, in Norway, and obviously there for some sinister reason. She was discovered by a Coastal Command aircraft while on a reconnaissance over Norwegian harbors. Flying high over Bergen, the pilot at once noticed a very large battleship and a cruiser anchored in the roads, and they were identified as *Bismarck* and *Prinz Eugen*, a *Hipper* class cruiser of 10,000 tons.

To naval men this was significant news, for the presence of such an important ship as *Bismarck* away from her home base could only mean that the tiger had come out of its lair for one purpose and that not a peaceful one. Therefore orders were given to watch the battleship, since it was surmised that she was bound on a raiding cruise. For several days the two warships lay in Bergen harbor, but one morning a naval aircraft found that the enemy had disappeared. The two warships had slipped away under cover of darkness, but in which direction it was impossible to tell. Those gentlemen of the Admiralty who order the movements of His Majesty's ships decided that the best guess was the North Atlantic and accordingly sent secret orders to the cruisers *Norfolk* (Captain A. J. L. Phillips), wearing the flag of Rear-Admiral W. F. Wake-Walker, and *Suffolk* (Captain R. M. Ellis) to take up positions in Denmark Strait, between Iceland and Greenland. As Denmark Strait is over two hundred miles wide at its narrowest point the prospect of intercepting any ship passing through those waters seemed extremely remote, especially as the weather at that period (late in May) was known to be bad, with visibility down to a mile or less. Ice-floes broken away from the polar ice-pack, and forming a menace to navigation, were still coming down from the Arctic Ocean, thus giving the cruisers' company an added incentive to keep a sharp look-out.

It was not forgotten that if *Bismarck* and her consort were heading for the North Atlantic convoy lanes, sailing on a Great Circle course between American and Canadian ports and Britain, they might pass through the even wider stretch of ocean between Scotland and Iceland, and all naval ships operating in those waters were warned to keep a look-out. There were, indeed, at that time so many big ships of the Royal Navy in the Atlantic that the enemy had little chance of avoiding discovery for long.

At this point it will assist us to visualize the situation if the names of the warships and their dispositions are set down, so that they may be referred to in following the action that took place when the enemy was encountered.

Norfolk and *Suffolk*, as we have seen, were watching Denmark Strait. They were both heavy cruisers of about 10,-000 tons displacement. South of Iceland were *Hood* and *Prince of Wales*, the latter one of the new 35,000-ton battleships commissioned in 1941 and later sunk by a Japanese torpedo attack in the Far East. South of Greenland the new 23,000-ton aircraft-carrier *Victorious* was cruising with her destroyer escort, and several hundred miles to the east another new 35,000-ton battleship, *King George V*, wearing the flag of the Commander-in-Chief, Admiral Sir John Tovey, was also cruising in search of the enemy. Two hundred miles south of the flagship was the battleship *Rodney* (34,000 tons), one of the most powerful ships in the Navy. And later this formidable armada was joined by a force comprising the 32,000-ton battle-cruiser *Renown*, the aircraft-carrier *Ark Royal*, and the heavy cruiser *Sheffield*, under the command of Admiral Somerville. A grand total of six capital ships, two aircraft-carriers, and four cruisers, also a number of destroyers. This widespread patrol over the vast wastes of the North Atlantic proved that the Navy was sparing no effort to catch and destroy the enemy before he had an opportunity to do any harm. These vessels were scattered apart over thousands of square miles of ocean.

Let us return to the Denmark Strait, where *Norfolk* and *Suffolk* were cruising in company with every look-out station manned and decks cleared for action. On Friday, May 23, dawn broke over a gray and stormy sea with the two cruisers rolling their decks under and the look-outs muffled up in duffle coats as they peered out through the driving snow and rain-squalls. It was a cold and lonely job, and, though the chances of finding the enemy so far north seemed poor indeed, the Navy could not afford to relax its vigilance, for there was also the peril of U-boats, and a keen watch was kept for the elusive periscope almost impossible to detect in such steep seas. The visibility during the day varied as snow-squalls blotted out the horizon. The two cruisers frequently lost sight of each other, and, though they were always in touch by radio, this was used as little as possible in order to avoid giving their presence away to the enemy.

The day wore on without sight of a ship, but about half-past seven in the evening the rain cleared, and there, about six miles away, appeared the gray mass of a monster battleship and another warship, recognized as a cruiser, pushing through the seas at high speed on a south-westerly course. Admiral Wake-Walker immediately sent out a radio to the Commander-in-Chief of all units of the Navy in the North Atlantic that *Bismarck* and *Prinz Eugen* had been sighted in Denmark Strait heading south-west at high speed. The two ships were soon lost in the mists, but *Suffolk* and *Norfolk* managed to shadow them all that night in spite of bad visibility and rough seas. Shadowing such a big ship as *Bismarck* had its risks, for there was always the danger of running into range of the battleship's 15-inch guns, since it was impossible to keep a fixed distance in the changing visibility. Although the enemy could hardly have failed to see the two shadowing cruisers, he made no attempt to attack them, probably because he suspected a trap such as that laid to decoy the Italian squadron towards Admiral Cunningham's heavy ships in the Battle of Matapan. The Germans continued to steam at high speed on the same course with the probable expectation of losing themselves in the wide Atlantic. Their object was to destroy convoys, not to risk action with the British battle fleet.

As Admiral Lutjens speeded southward he was not aware that *Hood* and *Prince of Wales* were approaching him from the east, that the aircraft-carrier *Victorious* lay in wait farther south, and that other big ships were hurrying to intercept him. When he left Norway to raid convoys in the Atlantic he doubtless felt that with luck he could avoid decisive action with superior forces, but, as we shall see, his chances of escape were almost nil. It was a bold action for a lone battleship (we can discount the presence of the cruiser) to steam into an area certain to be bristling with enemy warships. Modern aircraft-carriers, with their radio-equipped planes, able to watch every square mile of the ocean, make it impossible for any ship to remain at sea undetected. Much time and money have been spent in experiments to discover the perfect camouflage, but there is no means of concealing the telltale smoke and the white wake which trails behind any ship that is under way.

During the night H.M.S. *Hood* (Captain R. Kerr), wearing the flag of Vice-Admiral L. E. Holland, and *Prince of Wales* (Captain J. C. Leach) speeded westward at forced draught to intercept the enemy. As they plunged into the heavy seas the bows and fore-deck were swept with cascades of white water. At dawn officers and men were ordered to action stations, and a sharp look-out was kept for the enemy believed to be somewhere in the driving mists to windward. Officers and ratings, as is the custom before going into action, put on clean underwear and outer clothes, and in the cabins they stowed away all loose breakable objects such as framed photographs, glass, or anything that would splinter at the shock of the first broadside. Men in gun-turrets and on the bridge and control-tower put on lifebelts, anti-flash hoods, and steel helmets. Mugs of hot cocoa were brought up, and the hot drink was gratefully gulped down by men who were chilled through after long hours of watch duty. Through the narrow slits in the armored turrets and look-out towers powdery snow found its way, for the air was full of driving snow. Visibility had dropped to a hundred yards. The escorting destroyers whose duty it is to screen the costly battleships from torpedo attack were unable to keep station in the mountainous waves and had dropped out of sight astern. The battleships, however, seemed to disdain the gale and tore through the steep seas at a rate of nearly thirty knots. The eggshell hulls of the destroyers could not have stood up to the buffeting of the seas at that speed, and until the weather improved the battleships would go on alone and chance U-boats, for at all risks the foe must be met and challenged.

Shortly after dawn the skies cleared, though the seas were running high. The low clouds lifted, the snow-squalls had gone, and the horizon became a sharp black edge against a band of pale yellow sky. The visibility was perfect, and eager eyes aloft scanned the horizon for the first sign of the enemy. Suddenly the shrill voice of a boy in the highest look-out station of *Prince of Wales* was heard above the roar of the wind: "Enemy in sight!" And there on the northern horizon, clear and sharp, was silhouetted a monster battleship, followed by a smaller cruiser, steaming in line ahead and showing no smoke. The first impression of everyone who saw *Bismarck* was of her tremendous size. This impression seems to have been unanimous among the British sailors.

The range was estimated at thirteen miles. The long barrels of the big guns of *Hood* and *Prince of Wales* were trained on the enemy, and a few seconds later the signal came from the flagship to open fire. Instantly bright orange flashes spurted from the guns of the forward turrets of *Hood* as she fired the first salvo. Two seconds later *Prince of Wales'* 14-inch guns crashed out a deafening salvo, just as *Bismarck* opened fire. The German shooting was good, and the first salvo fell uncomfortably close to the British ships. *Hood* and *Prince of Wales* were speeding toward the enemy on parallel courses firing salvos from the big forward guns as fast as they could be reloaded. Then the monstrous and inconceivable thing happened, the fatal hit which destroyed the pride of the Royal Navy. Observers from *Prince of Wales*, which was herself hit by a 15-inch shell from *Bismarck*, saw a great flame shoot up from the boat-deck of *Hood*, which was amidships. At the same time a signal was hoisted ordering *Prince of Wales* to carry on with the pre-arranged maneuver. *Hood* was in serious danger, though the watchers from *Prince of Wales*, who had their own hands full, did not yet fully realize how serious was the state of things in the flagship. The great fire amidships was shooting up tongues of flame in the center of a vast cloud of yellowish smoke hundreds of feet high. From the heart of the fire huge pieces of metal were hurled high above the stricken battleship. A second later she was almost totally obscured by a great cloud of smoke, through which her forward guns were still gamely firing. Suddenly a shattering explosion seemed to lift the 42,000-ton monster out of the sea, and when the smoke had cleared away *Hood* was gone.

Within a few minutes of the opening of the battle the flagship was lost, and with her 1418 officers and ratings, including Vice-Admiral Holland. There were only three survivors. They were picked up by one of the escorting destroyers which had arrived on the scene. The first phase of the battle was over, and the Royal Navy had received a serious blow. So far as could be seen, *Bismarck* was unharmed; certainly her fighting power remained untouched. How had the largest, most heavily armored, and supposedly most formidable fighting ship in the world been

Men of H.M. Submarine *Proteus* at action stations. The *Proteus* took heavy toll of Rommel's supply vessels while on service in the Mediterranean. *British Official Photograph.*

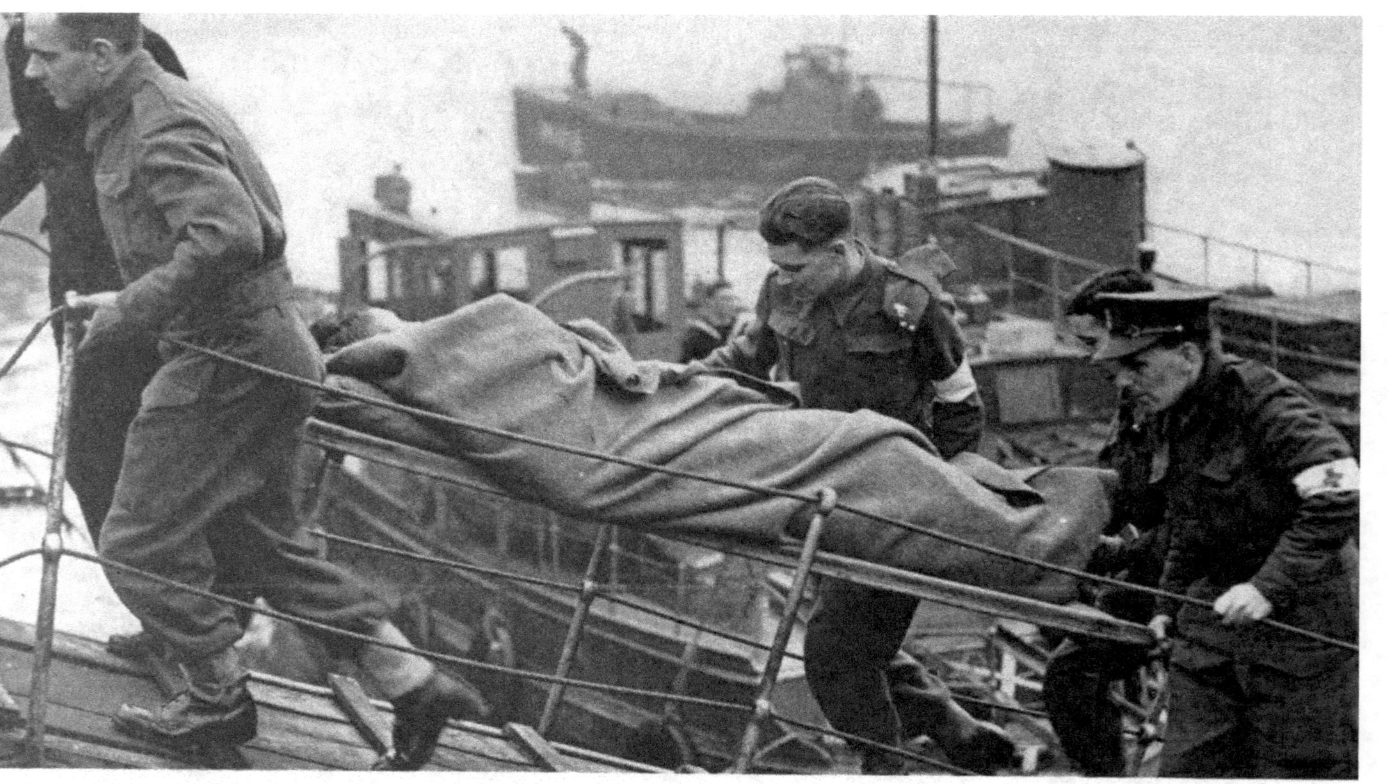

Survivors of the battleship *Bismarck* are brought ashore at a British port.
British Combine Photos.

destroyed by *Bismarck*'s guns at long range and within only a few minutes of the start of the action?

Was it through some inherent fault in construction, or some secret weapon of the enemy's such as a new type of armor-piercing shell? The probable explanation is simply that a 15-inch shell from *Bismarck* fired at a range of twelve miles by its necessarily high trajectory had dropped almost vertically on to the lightly armored section of the deck amidships, causing a fire in a magazine which spread to one of the main magazines with the inevitable consequences. Even giving the enemy his due for good shooting at such a long range when it is quite impossible to hit a given spot with certainty, it can surely be counted as simply a lucky shot, and the enemy must have had as big a surprise at the sudden disintegration of *Hood* as did the watchers on board *Prince of Wales*, which meanwhile continued firing, although she herself was in difficulties from a direct hit aft and had eventually to take avoiding action while temporary repairs were carried out. Meanwhile *Suffolk* and *Norfolk* hung on to the enemy, who altered his course to due south and was steaming at about twenty-five knots, obviously anxious to get away.

The weather had worsened again, and snow-squalls had shortened visibility to a mile. During the day *Prince of Wales* resumed the chase, and at midday both cruisers and the battleship opened fire on the enemy, without, however, being able to see if any hits were scored. The weather favored the enemy, giving concealment with swirling veils of snow and rain throughout that first day of pursuit.

When capital ships are firing at each other at extreme range it is not always possible to tell whether a hit is scored, though if no splash is seen it is presumed that the salvo has found the target. At such ranges, with a pair of binoculars, the observer will see a copper-red glow appear when a big shell strikes armor-plate, but nothing more unless an explosion follows the hit. Although it was not known at the time, *Prince of Wales* had permanently reduced *Bismarck*'s speed by a hit in the engine-room.

The first day of the chase ended with *Bismarck* steaming due south and *Suffolk, Norfolk,* and *Prince of Wales* in hot pursuit. The enemy was proceeding on a course that would bring athwart the aircraft-carrier *Victorious,* which was hurrying from the west to intercept him with torpedo-carrying planes. Just after midnight (in those latitudes in May it never really gets dark) the huge, rocky shape of *Victorious* rose above the western horizon, appearing through the mists to be twice its actual size. Through the glasses look-outs in the control-tower of *Prince of Wales* could see tiny planes—Albacores—leaving her deck, looking at that distance no larger than gnats. But each plane carried, slung beneath the fuselage, a deadly 18-inch torpedo. A few minutes later the planes, flying a few hundred feet above the sea, went in to attack the enemy. A white fountain of water alongside *Bismarck* told the watchers that at least one torpedo had found its mark. But obviously it was not in a vital spot, for the great battleship continued on her course without showing any outward signs of distress. It was learned that the appearance of *Victorious* and the subsequent torpedo attack seriously worried Admiral Lutjens, of *Bismarck,* and it was this which decided him to alter course and endeavor to reach the safety of the occupied French naval base of Brest.

Up to this time *Prinz Eugen* had kept company with *Bismarck,* but when the latter was next seen the cruiser was not with her. *Prinz Eugen* successfully evaded pursuit and eventually reached Brest. Bad weather and the failing light and the heavy anti-aircraft defence of the enemy made any further attacks by planes inadvisable, but the pursuing ships continued to shadow her until three in the morning, when the visibility dropped to a few hundred yards and contact was lost. The position was then 350 miles south-south-east of the southernmost cape of Greenland. The news that *Bismarck* had escaped greatly depressed the British people, and everywhere was heard bitter comment on those responsible for allowing the vanquisher of *Hood* to escape. It seemed as though Britain was always to have more than its share of misfortune. Meanwhile the Commander-in-Chief, Admiral Sir John Tovey, on board the new battleship *King George V*, was closing in from the east.

The quarry was lost, but the Navy did not intend her to get away, and every warship in the North Atlantic joined in the hunt. Here was the chance for aircraft-carriers to prove their value again, for planes had a far greater range of visibility than observers from the decks of ships, and furthermore a plane could cover an area ten times greater in a given time than the fastest ship. Both *Victorious* and *Ark Royal* were at sea, but a wide search was being carried out by land planes of the Royal Canadian Air Force from aerodromes in Newfoundland. It was, however, none of these which at last found *Bismarck* after all contact with her had been lost in the early hours of May 25.

At 10.30 A.M. on May 26, thirty-three hours after she had disappeared, *Bismarck* was sighted by Flying Officer D. A. Briggs in an American-built Catalina flying boat of Coastal Command 550 miles west of Land's End. *Bismarck* was alone, and the position showed plainly enough that she was trying to escape to Brest. Those units coming up from Gibraltar—*Renown, Ark Royal,* and *Sheffield*—immediately opened out to intercept her. Despite bad weather and a withering hail of anti-aircraft fire from

Bismarck, Flying Officer Briggs kept her under observation for half an hour, until he lost touch owing to bad visibility. All this time the Catalina's wireless operator was sending out *Bismarck's* position, and to such good purpose that by 11.15 A.M. British naval forces had come up to the quarry. The Catalina had doggedly hung on to the foe in spite of getting badly shot up by her fire. The hull was holed in several places, but the crew succeeded in plugging the holes with rubber, and the boat eventually reached a British base. For this feat Flying Officer Briggs was awarded the Distinguished Flying Cross.

Ark Royal's aircraft were the first units of the Navy to regain touch with the enemy, but the weather was too bad for a torpedo attack, and Vice-Admiral Somerville detached the cruiser *Sheffield* to shadow *Bismarck* until conditions were more favorable. During the afternoon *Ark Royal* sent off torpedo-carrying planes, but they were so buffeted about by the weather they had to return without attacking and made a very difficult landing on the carrier. The Commander-in-Chief fully realized the necessity of slowing up *Bismarck* by torpedo attacks before she had drawn the British ships within range of enemy land-based bombers.

In the evening, while *Sheffield* continued to shadow *Bismarck,* a second striking force from *Ark Royal* made a determined effort to torpedo the German, and this time was successful. Two hits were scored, one amidships and the other on the quarter. The second one smashed *Bismarck's* rudder and one propeller, and she was observed to be out of control and to steam in two complete circles before some measure of control could be regained.

The smashing of *Bismarck's* rudder and propeller was the beginning of the end. She was now within four hundred miles of Brest, but with the dice loaded so heavily against her there was no chance whatever of her escaping. Admiral Lutjens realized this that fateful night when he radioed a message to the Nazi High Command at 11.42 P.M.:

Ship incapable of maneuvering. Will fight to the last. Long live the Fuehrer.

LUTJENS
Commander-in-Chief of the Fleet

Less than an hour before he had sent this tragic message a Polish destroyer played a very gallant part during a torpedo attack on the enemy. A force of the big "Tribal" class destroyers—*Maori, Zulu, Tartar, Cossack, Mashona, Sikh,* and the Polish destroyer *Piorun,* all under the command of Captain P. L. Vian, D.S.O.—approached the enemy after dark to make a torpedo attack. Commander Eugeniusz Plawski, of *Piorun,* first sighted *Bismarck* at half-past ten and at once, with great daring, closed in to launch his torpedoes. One heavy shell from *Bismarck* could have blown the destroyer out of the water, but fortune favored the daring commander. *Piorun* was seen and immediately ran into heavy shell-fire, but Commander Plawski by cool and skilful seamanship took avoiding action while the destroyer's gunners audaciously fired back at the giant with their small guns. After the skirmish Captain Vian signaled his congratulations to the Polish commander.

Throughout the night the destroyers harried their prey. About 1.30 A.M. (May 27), *Zulu, Maori,* and *Cossack* got in close enough for each to launch a torpedo. The latter two destroyers scored hits, and across the dark sea bright flames appeared on the fore-deck of *Bismarck,* but as they shortly afterwards subsided it was evident that the Germans had got the fire under control. Between two and three in the morning the crippled battleship stopped, but shortly afterwards her people got her under way again, and when dawn broke with a leaden sky periodically blotted out with snow- and sleet-squalls the quarry was seen to be twelve miles to the eastward, limping along at a mere eight knots. To all those sailors who witnessed her in this plight—in spite of their knowledge that she would have had no mercy on any British ship—she was a tragic sight. Admiral Lutjens lived up to his promise to fight to the end, for his guns replied vigorously to the British fire, though it was noticed that his aim was erratic and no damage was done to the pursuing warships. *King George V* had come up, and on the eastern horizon, silhouetted against the cold morning light, was the long, rakish, three-funneled silhouette of the cruiser *Norfolk*. The position was approximately four hundred miles from Brest. The quarry had been brought to bay after a chase of eighteen hundred miles.

The third and last phase opened at dawn on Tuesday, May 27. The weather continued bad, and a second striking force from *Ark Royal* had to return to the carrier unsuccessful owing to the extremely poor visibility. But the hour of reckoning was near, and it was now a mathematical certainty that *Hood* would be avenged.

It was, of course, an unequal fight, but the Navy could not afford to take chances now. The chase must not move any nearer the French coast. The lives of British sailors could not be risked in order to play a gentleman's game with an enemy who would have taken advantage of any such gesture. It was a fight to a finish with no quarter given or expected. Consider what *Bismarck* was up against. In sight were the flagship *King George V*, the giant *Rodney* (sister-ship to *Nelson*), the aircraft-carrier *Ark Royal*, the battle-cruiser *Renown*, the heavy cruisers *Norfolk* and *Dorsetshire*, and a number of "Tribal" class destroyers.

As the sky in the east grew lighter *Bismarck* and *King*

George V were seen approaching each other, head on, and both ships firing their forward guns. To port, ten miles away, the 16-inch guns of the giant *Rodney* were booming salvos. *Bismarck* was firing four 15-inch guns from the two forward turrets, but the shots, which were aimed at *Rodney*, were erratic, and none hit the British ship.

The Royal Navy seemed to be doing better, for with twenty shells only two splashes were seen. The rest must have bored their way through the heavy armor of *Bismarck*, doing fearful damage to her vitals. At this time an aircraft from *Ark Royal* reported that the sea in the wake of the enemy was covered with oil, a sign that her oil-fuel tanks were holed. *Bismarck* now turned northward at a speed of about eight knots, and the two British battleships were rapidly overhauling her. The cruiser *Norfolk*, which had kept up the chase, was firing her 8-inch guns, which, however, were of uncertain value at that range.

The enemy's fire improved now that the range had shortened, and *King George V* and *Rodney* began zigzagging to confuse the German gun-layers. Rain-squalls, heavy seas, with the wild rolling of the ships made accurate gun-laying difficult and aided both sides, and the Navy closed in for the *coup de grâce*, but it was deemed wise not to take unnecessary risks, for the crippled battleship was fighting back gamely with her after-turrets and secondary armament. The back of her upper forward turret was seen to be torn away and the 15-inch guns cocked up at crazy angles. A fierce fire was blazing on the fo'c'sle, and the ship began to steer erratically as though the rudder was again damaged. British sailors who witnessed the end of *Bismarck* afterwards said, in interviews, that they could not help feeling sorry for the beaten adversary, but this was total war and their duty was to sink her since she refused to strike her flag. *King George V* and *Rodney* kept up a merciless fire which ripped and tore through the hull and superstructure, throwing jagged pieces of metal high in the air. *Bismarck* seemed now to be trying to conceal herself in clouds of smoke, but the strong wind immediately blew the smoke away, leaving her exposed to the pitiless salvos from the British ships. The action had lasted about twenty-five minutes when the flames on the fo'c'sle were seen suddenly to increase in size to one vast flame which licked over the bridge and enveloped the control-tower in a searing heat that must have roasted alive every living creature there. Her remaining guns were now firing wildly, and the fact that they were firing at all showed the desperate resolve of the German commander to go down fighting.

King George V's and *Rodney*'s salvos were firing in a rising crescendo of shattering crashes and the screaming whine of projectiles as the two battleships went in for the kill. The range was ten miles, but through the glasses men on the decks of *Bismarck* could be seen running aft and jumping overboard as though to escape an even worse fate.

The battered enemy began to show a list to port, though she was still slowly moving. Her flags were flying defiantly, but her last gun had been silenced. The Navy's heavy ships had done their work—it only remained to finish her off with a torpedo. But the Commander-in-Chief saw no reason for risking one of his capital ships, for the enemy might still have a sting in his tail, and so the cruiser *Dorsetshire* was ordered to close in and finish *Bismarck* with torpedoes. It should be explained that, although the enemy could, of course, have been sunk by gunfire, torpedoes were more economical and quicker, since it might have cost a thousand rounds of the heaviest shells to sink such a stoutly armored ship. *Dorsetshire's* first two torpedoes sped across the miles of intervening sea, and geysers of water told that they had reached their mark. But they did not appear to have affected the huge ship, so the cruiser steamed round to the opposite side and fired another torpedo. When this struck, *Bismarck* began to list, and at 11 A.M. precisely the great battleship was seen to roll slowly over to port, and float bottom up for a half-minute, before lifting her bows and slipping out **of** sight. She went down with her flag still flying.

As she rolled over, men were seen crawling all over the hull like ants on a sinking log. Where she had floated the surface of the sea was dotted with the dark heads of swimming men. *Dorsetshire* and two destroyers approached the spot and began picking up the Germans, and had safely hauled out of the water about a hundred men when the cruiser's look-outs reported the presence of U-boats. The ships were left no alternative but to withdraw—the enemy habit of sinking ships which stopped to rescue torpedoed sailors had taught the Navy a bitter lesson, and the Admiralty reluctantly made it a rule that a ship must not stop to pick up survivors if U-boats were known to be in the vicinity.

The hunt was ended, and all units were ordered to disperse to their stations, some to shore bases and others to resume their interrupted convoy duties. Meanwhile the enemy, thirsting for revenge, had sent out from France Focke-Wulf bombers to attack the British ships. Two of the big "Tribal" destroyers, *Tartar* and *Mashona*, were steaming together when the bombers sighted them and dived to attack. Wave after wave of bombers beset the two destroyers throughout the day, and, though they fought back gamely with every A.A. gun they had and zigzagged to such good purpose that they dodged most of the bombs,

Mashona received a direct hit from a heavy bomb and went down very quickly. *Tartar* took the risk of standing by to pick up survivors, defying torpedoes and bombs. Heroic feats of rescue were carried out by the crews of both ships, the medical officer of *Mashona* particularly distinguishing himself for his coolness and efficiency in saving some of the wounded.

Tartar was now alone to face the air attacks, but early in the afternoon she was joined by two more destroyers, and although the enemy kept up his air attacks until midnight there were no more casualties and the destroyers were able to make a British port.

Bismarck was destroyed, and the Royal Navy had lost *Hood* and the destroyer *Mashona*. It would hardly seem a fair exchange, but it may be pointed out that the enemy's loss was greater in proportion, since his naval tonnage was only a fraction of that of the British. As a sad sequel to this titanic drama *Prince of Wales* and *Ark Royal* were both within a few months lost in enemy action—the former in the Far East, the latter in the Mediterranean.

The purpose of the sortie of *Bismarck* and *Prinz Eugen* was obviously to destroy Atlantic convoys. They planned to keep at sea, receiving their supplies from Nazi ships, including oil-tankers, sent out from neutral ports. A week after *Bismarck* was sunk British naval forces intercepted and sank three enemy supply ships and an armed trawler in the North Atlantic. Others were suspected to be at sea, and the search continued, with result that on June 23 the German motor-ship *Babitonga* (4400 tons), disguised as a Dutch tramp, was caught heading for Brest. She carried one thousand tons of Diesel oil in drums convenient for transferring to U-boats. The cruiser *Prinz Eugen*, which had suffered some damage from *Prince of Wales* in the

Denkar Straits action, was located in dock at Brest by R.A.F. reconnaissance aircraft.

To sum up the *Bismarck* action, certain valuable lessons were learned by the Royal Navy, and the loss of *Hood* was not without a useful moral. The Navy learned that the German gunnery was very good at first, though it inevitably deteriorated after the ship had been damaged. Her crew, though made up mostly of very young men, nearly untried in battle, proved tough and fought bravely. *Bismarck* absorbed at least seven torpedo hits without either blowing up or sinking, a proof of the wisdom of her designers in dividing the hull up into an unusual number of watertight compartments. It was either this or the enormous thickness of her armor belt that enabled her to keep afloat after taking so much punishment. Another lesson learned was the value of torpedo attacks from the air on capital ships. The smaller (18-inch) torpedoes carried by the Albacores were deadly enough to cripple the leviathan. The lesson of Taranto and Matapan had been amply verified. Later the Japanese were to profit by this example in their attacks on the American fleet at Pearl Harbor and on *Prince of Wales* and *Repulse* in the Far East. Finally, the shooting of *King George V* and *Rodney* had proved to be good, especially in the third phase of the battle, as shown by the absence of shell splashes from the British salvos.

CHAPTER II

The Immortal Story of *Illustrious*

AT THE beginning of the war Great Britain possessed six aircraft-carriers—*Ark Royal, Courageous, Glorious, Furious, Eagle,* and *Hermes*—with another, *Argus,* used as a training ship. There were six others besides, building, their names given in *Jane's Fighting Ships* as *Illustrious, Victorious, Formidable, Indomitable, Implacable,* and *Indefatigable,* all big ships. The first four were laid down in 1937 and were due for completion in 1940–41. Since *Illustrious* and *Victorious* and *Formidable* figured in the news before June 1941, it was then known that the first three of these four were completed and on active service. *Courageous,* sister-ship of *Glorious,* was the first major naval casualty of the war. She was torpedoed in September 1939 by an enemy submarine. *Glorious* was sunk by shell-fire from the German battleships *Scharnhorst* and *Gneisenau* off Norway in June 1940. They were both designed as cruisers during the World War of 1914–18 for operations in the Baltic—hence their shallow draught. After the war the cruisers were converted to aircraft-carriers and were ready for their new role in 1930.

The first aircraft-carriers, commissioned during the World War of 1914–18, were called 'the hush-hush ships' as their building was kept secret. They were converted from cruisers and were the original *Furious* and *Argus.* The first carrier to be built expressly for that purpose was

H.M.S. *Hermes*. She was fitted to carry twenty airplanes, and was the first carrier to have a flight-deck extending the full length of the ship without a break. Her superstructure —funnel, bridge, and signaling mast—was built on the starboard side, a practice that was adopted in all subsequent vessels of this type. In 1913 there was laid down at Armstrong Whitworth's yard at Tyneside a battleship for the Chilean government to be named *Almirante Cochrane*, but all work on the ship ceased in August 1914. In 1917 the British government purchased her from Chile for £1,334,358, and put the half-built ship in hand at Portsmouth Dockyard for conversion to an aircraft-carrier. As H.M.S. *Eagle* (22,600 tons displacement, and the largest vessel of its kind in the world) she was finally completed in 1924. Two more hush-hush cruisers, H.M.S. *Courageous* and H.M.S. *Glorious*, as we have said, were converted into aircraft-carriers and completed in 1928 and 1930.

Illustrious was laid down in the yards of Vickers Armstrong at Barrow-in-Furness on April 4, 1937, as one of the big carriers budgeted for in the rearmament programme following the long sleep of the British government after the Treaty of Versailles. With a displacement of 23,000 tons, she was bigger than *Ark Royal*, which was completed in November 1938. Her length was 753 feet, and the width of the flight-deck 95¾ feet. Like her sister-ships, her full complement was 1600 men. Space for seventy airplanes was provided for, though sixty was accepted as a more practical figure for operational purposes. Her defensive armament consisted of sixteen 4.5 dual-purpose guns mounted on sponsons along either side, flush with the flight-deck. Besides these guns she carried the usual batteries of multiple pom-poms. Japan and the United States equipped their carriers with 8-inch guns, but the Admiralty, moved by the principle that aircraft-carriers should not be risked in offensive operations, had adhered to the policy of defensive armament only.

Put into commission in the autumn of 1940, *Illustrious* was sent almost before her paint was dry to assist the over-worked Mediterranean Fleet. Her commander, Captain D. W. Boyd, C.B.E., D.S.C., was a naval officer of long experience, and before this cruise was over the wisdom of the Admiralty's choice was to be amply justified. Under sealed orders the biggest and newest of the Royal Navy's aircraft-carriers left Britain, and after an uneventful voyage through the 'Bay' passed the Straits of Gibraltar and entered the Mediterranean, where her captain had instructions to keep his planes busy watching the skies and the seas for Axis aircraft and surface craft. Up to then the Navy had been unable to spare a modern carrier for these waters, and the arrival of *Illustrious* was a great relief to every British naval officer and rating in the Mediterranean. Axis planes had done much mischief among convoys, and at any moment the home-keeping Italian Navy might come out of their bases and challenge the Royal Navy. The presence of *Illustrious* soon began to be felt by the enemy, for her planes swept the skies and gave the Navy the freedom of movement it so desperately needed to protect convoys and the Suez Canal. But this was not spectacular work, and very few people in Britain were even aware that such a ship as *Illustrious* existed. Then came the famous raid on Taranto harbor, and her name appeared for the first time in the news.

On the night of November 11–12, 1940, the great naval base inside the heel of Italy was raided by torpedo-carrying aircraft from H.M.S. *Illustrious* and H.M.S. *Eagle*, an old ship. It was no coincidence that this most determined attack was carried out on the anniversary of the Armistice after the World War of 1914–18. In the harbor lay the main Italian battle fleet, comprising the two new battle-ships *Littorio* and *Vittorio Veneto* and four others of the *Cavour* class as well as a number of cruisers and auxiliary craft. The attack was so carefully planned that the enemy was caught off his guard with such successful results for the Royal Navy that the balance of naval power was decisively altered in favor of Britain. In one night torpedo-carrying Swordfish and Skua dive-bombers flying from *Illustrious* and *Eagle* at sea forty miles away wrought fearful destruction. The Swordfishes, coming in low over the water, dropped their torpedoes at point-blank range, leaving two battleships (one of 35,000 tons and the other of 23,000 tons) severely handled and half submerged in the harbor. Another battleship was badly damaged, and two cruisers had taken a heavy list to starboard. A daylight reconnaissance carried out the next day showed two of the *Cavour* class battleships to be aground, another partly submerged and abandoned, and a big 35,000-ton *Littorio* battleship with her stern under water and surrounded by salvage craft. Several smaller vessels could be detected lying under water in the inner harbor. This single raid had put out of action half the Italian battle fleet at the cost of two British planes. For the first time in war the aircraft-carrier had scored a major victory, and in doing so she had thoroughly justified herself.

So incensed were the German and Italian High Commands at this audacious raid that they issued orders that at any cost the aircraft-carrier *Illustrious* must be destroyed. All other operations in the Mediterranean were to take second place in importance to this urgent and supreme necessity. For weeks German and Italian bomber planes searched for her, but it was not until January 10 that they caught her, south of Malta, and with all the pent-up fury of thwarted hunters did their best to sink the giant ship. *Illustrious* was part of a squadron covering the passage of a convoy of ships taking supplies to Greece. The attack took place in the Sicilian Channel, the bottle-neck of the Mediterranean which lies between the island of Sicily and Cape Bon, on the African coast. Almost mid-way in the channel lies the small Italian island-fortress of Pantelleria, which had a small aerodrome and a base for U-boats. As the narrowest part of the Mediterranean it was the danger spot for convoys—a fact that the enemy did not fail to take advantage of.

The first news of the attack published in the more mod-erate British newspapers was a masterpiece of under-statement. After announcing that a sea and air action had taken place in the Mediterranean, in which three British ships had been hit and damaged and twelve Axis planes had been brought down, and that the destroyer *Gallant* had been damaged but reached port, the London *Times* stated that the aircraft-carrier had been hit and had re-ceived some damage. War-time censorship of necessity waters down spectacular news, and for weeks, if not months, the story of the hell *Illustrious* had been through was suppressed. But, piecing together the events of that dramatic day from official communiqués and from eye-witness accounts, we can get a whole picture.

The convoy, escorted by warships, was half-way through the Sicilian Channel and heading eastward at dawn on January 10. Just as the first streaks of dawn were rising from the eastern horizon a star shell was seen curving up from a British destroyer which had sighted the dark shapes of two Italian destroyers several miles away. At the signal British cruisers and destroyers raced to over-take the enemy, firing salvos as they took up the chase. One of the enemy destroyers managed to escape to the north, but the other, a *Spica* class destroyer, crippled by

The aircraft carrier *Illustrious* at speed for flying. A Swordfish has just landed and is being taken to the forward lift. *British Combine Photos.*

Pom-pom crew at action stations on H.M.S. *Illustrious*. *British Combine Photos.*

the British guns, slowed down and was sent to the bottom by a British destroyer, which went in and finished her with a torpedo.

As the escorting destroyers were tearing about, the drone of enemy aircraft was heard, and high up in the winter sky unidentified enemy planes were seen approaching. *Illustrious* at once sent off a squadron of her own planes, which roared up and chased the enemy away. These planes turned out to be Italian machines from Sicily, and though they were driven off, it was not before they had radioed a report of the presence of the British convoy and its size. One hour later—at 12.15 P.M.—two Italian torpedo-bombers, coming out of the sun, dived at *Illustrious* and dropped their 'tin fish.' The vicious anti-aircraft fire from *Illustrious* and other ships undoubtedly upset their aim, for both torpedoes missed, but one passed too close astern for comfort. The carrier had eighteen of her own planes in the air during this attack, but no others were able to leave her spacious flight-deck that day, for a quarter of an hour later a large force (as many as forty-five were counted) of German and Italian dive-bombers appeared and dived straight at *Illustrious*, leaving no doubt at all that their instructions were to concentrate on this ship and destroy her at whatever the cost.

With reckless courage they came straight in, ignoring the almost solid wall of anti-aircraft shells that screamed up to stop them. With daring and skill the attack was pressed home, though planes fell out of the sky like winged ducks. Hell broke loose over and around the victim of their fury. The sea was churned up into spouting columns of water and plumed spray as the Stukas rained down a torrent of bursting steel. Goggled pilots frowning down at the oblong shape of the carrier a thousand feet below, fatalistically ignoring the vicious, spitting anti-aircraft guns, were bent almost impersonally on one relentless purpose—to destroy that hated symbol of Britain's sea-power.

Hammering her implacably with showers of heavy high-explosives, indifferent to the wholesale slaughter of those British sailors, human beings like themselves, but turned enemies by the accident of war, the Nazi pilots pressed their attack with all the concentrated fury of their fanatical desire to destroy without mercy. They had been told that it was the planes of this ship that had caused the greatest destruction among the ships of their Italian ally at Taranto.

Other naval ships in the vicinity did what they could to protect the giant carrier, filling the blue Mediterranean sky with the dirty smudges of bursting A.A. shells. Watchers from the ships could see that *Illustrious* was taking terrible punishment and had received at least one direct hit on the flight-deck by a bomb of heavy caliber. Sometimes the carrier was entirely blotted out by the columns of water and smoke from bursting bombs, but she was still fighting back gamely, her gunners remaining at their posts on the exposed gun-platforms in spite of appalling casualties. Wave after wave of Stukas roared down on her, screaming like shells as they dived with their throttles wide open.

With jagged fragments of steel flying in every direction it was impossible for any of her crew to appear on deck. Still the gunners remained at their stations, though the crew of a multiple pom-pom were all killed when the gun received a direct hit from a bomb. A 1250-pound bomb, hitting the rear elevator hatch which was open and bringing up more planes, destroyed the planes and killed the crews.

At 1.30 p.m. a second wave of thirty-five Stukas approached, flying high, and when over the carrier broke into flights of three, and with throttles wide open dived to attack. Good bomb-sights or good luck got them another direct hit on the unfortunate ship. This time the after-part of the flight-deck was hit, and a huge, ragged hole torn in the steel. The bomb burst in the hangar-deck below, utterly destroying the closely packed planes and blowing the wreckage into a chaotic mess at one end of the vast hangar. Thousands of gallons of escaping gasoline from burst tanks caught fire, and the burning spirit running down openings in the deck started numerous fires below. Bomb-splinters which penetrated steam pipes filled the engine-room with scalding steam.

Although half the men there were wounded, superhuman efforts were made to quench the fires and suppress the escaping steam. These men, imprisoned in a flaming inferno, fought with selfless valor to save their ship—and succeeded. Dragging the dead aside, they rigged and manned the fire-fighting apparatus, and, while the great ship rocked with the titanic concussion of explosions, they remained at their posts in the face of what appeared certain death. As the electric generating system was disabled and cables cut, all lights went out, and the heroic fire-fighters worked by the light of the flames. To add to the hell between decks, bombs bursting below the water-line buckled plating and let in torrents of sea-water which flooded the holds.

During action collision-mats were dragged over the hole by men struggling up to their waists in water. Above the crash of gunfire and bursting bombs outside the men could hear from loud-speakers throughout the ship the calm and measured words of the chaplain, who was describing the battle. He stood on the exposed bridge with a microphone to his lips all that day, telling the men below what was happening. For the first time in naval war-fare the engine-room staff were given a minute-to-minute account of what was happening outside. The heroic chaplain was afterwards awarded the Distinguished Service Order.

At four in the afternoon another wave of dive-bombers attacked, and it was then that a direct hit on an octuple pom-pom killed the entire crew, blowing the bodies overboard. Immediately afterwards a large bomb penetrated the overhanging flight-deck at the bows, ripping up the thick steel deck as though it were a tin can, leaving a vast hole with edges curling up like the petals of some fabulous flower. The design of aircraft-carriers permits of little protection to the gun-crews, but for six hours the heroic gunners remained at their stations. Though blackened by smoke and deaf from concussion, they fought back, firing from their high-angle A.A. guns thousands of rounds of 4.5 shell and pom-pom ammunition. A direct hit on a pom-pom station drove the body of one of the gunners through the deck. The enemy dived to the level of the flight-deck and, sweeping along the full length of the ship in the face of terrific fire, machine-gunned the pom-pom stations, killing many of the crews.

Observers on other ships, appalled at the terrible battering *Illustrious* was getting, abandoned hope for her. Aircraft-carriers, without the armored decks of battleships, are not built to withstand direct vertical hits, but *Illustrious* had received three such hits and still floated. She had also sustained several of those near-misses which, bursting in the water alongside, put a pressure on the hull that buckles the heaviest plating, and hurls jagged fragments of steel into the ship. Over a thousand such splinters, some making holes big enough for a man to crawl into, pierced the carrier's sides, cutting and ripping through electric cables, voice pipes, and steam and water pipes, and killing members of the crew. A direct hit on the stern had put the steering-gear out, and for the rest of the action she steered with her engines—that is to say, by the alternate use of her propellers. At times the 750-foot hull was completely hidden in clouds of smoke and fountains of spray. A photograph taken from the deck of a cruiser less than a mile away at the moment she received a direct hit shows nothing but a mushrooming cloud of smoke billowing darkly over the sea.

On board *Illustrious* the undaunted defenders of their ship were still manning the guns, still fighting the fires and the inrush of water below, removing the dead and attending to the wounded. The hospital deep in the interior of the ship was crowded with wounded men, and the surgeon and his assistants were working without rest in the sickening atmosphere of ether and cordite fumes. Wounded men lay on the decks in rows waiting their turn for emergency operations. Above on the 'island'— the bridge and control-tower—Captain Boyd and his officers remained directing the ship. Many missed death by the narrowest margin of chance, but many lost their lives. The heavy bronze ship's bell was perforated and ripped by shell fragments, till it resembled rat-eaten cheese, and the bride-island plating was holed in a hundred places. A bomb fragment weighing ten pounds pierced the control-tower, missing seven men stationed there. Though the gallant ship seemed to be taking all the punishment, she was making the enemy pay heavily for it. Her gunners are believed to have shot down nearly fifty of the attacking bombers, and at least one Stuka was blown to pieces by the upward blast of the bomb it had just dropped on the flight-deck of the carrier. The fight of *Illustrious*, as bloody and brave as any in the history of the British Navy, can be compared to the fight of Sir Richard Grenville's *Revenge.*

At half-past five, in the fading light, the enemy returned to make his last attack. About thirty-five Stukas roared down one after another to within a hundred feet before leveling off to drop their bombs, but so fierce was the anti-aircraft fire from *Illustrious* and other ships that, the enemy's aim being persistently obstructed, the bombs fell wide and the battered ship escaped further damage. But she had had enough. In the savage all-day bombardments she had absorbed more punishment, still floating, than any ship in the war to that date. Her flight-deck was torn up by four great jagged craters; her hangar-deck was burned out and all her planes destroyed; her steering-gear was disabled and her engine-room in chaos. Her funnel and bridge-island superstructure were perforated with a hundred holes; searchlights, rail stanchions, steam pipes, Carley floats, ladders, and all the complicated mass of gear belonging to the superstructure were twisted and bent into a ghastly tangle of scrap steel. When the roll was called her casualties were found to be 14 officers and 107 men killed and over 400 wounded.

During the attack the convoy had scattered, though some of the escorting warships had remained with *Illustrious* and had not escaped damage. Although the enemy had failed to achieve their main purpose—to sink the carrier—they had put her out of action for months, and so damaged the 9000-ton cruiser *Southampton* that she became a total loss. Heroic efforts were made to save her, on fire and out of control, but after hours of titanic effort the survivors of her crew were taken off and she was sunk by British forces. Most of the crew were saved.

Illustrious, though still afloat, was too badly hurt to continue at sea, and her captain decided to make under cover of darkness for the refuge of Malta, about 150 miles away. This naval base, close to enemy territory and subject to frequent bombing, was not an ideal sanctuary for the battered ship. Alexandria would have been far preferable, but *Illustrious* was in no condition to withstand the 1000-mile voyage, and so Malta was the inevitable choice, though the enemy was bound to find her there and make further attacks. The crippled ship, escorted by screening destroyers, limped into Valetta naval harbor the next morning.

At Valetta were well-equipped machine shops, heavy cranes, and everything necessary to carry out extensive repairs to the damaged carrier, but the enemy had no intention of permitting their victim to recover, and after a search of the Sicilian Channel they found her in the naval dock. Her dead and wounded had already been taken ashore, and scores of mechanics had invaded the ship to begin temporary repairs. Towering over her swung the giant crane ready to lift out damaged machinery and torn plating. The work had already begun when the first enemy planes, flying at a great height, came over. The sound of air-raid sirens had scarcely died away when the first bombs fell. As usual in enemy raids on ports and dockyards, most of the bombs fell on the town, but some fell on the dockyard, one stick blowing up a row of warehouses and workshops close to *Illustrious*. Towering clouds of dark smoke rolled up from the town, and falling fragments of A.A. shells kicked up spurts of water on the sunlit harbor. The bombers, coming over in waves, roared across like angry hornets, twisting and climbing to avoid the A.A. fire from the harbor defences. The enemy's aim was, under the circumstances, very good. Within the space of ten minutes bombs had hit the dock sheds, the dock, and the ship herself. The bomb that fell on the quay did some superficial damage to the ship from flying fragments, but a moment later a direct hit down the rear elevator hatch rocked the vast hull as in an earthquake, and caused further destruction to the interior of the already wrecked 'tween decks.

After the enemy had gone and the new dead and wounded were removed it seemed as though *Illustrious* was damaged beyond hope of repair. The German pilots, seeing the direct hit, must have thought so, but with Teutonic thoroughness they came again and again. In two weeks *Illustrious* was attacked four times as she lay alongside the dock at Valetta. The enemy caused wanton destruction in the town and considerable damage on the dock, but they failed to destroy *Illustrious*. They came over and took photographs, and when their expert annotators studied the results they had to admit that the ship was still upright, though she was certainly full of water and resting on the harbor bed. She could not conceivably be of any further use to the British Navy. Meanwhile down in the battered interior of the ship the engine-room staff, ignoring the falling bombs, had struggled night and day to carry out temporary repairs. New sections were put in broken steam pipes, electric cables were spliced, the smashed steering-gear repaired and steel plates riveted over the holes in the hull. Thus patched up, and with steam again in her boilers, she slipped out of the harbor under cover of night and put to sea under her own power on a course for Alexandria. It was the Navy's only hope of saving the ship, but a hard choice, for the 1000-mile voyage for a crippled ship crawling along at half-speed in waters infested with enemy submarines was not a comforting alternative. But if *Illustrious* could get to the Egyptian base she would be comparatively safe, as it was too far from Axis airfields to be in any danger from heavy air raids.

Steaming eastward with an escorting destroyer screen, the wounded giant slowly crawled towards the sanctuary. She had got away from Malta in such secrecy that even the people of Valetta were surprised when they woke up and found her gone. So, too, was the enemy when one of his reconnaissance planes discovered the empty dock. When photographs disclosed that *Illustrious* had not sunk but had actually departed the Luftwaffe was ordered to find and destroy her. She could not have got far away in her crippled condition, nor were the enemy long in finding her. But she was well protected by escorts, and now, some hundreds of miles from Malta, she was slowly drawing out of effective bombing range. The enemy attacked her, but without the ferocious persistence of that dreadful day when they all but put an end to her career, and as she drew farther away from the land the attacks ceased, and she was permitted to reach Alexandria without any damage.

At once the dockyard repair gangs took her over and began further temporary repairs. Captain Boyd, who had brought *Illustrious* through her bloody ordeal, was promoted to the rank of Rear-Admiral, and he was succeeded in command by Captain G. Seymour Tuck, late executive officer of the ship. Meanwhile the British government, gratefully taking advantage of an agreement with the United States permitting ships of the Royal Navy to be repaired in American yards, was in touch with Washington about getting the damaged carrier repaired in a United States navy yard. While temporary repairs to her were being done at Alexandria her captain received orders to take her to Norfolk, Virginia, as soon as she was ready to put to sea. The route was, of course, a secret, as also was her departure from Alexandria. With her flight-deck patched up, and a few planes for self-defense, she slipped out of the Egyptian port one morning in the early spring bound on her long and perilous voyage. Steaming at reduced speed, she turned east for Suez and the Red Sea, since the shorter voyage westward through the whole length of the Mediterranean would have been suicidal in the ship's crippled condition. Through the Straits of Bab-el-Mandeb (the Arab "Gate of Tears") *Illustrious* turned eastward to Cape Guardafui and thence south along the coast of Somaliland and Portuguese East Africa to Capetown. From there she limped up the South Atlantic to her destination, the great United States navy yard at Norfolk, Virginia, where she arrived in the middle of May 1941, four months after the bloody battle in the Sicilian Straits.

At Portsmouth navy yard American workmen began stripping out the damaged machinery and plating while her crew, with well-earned shore leave, fraternized with the hospitable people of Norfolk. The Americans gave them a wholehearted welcome. Three months after the arrival of the ship at Norfolk Captain Tuck, who had received the D.S.O. for his part in the battle, was promoted to a higher command, and Captain Lord Louis Mountbatten, who had commanded the torpedoed destroyer *Kelly*, took over the rebuilt carrier in a formal navy ceremony on the flight-deck. In dazzling sunlight and in white tropical duck the surviving officers and crew watched Captain Tuck hand over his command to their new commander, the tall and handsome cousin of the King. The deafening clamor of riveting hammers and all the accompanying noises of the shipyard were stilled while the brief ceremony was carried out, and when this was over the work on the ship proceeded, for there was no time to lose. With the Royal Navy spread dangerously thin over the Seven Seas every ship was needed, and before the winter came *Illustrious* was at sea again and as good as new. The enemy had failed in his sworn resolve to sink the hated ship which was mainly responsible for the Italian disaster at Taranto.

Students of modern naval warfare have read many significant lessons in the epic fight of *Illustrious*. The ship had taken several direct hits from the heaviest bombs, but could she have survived a torpedo? The fate of *Ark Royal, Prince of Wales,* and *Repulse* seems to suggest that she could not have done so. The two latter ships with an extra thick armor belt had been sunk by the smaller 18-inch torpedoes that planes carry, not the 21-inch size carried in ships and submarines. The two battleships, moreover, were much more heavily armored than *Illustrious,* though this did not save them. The most important lesson seemed to be that torpedo- and bomb-carrying aircraft in the hands of skilled and daring pilots will always be a grave menace to even the heaviest surface craft. So far *Illustrious* had survived, but would she be so lucky against a torpedo? She had survived as much through the undying heroism of the British sailors who manned her as by the sturdiness of her construction. No ship or crew in the war had taken such fearful punishment and escaped. The experience of *Illustrious* makes grim reading, but it stirs the pulse of all those who belong to the same race as these men, for what is a man worth without courage? And these bluejackets of *Illustrious* had courage of the highest order. But courage alone could never win a total war, and the courage of those men who set out in motor torpedo-boats to try to sink the big German warships after their escape from Brest did not stop the enemy. It only proved that courage without intelligent planning is needless and tragic sacrifice.

CHAPTER III

The Remarkable Capture of a U-Boat

THE ADMIRALTY had made it a rule not to announce particular sinkings of U-boats [1] in order to avoid giving away information that might be helpful to the enemy. It had been found from the experience of the last war that when the enemy was kept in ignorance of how and where his submarines had been destroyed he was denied valuable information. Also it was believed that the mystery surrounding the loss of U-boats had a harmful effect on the morale of other enemy U-boat crews. Whether in practice this was so or not, the Admiralty kept to its policy of not announcing definite U-boat losses—except where the circumstances were of such an unusual or remarkable character that the facts were, shall we say, too good to keep.

Then the Lords of the Admiralty, or the Censors, became human and gave the news-hungry public the story. Such a story was the capture of a U-boat and her crew in the North Atlantic in September 1941. Some U-boats had been captured intact by surface craft, notably an Italian submarine in the Mediterranean earlier in the year, but none in the history of submarine warfare had been taken in such a remarkable fashion as the U-boat in question. The honors for the capture must primarily go to a Coastal Command plane, but the Navy had a share in the

[1] Unterseebooten.

exploit, and we are therefore justified by this, if by no other reason, in including the story here.

When the Germans commenced their rearmament programme the shipyards at Kiel, Hamburg, and Bremen began building a large number of submarines, ranging in size from small coastal boats of 250 tons to big long-range ocean-going 1000-ton mine-laying craft. The boats of the Nazi submarine navy were numbered from one onward, and U1, a small 250-ton boat, was completed by the Deutsche Werke at Kiel in 1935. The first 500-ton U-boat, U27, was launched in the following year. It was an improved boat of this class which was cruising at periscope-depth in the North Atlantic, in the first week of September 1941, when its long, slender shape was spotted by the pilot of an American-built Lockheed Hudson of the Coastal Command. In clear water a submarine can be seen when several fathoms below the surface, generally as a long, cigar-shaped mass, darker than the water. If the surface of the sea is not too rough a wake of escaping air bubbles also is visible. Closer observation will reveal the 'feather' of white water caused by the moving periscope-tube.

The American-built Lockheed Hudson that discovered the U-boat was in command of Acting Squadron Leader J. H. Thompson, a forty-three-year-old native of Hull. His second pilot and navigator was Flying Officer W. J. O. Coleman, of Berkhamsted, Hertfordshire. The rear gunner had in peacetime been an agricultural student at Oxford. The wireless operator was a twenty-one-year-old native of London.

The Hudson was on routine patrol out on the Atlantic in the area known in the Navy as the Western Approaches —a significant descriptive name in war-time—when the navigator caught sight of something about 1200 yards away—something every Coastal Command flyer would give a month's pay to see. He gave a sudden shout and pointed excitedly below.

The submarine's periscope, an imperfect instrument considering its limited field of vision, though well adapted for conning the surface of the sea, was not constructed to survey lurking dangers above, and the first warning the Nazi commander, sitting at the eyepiece of his periscope, had of the peril was the under-water rumble of an exploding bomb and the violent shuddering of the boat. The Hudson swooping down on the unwary craft had dropped its bombs so close that the U-boat was temporarily disabled. In the darkness, for all lights had been put out in the boat's interior, commands were shouted to surface at once. The plating had been started, water was squirting through strained rivet-holes, and the boat could not possibly stand the tremendous pressure put on her if she dived to escape. The only hope was to surface the boat and take a chance with the unseen attacker. The enemy believed that they had been depth-bombed by a surface craft of the hated Englanders, but they were soon to be disillusioned of this natural assumption.

Banking steeply in tight turns a few hundred feet overhead to keep the U-boat in sight, the Hudson roared like a gargantuan eagle hovering over its prey. The crew peering down from the Perspex windows saw the long steel shape break surface. Torrents of white water cascaded off her narrow deck and through the rows of drain scuppers in her superstructure as the sinister snout of the boat slowly rose above the surface of the sea. A full gale was blowing, and sheets of spray and flying spume dashed over the conning-tower, half burying the craft as she rolled sluggishly in the heaving seas. The ocean was covered with white caps, and rain-squalls so reduced the visibility that had the crew lost sight of the U-boat it is doubtful if they would have found her again. Knowing the character of the enemy, Squadron Leader Thompson dived towards the boat with all forward guns blazing.

The steel-nosed bullets spattered conning-tower and superstructure with a devil's tattoo that must have sounded like the call of doom to those men inside the U-boat. Anxious to escape from their steel tomb, they threw open the conning-tower upper-hatch cover and began tumbling out on to the tiny bridge and the narrow fore-deck. When the gunners of the Hudson saw the Germans piling out of the conning-tower they naturally assumed that the enemy was going to man the guns. On deck forward of the conning-tower was one 3.5 gun and one 1-pounder anti-aircraft rifle, the latter a handy weapon for bringing down the Hudson. In total war, where no quarter is given or expected, there is no room for old-fashioned chivalry, and the natural instincts of the British flyers, labeled soft and decadent by their enemies, were steeled to shoot these fellow-humans before they reached their guns. The bright orange sparks of tracer bullets splashed across the conning-tower plating leaving a line of neatly drilled holes, and cutting grooves in the wooden deck planking on the superstructure. The result was that the Nazis who had descended to the deck now scrambled back on to the conning-tower to find shelter inside the boat, only to meet others who were frantically scrambling up the ladder to escape. The observers from the plane could see those outside hatless and wearing bright yellow life-saving jackets, struggling frantically to push past the mob fighting to get out of the conning-tower hatch.

The Hudson swept four times over the length of the boat a hundred feet above it, and was banking round to make a fifth attack when the wireless operator shouted through the intercommunicating telephone, "They're waving a white flag"—a euphemism in fact, for they were actually waving a white shirt. Then, as though to make sure, they held up a white-painted board. This was the first time a submarine had ever surrendered to an airplane. It raised a curious problem for Squadron Leader Thompson, since a Hudson is a land plane and could not descend on the water to take possession of the prize. It flies at a comparatively high speed—not therefore an economical speed, and its capacity to remain in the air was strictly limited. It could only for a few hours at most remain with its prize, and unless relief came the captive U-boat might get away. A strange situation. The enemy, for fear of further machine-gunning, had abjectly surrendered, but the victor was unable to arrest him. It was as though a swimmer were held captive by an eagle.

Down below the long gray rust-stained hull of the U-boat wallowed in the trough of the seas which continually broke over her in sheets of green water and drenching spray. She lay slightly down by the bows as though her forward tanks were partly flooded. The tiny railed bridge abaft the conning-tower was packed with men, their white faces staring up at the huge twin-engined plane circling no more than fifty feet overhead. Up there in the Hudson the radio operator at his transmitting instrument was busy sending out calls to all aircraft and naval ships in the vicinity. The fuel gauge indicated about four hours' more flying-time. The young radio operator sat at his key, the headphones to his ears, while he tapped out the news of the capture and the urgent request for assistance. Coastal Command bases and ships at sea picked up the astonishing news that a Hudson in latitude and longitude so-and-so had captured a U-boat, and urgently needed surface ships to take over. But the nearest armed

A Catalina patrols over the U-boat captured by a Hudson aircraft, while a British ship stands by, unable to lower boats in the heavy seas. *British Official Photograph.*

A Coastal Command Whitley destroys a U-boat in the Bay of Biscay. Bombs explode; the U-boat is forced to the surface; oil spreads over the spot.
British Official Photograph.

vessel was over a hundred miles away, and the first craft to arrive was a Catalina flying-boat of Coastal Command which appeared about three and a half hours after the radio message was sent out. All that time the Hudson flew in tight circles over the U-boat, never getting far away for fear of losing sight of her in the rainstorms. The weather grew worse as the day wore on, with lowered visibility, which caused the air crew much anxiety lest they should lose the prize. Squadron Leader Thompson, after returning to base, complained of a severe stiff neck, so bad that he could not turn his head, a condition resulting from his long watching of the U-boat as the Hudson circled over it.

The Catalina, being a flying-boat, could, if necessary, alight on the sea, and as it had a much longer cruising range than the Hudson it was the ideal craft to keep watch on the enemy until surface ships could arrive. Squadron Leader Thompson waved to the Catalina's pilot and left the latter to take over. As the Hudson flew toward its distant base other planes were met and passed flying toward the position of the captured U-boat. All air and surface craft had been diverted to help, and dozens of planes and ships were rushing from every quarter of the compass to the focal point. The planes, however, were not needed, since the Catalina was fully capable of handling the situation until the arrival of warships which were hourly drawing nearer. But to the flying men accustomed to speeds of over two hundred miles an hour the twenty-five or thirty knots of the surface craft was maddeningly slow. They were all a long way off, and the nearest ship could not arrive much before dark. Once it got dark it would be impossible to keep contact with the U-boat. Hour after hour the giant flying-boat thundered overhead, its guns trained on the U-boat for any sign of treachery. But the unlucky crew, shivering in their wet clothes, huddled together on the little platform abaft the conning-tower and made no attempt to man their guns. The German creed of scuttling their ships rather than letting them be taken could not in this case be carried out for obvious reasons. To make any attempt to man the U-boat's two guns would have been equally suicidal, so it is clear that the Nazis had no choice but to follow the course they did. A submarine exposed to bombing and machine-gunning is, when on the surface, utterly helpless, since she cannot submerge quickly enough to escape and her deck-gun is not adapted for high-angle anti-aircraft defence.

The Catalina had been flying over the U-boat for nearly ten hours when out of the dusk appeared a destroyer, one of the four-funneled flush-decked ex-American destroyers handed to Britain in exchange for island bases in the Atlantic. Sending up rocket signals, she approached to within a hundred yards of the U-boat, which she flooded with light from her searchlight. It was an eerie scene—a U-boat on the surface brilliantly lit up against the darkness by a destroyer's searchlight while overhead roared the powerful engines of a huge flying-boat.

A full gale was blowing and making it impossible to take off the prisoners and put a prize crew on board. The Catalina which had been keeping guard all day signaled that it was returning to base, but during the night another Catalina arrived to patrol the spot. The night was intensely black, and it became difficult, even impossible at times, to see the side-lights of the U-boat. The searchlight could not safely be used during the night because of the danger of attracting the attention of lurking U-boats or other enemy craft. Sometimes the U-boat's lights would be lost for as long as a quarter of an hour, but they were never permanently lost, and when the chilly rays of dawn spread over the leaden seas the destroyer was seen lying head to the wind a couple of hundred yards from the captured U-boat. Now other ships could be sighted approaching. They had been lying-to all night, waiting for daylight to check their position, only to find themselves sitting practically on the spot. For forty hours more Coastal Command aircraft soared over the captive U-boat, but their work was virtually done. The job was now in the hands of the Navy. As for the pilots of the Hudson who first sighted the U-boat—Squadron Leader Thompson and Flying Officer Coleman—they were both awarded the Distinguished Flying Cross for their valuable services.

From the decks of the ships standing by, the U-boat was frequently hidden in the trough of the giant Atlantic rollers, the seas so rough, indeed, that it was humanly impossible to launch a boat, and it was necessary to wait until the sea had moderated before a boarding party could attempt the short passage. During the long wait captors and captives rolled and pitched in the angry seas. In the broken water the U-boat rolled like a half-submerged log, the unhappy little group of men who were her crew watching their jailers with what feelings in their hearts only those who have been taken prisoner can know. In the afternoon the commander of the destroyer in charge of operations decided to send two officers over in a Carley float, since the sea was still too rough to allow them to bring a lifeboat alongside the prize. A submarine's deck rises vertically from the cylindrical shape of the hull, which makes it impossible for a boat to come close alongside the superstructure. But a Carley float—an oblong frame of 12-inch copper tube with rounded ends and a slatted platform which is submerged when afloat—can, because it is nothing more than a raft, come alongside a shelving surface without the risk involved in attempting the same operation in a boat. The float was paddled across, and a German sailor on the U-boat took the line thrown and made it fast.

The final surrender was almost an anticlimax after the stormy drama of the previous day when the Hudson roared overhead spraying the boat with machine-gun fire. The forty unhappy men, most of them wearing the easily visible orange-colored life-saving jacket, made no attempt to interfere with the two British officers who had come aboard. The two British officers stood among forty hostile men who hated them with a fanatical hatred. The moment was a delicate one, but the U-boat commander received them with frigid politeness and formally surrendered. After a brief examination of the boat the British officer in charge of the boarding party signaled across to the destroyer, and presently a lifeboat was safely got across. It brought over a prize crew from the destroyer and returned with prisoners.

The U-boat bore no distinguishing numbers, but after examination was identified as the U570, a 500-ton boat with one stern and four bow torpedo-tubes. Of a new design, an improvement on the earlier (1936) type, she was found to be 220 feet long and carried a crew of thirty-five men. She was apparently undamaged except for the marks of bullets from the Hudson's machine-guns. Patches of rust all over the superstructure suggested that she had been at sea for some weeks. On the fore-side of the conning-tower were screwed two horseshoes, upside down, but whether they were merely there for luck, or to indicate that the U-boat had sunk two ships, the Nazi seamen refused to say.

Lieutenant George Colvin was put in charge and Warrant Engineer Jordan took over the engine-room. Both were experienced submarine men, and Lieutenant Colvin, a thirty-year-old, red-bearded man hailing from the London suburb of Wimbledon, had formerly been in *Swordfish*, a British submarine which had figured in several notable exploits during the war. Assisted by a small British crew, he began the task of examining the prize thoroughly and found his task enormously interesting.

On general principles, submarines of all navies are alike in design, but the experts found many little differences, little fittings and gadgets that provided them with plenty of entertainment during the journey to base. An examination of the provisions on board disclosed the interesting facts that the Nazi submarine crews were well looked after, and also that the Nazi larder and granary were the whole of conquered and starving Europe. Norwegian tinned delicacies, Danish eggs, hams, and butter, and bottles of Spanish wine were found in the provision lockers among other stores.

On Friday, October 3, 1941, she entered port with the British ensign flying from the conning-tower and her crew, in white sweaters and duffle coats, lined up on the narrow deck. Lieutenant Colvin reported that the prize had behaved very badly, and his men had had scarcely any rest during the passage. After a short and stormy life the U570 would fight no more. And if her end had been an inglorious one she had at least earned a unique position in the story of naval warfare as being the only submarine that had as it were been 'taken alive' by an airplane. But without the Navy the captive could not have been held, and the honors of the capture must go equally to the two services.

CHAPTER IV

The Little Ships

IN THE First World War it was found that the trawlers of the fishing fleets made the best minesweepers because they are designed to steam slowly ahead in a rough sea, towing from a powerful winch in the stern a heavy trawl sweep, and hundreds of those sturdy little vessels were taken from their peace-time work to sweep up mines laid by the enemy in British sea lanes. The Admiralty augmented this fleet with trawlers specially built for the Navy and henceforth known as fleet sweepers. Vessels of 1100 tons called "Flower" class escorts were also built in large numbers, but at the beginning of the Second World War only three of these, *Lupin, Rosemary,* and *Foxglove,* were in commission.

When the war started in 1939 a new fleet of specially designed sweepers and patrol ships was commissioned. These were of the familiar trawler lines—high, flaring bow, engines and boiler well aft. Their average displacement was 850 tons and their crew eighty men. They worked in pairs, towing the heavy sweep between them. Several hundred of these ships were put into service, and all, of course, were armed—a four-inch gun in the bows and machine-guns aft. Some were equipped for mine-laying, and most of them carried depth-bombs. *Lady Shirley,* whose successful encounter with a U-boat is described in this chapter, was a typical armed trawler.

The work of minesweepers and trawlers is rightly said to be the most dangerous work in the Navy. The grim truth of this is shown by a few simple figures. In the first seventeen months of war 103 armed trawlers and drifters were lost. Twenty of these were sunk during the evacuation of the British Expeditionary Force at Dunkirk. Mines destroyed forty of these little ships, and twenty-eight were sunk by aerial attack. Thirty-three more were lost from various causes. In short, the percentage of losses in the trawler fleet was far higher than among any other type of naval craft. The figures show that mines constituted the greatest danger.

Armed trawlers are described variously, according to their functions, as minesweepers, fleet sweepers, patrol trawlers, antisubmarine trawlers. The fleet sweepers proceed ahead of the fleet, or individual ships, sweeping a channel clear of mines or destroying those previously brought to the surface by trawlers. British minefields were laid off the East Coast from the North Foreland to the Orkneys, across the western approach to the English Channel, and across the entrance to the Irish Channel. Minefields were also laid from the north of Scotland to Iceland. Probably the longest minefield that had ever been laid was that off the East Coast of Britain.

Mines are placed so that they remain below the surface where they cannot be seen and are held down by a heavy weight. They may be likened to a toy balloon held down by its string. The chain of wire rope holding the mine is usually adjusted so that the mine swings to its anchorage eighteen feet below the surface; thus shallow-draught vessels can pass harmlessly over a minefield.

The minesweepers, which always work together in pairs, have attached to each side of the bows a strong wire cable towing the device known as the Oropesa float and named after H.M. trawler *Oropesa*, which first used it. This float, which is shaped something like a torpedo, has on its sides planes which force it out away from the vessel's side and so hold the sweep wires out to form a huge arrowhead or a letter V as the trawler moves through the minefield. The wire catches the mooring of the mine, and as it slides along the wire it is met by a knife-edged cutter, which severs the mooring and allows the released mine to bob to the surface, where it is destroyed by fleet sweepers. Mines are usually destroyed by rifle-fire, and it is said to take, on an average, over a hundred rounds to destroy each mine. The trawlers steam along *en échelon,* or in overlapping formation, to ensure that the sweep area is covered. Sweeps are never carried out at night or in a fog, since it would be at these times impossible to see any mines brought up. Nor are sweeps carried out at low tide, as the mines are then too close to the surface even for a light-draught trawler to pass safely over them. When the Germans dropped (by airplane in the Thames Estuary) the first magnetic mines they were believed to be the threatened secret weapon, but, whether they were or not, Lieutenant-Commander Ouvry, R.N., at the risk of his own life opened one and discovered its secret, and within a few weeks the antidote was found for this new peril. This was the famous degaussing apparatus, which 'neutralizes' the magnetic influence of a ship's hull on the mine and so renders it harmless. Later the enemy brought out the acoustic mine, a more difficult problem, for it was set off by the sound waves of a ship's propeller acting on a delicately adjusted microphone within the mine.

If the mine is the worst hazard for minesweepers the next greatest menace is the bombing airplane, as the figures for trawler losses show. In the first seventeen months of war just over 40 per cent of the losses were due to mines and 28 per cent to attacks from the air. The third risk was from E-boats, the large torpedo-carrying speed-boats, called *Schnellbooten* (*schnell*, quick, fast) by the Germans. They had an approximate speed of fifty miles an hour, a range of 600 miles, carried two torpedo-tubes (one on either side of the bows), and were armed with automatic 1.5-inch guns. Strangely enough, the least risk seemed to have been the submarine. Only one trawler out of the first hundred lost was sent to the bottom by a U-boat. On the other hand, more than one enemy submarine was destroyed by trawlers. Here is a brief account of two submarines, one captured and the other sunk by two British trawlers, *Moonstone* and *Lady Shirley*.

In the middle of January 1942 the Admiralty announced with regret that the 470-ton naval trawler *Lady Shirley* was overdue and must be considered lost. It was presumed that her skipper, Lieutenant-Commander A. H. Callaway, of the Royal Australian Volunteer Reserve, and the crew of thirty officers and men were lost with her. The loss of the trawler would scarcely have attracted special notice had it not been that *Lady Shirley* had in the previous autumn figured in a remarkable adventure, an adventure that had earned Lieutenant-Commander Callaway the D.S.O. and other awards for fourteen of his crew. Only once before had a trawler beaten a submarine, and that was just after Italy entered the war. The Italian 880-ton submarine *Galileo Galilei* was unlucky enough to encounter H.M. trawler *Moonstone* in the Gulf of Aden. *Moonstone*, one of the class of Gem trawlers, was 152 feet long, with a displacement of 615 tons. She was armed with one 4-inch gun, and it is interesting to compare this with the armament of the submarine. The submarine—one of the *Archimede* class, 231 feet long, with a crew of fifty, and armed with two 3.9-inch guns and eight 21-inch torpedo-tubes—although larger and better armed than the trawler, was beaten in a gun duel with the latter after being brought to the surface with depth-charges. In the ensuing fight the submarine's commander and some of his officers were killed. As the boat was too big for the trawler to handle after she had surrendered, a destroyer took her in tow and brought her into Aden.

Lady Shirley—one of a hundred such craft, a typical naval trawler with one 4-inch gun on a raised circular platform on the fo'c'sle, a pair of machine-guns aft, and a good supply of depth-charges which could be released on a special chute over the stern—was on patrol in the Western Mediterranean when she sighted a mile away the periscope of a U-boat. Lieutenant-Commander Callaway, one of Australia's "Wavy Navy" [1] officers, a brawny, dark-bearded sailor from Sydney, at once ordered the helmsman to alter course to ram the enemy. But evidently the U-boat captain had seen the trawler, for he immediately crash-dived, and when *Lady Shirley* rushed over the spot he was several fathoms deep. In the stern of the trawler a little group of men standing by the depth-charges lost no time in releasing these deadly cylinders, which slid down the guide rails and exploded one after another, throwing up hundred-foot fountains of water. Deep below the surface the terrific concussions rocked the U-boat, putting out all lights and damaging the delicate machinery. This boat, a newly built craft, out on her second operational cruise, was the U111, built at Bremen, an ocean-going submarine of 740 tons, and 244 feet long. She carried a crew of between forty and fifty, and was armed with one 4.1-inch gun, two 1-pounder A.A. guns, and six 21-inch torpedo-tubes. Her commander, thirty-four-year-old

---

[1] So called from the wavy stripe around the cuffs and on shoulder straps of R.N.V.R. officers.

Wilhelm Kleinschmidt, had a guest on board, Commander Hans Joachim Keinecke, who had come along to get submarine experience before taking over a U-boat himself. Thus the humble little trawler was responsible for the loss to Germany of two U-boat commanders.

In the center of the area of swirling foam caused by the depth-charges the conning-tower of the submarine broke surface. To the crew of the 470-ton trawler she looked enormous, and Commander Callaway knew he must act promptly and with the utmost resolution before it was too late. Even while the sea was pouring off the conning-tower the U-boat's crew were scrambling out of the upper hatch to get at the deck-gun and smash their British opponent. Callaway, fully awake to the danger, swung his tubby little vessel round to bring his 4-inch gun and two machine-guns to bear on the enemy. The huge submarine lay on the surface a perfect target less than a mile away, a Goliath to the trawler's David. *Lady Shirley's* machine-guns opened fire before the Germans could get to their own guns, and the U-boat's men could be seen falling under the vicious stream of steel. Her gunners tried to get to their deck-gun, but they never reached it. At the trawler's machine-guns were Seamen Windsor and Halcrow, and the gun-layer at the 4-inch gun was Seaman L. W. Pizzey. Depressing the gun to bear on the target, he began hitting the U-boat above and below the water-line. The shells could quite clearly be seen boring through the light plating of the U-boat. Pizzey fired his gun as fast as it could be reloaded, and the two machine-gunners aft swung their guns slowly round in wide arcs, spraying the enemy with a deadly rain of bullets. Though doomed, he fought back bravely. Two of the German seamen managed, before they were hit, to reach their machine-guns and direct one burst of rapid fire at the crew of *Lady Shir-*

ley's 4-inch gun. Seaman Pizzey was killed instantly, but his place was taken by the second-in-command, Sub-Lieutenant F. E. French, R.N.R., who, with calm disregard of the enemy machine-guns, continued to fire and score repeated hits with the 4-inch gun. Though the British seemed to be masters of the situation, it was by no means an easy victory, for the enemy continued to fire their machine-guns until the U-boat sank. They managed to wound the trawler's two machine-gunners, Seamen Windsor and Halcrow, though this tough pair continued to fire their guns like men possessed. This was a battle in which neither side expected or would give any quarter; a fight to a finish between the wolf and the fox. And the fox triumphed because he had been more agile than the wolf. The little trawler had, thanks to a finely trained crew and an alert commander, got in the first blow, had taken and held the offensive. She had been quick enough to prevent the U-boat from escaping by dropping depth-charges, and quick enough to get in the first deadly shots when the enemy appeared on the surface. She had, in fact, prevented him from getting in a single telling blow, and her triumph was due entirely to the speedy team work of her crew. The intensive fire was too much for the Germans, and after a few minutes they could be seen putting their hands up in token of surrender. Their boat was already sinking and lay ominously down by the stern, her four bow caps showing above the sea.

A boat of *Lady Shirley* was lowered to pick up the survivors, and forty-four men were thus rescued. Some of them, far from being grateful for the humane treatment they received on board the trawler, were truculent and openly contemptuous of their British captors, but all of them, without exception, were frankly dumbfounded that a trawler 177 feet long had outfought a submarine 250 feet long and with nearly twice her opponent's tonnage.

The forty-four prisoners were taken to Gibraltar and handed over to the naval authorities. Lieutenant-Commander Callaway was awarded the D.S.O. for bringing about the destruction of the U-boat. Two of his officers were awarded the D.S.C., and one rating received the Conspicuous Gallantry Medal and six others the Distinguished Service Medal.

Among the little ships that faced the hazards of war were the minesweepers' civilian sisters of the fishing fleets —the trawlers which sometimes brought up mines with their catch of fish. The men of the East Coast fishing fleets were almost daily machine-gunned and bombed by Nazi planes; but the fishing went on, for the country had to be fed, and if the price of fish soared who can say the fishermen did not earn their money, and who among the complaining landsmen would have cared to step into the fisherman's place?

The least spectacular of all the sea hazards was the work of the Trinity House lightship-keepers and relief men. Lightships are for the safety of all who go to sea, friend and foe alike, and in all past naval wars lighthouse- and lightship-keepers were left alone. There is a story about Louis XIV of France, who ordered that two English lighthouse-keepers, taken prisoner by a French frigate, should be returned to their own country, since he did not make war on those who served all humanity. But such scruples were regarded by young Nazi air pilots as a sign of weakness and decadence, and from the beginning of the war they shocked the so-called decadent democracies by attacking lightships. After several famous British lightships off the East Coast were savagely attacked, the Admiralty ordered all manned lightships to be withdrawn and replaced them with the modern automatic type or with light buoys and other navigational marks which needed no crews.

During the early months of 1940, before the manned lightships were removed, there were almost daily attacks on these vessels, and a number of men were killed. Early in January the Trinity House tender *Reculver* was on the way out with reliefs for various East Coast lightships when she was attacked by a Heinkel bomber. To make her identity clear, which by International Law should have made her immune from attack, the Trinity House ensign, five feet by eight, was flying from the mast-head. Besides her own crew she was carrying about thirty men ready to relieve lightship crews who after a month's spell of duty would be taken ashore. The Heinkel came down almost to sea-level and sprayed *Reculver* with machine-gun fire. It then returned and dropped bombs on the helpless vessel, smashing all but one of the boats, and putting the engines and steering-gear out of action. Thirty-two men were wounded, but by a freak of chance only one man was killed.

Two days after this attack a Heinkel bombed another lightship. The next day lightship No. 85 was attacked from the air. A fishing ketch was hauling in her nets close by, and after the plane had sprayed the lightship with machine-gun bullets it flew over the ketch and dropped several bombs, with the result that this boat was blown to pieces and all her crew were killed. Then, on January 29, came the attack on the famous East Dudgeon lightship which indirectly caused the death of seven of the crew of eight. At 9.30 A.M. those on watch saw a large plane, which was identified as German, approaching. It passed over as though examining the lightship to see if she was armed, but no bombs were dropped. Turning back, it swooped down to eighty feet and flew over the vessel, giving it a three-second burst of machine-gun fire. At this the lightship crew, who had stood staring up at the enemy plane, ducked for cover. As the lightship was not armed she made a sitting target which the enemy could destroy at his leisure and at no risk whatever to himself. While the lightship crew crouched behind bulkheads waiting for another machine-gun attack there was a shattering explosion which, however, did no harm to the men or the ship. The plane had dropped a bomb in the sea about forty yards off the starboard beam. This trial shot fell wide, but the plane turned and flew over again, dropping three more bombs, which fell much closer and shook the vessel like a rat. Persisting in his intentions, the enemy returned twice more and only desisted when all his bombs were gone. He dropped nine bombs in all, and the ninth made a direct hit on the lightship. The concussion lifted the heavy ship out of the water, and she fell back with a force that sprung her plates and left her in a sinking condition. The bomb had hit the port lifeboat, blowing the bulwarks away and snapping off the mizen-mast like a straw. It set off several calcium flares whose smoke completely hid the vessel from the enemy until the wind blew the concealing vapors away.

When the bomb hit the lightship the crew of eight ran forward, crouching behind the bulwarks for what shelter they could get, but as the ship was settling beneath them they had no choice, in spite of the very steep seas that were running, but to attempt to launch the remaining lifeboat. Partly concealed by the drifting smoke from the still-burning calcium flares, they got the boat over and pushed away from the sinking vessel without capsizing. The enemy, satisfied that the lightship was destroyed, flew off, and with this danger over the men in the boat decided to return to their vessel for a keg of water and some provisions, since they could not tell how long they would be adrift. By exceptionally fine seamanship the boat was got alongside, and two men were able to climb aboard without difficulty as the vessel was by this time very low in the water. These men were getting provisions out of the lazarette when the plane returned. However, they were able once more to scramble back into the boat and pull away without being machine-gunned. The German pilot circled over once as though to reassure himself that his work was properly done and then flew off, this time for good.

After three hours in the boat the men saw a trawler in the distance and burned flares to attract her attention, but were not seen because of the mist and rain over the water. It was now early afternoon, and the men judged they must be nearing the coast, but in spite of a keen look-out the visibility was so poor that no signs of land could be seen. After hours of pulling at the heavy oars the men were so exhausted that the skipper decided to drop the anchor and give all hands a rest.

The water here was shallow enough to anchor, but the heavy ground swell raised such a confused sea that hardly had the hook caught the bottom than a wave caught the boat on the beam and rolled her over, spilling the tired men into the sea. Exhausted from rowing, and weighed down by their thick clothing and heavy seaboots, seven of the eight men were drowned, but Saunders, the lightship's fog-signal operator, who was a powerful swimmer, struck out in what he believed the right direction, resolved to die fighting rather than give up without a struggle, forlorn as the hope might be. But his thick, water-soaked clothing quickly hampered his swimming, and he lay on his back to float and so drifted for nearly an hour, he judged. Somewhat rested, he turned over to resume swimming,

Captain and look-out on the bridge of a minesweeper. The look-out has his rifle ready to sink any surfacing mine. *British Combine Photos*.

The sailors on this British minesweeper, drenched by crashing waves, are preparing
a Dan Buoy to mark the swept channels. *British Combine Photos.*

when he felt his feet touch bottom. At this astonishing discovery he stood up, shoulder-high in the water, and stared about him, to see through the mist breakers and sand-dunes a few hundred yards away. And so he returned home, the only survivor of the East Dudgeon lightship.

Another famous lightship to be attacked before the Admiralty replaced these vessels by navigational marks and automatic lights was the Outer Dowsing ship. One morning in March 1940, while it was still dark and the revolving light made a perfect beacon for an enemy, a plane was heard approaching, and a few seconds later a stick of five bombs dropped in the sea astern of the vessel and exploded with a deafening roar without, however, doing more than superficial damage to the lightship. The captain, with great presence of mind, instantly extinguished the light in the big revolving lantern, while the crew took what poor shelter they could. The plane meanwhile returned and, flying just over the mast-tops, dropped four more bombs, but without hitting the vessel. Apparently the enemy had used up all his bombs, for after this he flew away and did not return that day. But the next morning either this or another plane returned at the same time as on the previous day and dropped seven bombs, again without hitting the lightship. It was after this attack that the Admiralty decided to avoid uselessly risking the lives of lightship-keepers by withdrawing the vessels from service, so breaking a tradition that no naval war had ever before interrupted.

CHAPTER V

Submarines and U-Boats

THE SUBMARINE by its very nature must ever remain something of a mystery ship to all but those who serve in her. She lives under the sea, but, like a whale, must come up occasionally to recharge her lungs. Unlike the surface ship, she is designed to strike unseen and slip away undetected. Her work is the most dangerous in the Senior Service, and the ratio of losses in the "Phantom Navy" is far higher than of those among surface ships.

Like the airplane, the modern submarine owed its development to American inventors and engineers. Ironically the submarines in the British Navy are patterned after a type designed by John P. Holland, the Irish-American who found an outlet for his hatred for England in building a submarine which was dubbed the "Fenian Ram," because it was hoped to use it against the British Navy. Holland and Simon Lake, another American, were largely responsible for the development of the submarine which, with various modifications and improvements, is used in modern navies throughout the world.

For the reader with no initial knowledge of how submarines work it may not be out of place here to describe briefly their construction and working. They range in size from the small 250-ton craft carrying a complement of twenty-three up to the giant *Surcouf* [1] of the French Navy,

[1] This comparison omits the midget two-man submarines used by the Japanese at Pearl Harbor against the American fleet.

with a displacement of nearly 3000 tons and a complement of 150. The streamlined 'cigar' shape of the submarine is divided into three sections, the forward section carrying the torpedoes, which are discharged by the agency of compressed air into the sea through brass cylinders (torpedo-tubes) arranged in a set of four or six in the nose of the boat. When not in use the tubes are closed by lids called caps, which can be operated from inside the boat. The middle section is the control compartment. Here are the eyepieces of the periscopes, the electric switches and depth gauges, control levers and wheels for operating the boat. Here also are the Kingston valves for letting water in or out of the trimming tanks, the hydroplane and rudder controls, and the speaking-tubes leading to all parts of the boat.

The after section is the engine-room, and here are the electric motors for running when submerged, and the Diesel (heavy oil) engines, which consume air and can therefore be run only when the boat is on the surface. The Diesel engines also drive the dynamos which charge the huge accumulator batteries and which in turn drive the electric motors when cruising under the sea. The interior of a submarine is a labyrinth of machinery, electric cables, and dial gauges with very little room for the crew; hence the rule that when in port submarine crews live in depot ships—big, commodious vessels with the comforts and conveniences so conspicuously absent in even the largest submarines. The storage batteries, the compressed-air cylinders, and water-ballast (trimming) tanks are situated beneath the steel floor of the torpedo-, control-, and engine-rooms. The boat submerges by letting the sea into the tanks and trimming the horizontal rudders or hydroplanes which are situated at both the bows and the stern of the boat. She rises by driving the water out of her tanks with compressed air and again raising her hydroplanes. The hydroplanes are, of course, effective only when the boat has a forward way on her.

The periscope is simply a long telescopic brass tube with a prism at its upper opening and another at its lower opening (eyepiece) in the control-room. The modern submarine periscope is about twenty feet long, and is fitted with as many as sixteen prisms and lenses. The whole thing can be raised or lowered into itself by telescoping tubes without affecting the height of the eyepiece in the control-room. The prism at the upper 'eye' of the periscope reverses the image and reflects it downward through the various lenses and prisms to the eyepiece. The chief disadvantage of observation by periscope is that its horizontal field of vision is limited to 60 degrees, leaving the observer blind to the other 300 degrees of the horizon, thus rendering him liable to attack from this blind spot. He can, however, rotate the periscope round the horizon, though he can never see more than a field of 60 degrees at one time.

The maximum diving depth of a submarine is governed by the capacity of the hull to withstand the pressure of the sea. This maximum depth is roughly about 300 feet, but such a depth is never attempted, nor is it ever necessary. Before that depth was reached the terrific pressure of the sea outside the hull would probably begin forcing jets of water through rivet-joints and seams in the plating. In the outer shell of a submarine are a number of exhaust and intake openings, all of which can be opened or closed at will by turning the brass wheels of the Kingston valves in the main control station. Before the boat submerges the responsible officers have to make certain that all openings are closed. The Diesel engines exhaust their spent gases through ducts which must be closed before submerging.

All hatches have to be clamped shut, and failure to do this would cost the lives of every one in the boat, since the pressure of water rushing in would prevent any attempt to escape. The British submarine *Thetis* sank on her trials in June 1939 owing to water entering the forward torpedo-room when the rear cap of a torpedo-tube was opened when the bow cap was thought to be closed. All attempts to close the cap against a 21-inch torrent of water at high pressure were futile, and only four men out of over a hundred on board left that submarine alive.

Until shortly before the Second World War it was the Admiralty's policy to give British submarines a letter and a number; thus H29 was the twenty-ninth vessel of the H class. This system was abandoned in favor of the more picturesque one of giving His Majesty's submarines names such as *Swordfish, Ursula, Olympus, Pandora, Thunderbolt, Sealion,* and *Talisman,* to give a few examples. Incidentally, *Thunderbolt* was the name given the unlucky *Thetis* after she had been raised from the sea and repaired. Now that alphabetical letters are no longer used, submarines are grouped into classes according to name—thus the Olympus class with three boats; the Oberon class with two; the Triton class with sixteen boats, and the Sealion class with four.[2] The United States also adopted the policy of naming their submarines—thus *Porpoise, Narwhal, Cachalot, Salmon, Flying Fish, Nautilus, Argonaut.* France, on the other hand, had always given her submarines names instead of numbers—after fish or goddesses of Greek mythology or precious stones—thus: *Narval* (*Narwhal*), *Phoque* (*Seal*), *Méduse* (*Medusa*), *Diane* (*Diana*), *Emeraude* (*Emerald*), *Diamant* (*Diamond*), and *Rubis* (*Ruby*).

The submarine's main offensive weapon is the White-

---

[2] From *Jane's Fighting Ships,* 1940.

head torpedo, invented by an Englishman of that name. It is fired through a tube to project it clear of the boat, but once it is in the sea it is self-propelled. Rather like a miniature submarine, it is divided into three parts—the warhead, containing the explosive charge; the stern section, containing the engine; and the central and largest section, containing the compressed-air reservoir which drives the engine. This engine is a highly complicated mechanism which drives two propellers revolving in opposite directions to counteract the tendency of one propeller to drive the torpedo in circles. Also in the miniature engine-room is the gyroscope which governs the hydrostatic valve, which in turn keeps the torpedo at a predetermined depth. There is also the vertical rudder mechanism to keep the torpedo on its course and the heater device which heats the compressed air to give it higher pressure. To the nose of the torpedo is screwed a small propeller, which by unwinding itself off the percussion-pin while the torpedo is rushing through the water renders it 'alive' and ready to explode on contact. As a protection against torpedoes battleships were formerly fitted with steel nets hanging outboard from heavy booms, but for various reasons—one because the nets were cumbersome and interfered with the ship's speed, and another because a modern torpedo could cut through a steel net—the practice was abandoned.

For every ill there is generally an antidote, and the chief antidote for submarines is the depth-charge, a simple device which is designed to crush the plating of any submarine in the vicinity when the charge explodes. Even if the boat is not immediately destroyed the violence of the explosion will bring her to the surface, forcing her to surrender. The depth-charge, which is a form of submarine mine, is dropped from the stern or catapulted from the side of a ship, which must be traveling fast enough to be safely out of danger when the charge explodes. The principle on which it operates is extremely simple. Inside a steel cylindrical canister about the size of a domestic dustbin is a charge of about 300 pounds of high explosive, which is fired by a 'hydrostatic pistol.' This is actuated by water-pressure when the depth-charge has sunk to the required depth. The firing pistol is adjusted to a predetermined depth before it is dropped overboard.

On operational patrols the life of a submarine crew is uncomfortable and tedious, except, of course, when they go into action. Most of the crew seldom see the light of day during a cruise. The boat, when in enemy waters, remains submerged throughout the daylight hours, coming to the surface only to charge the batteries under cover of darkness. Only men of strong physique and in good health can stand the effects of living in air above atmospheric pressure. Submarine crews, besides being physically fit, must also possess a mental stability that is not easily disturbed by the inevitable strain of close contact with other men under conditions that 'nervy' people could not stand. In the British Navy submarine crews stand watches of two hours on and four hours off, instead of four hours on and eight off in surface ships, as the work is too concentrated, too much of a strain, for the men to be able to do more than two hours at a time without relief. Submarine crews are always volunteers and they receive extra pay for their dangerous work.

It does not do for a submarine commander to be tyrannized by his imagination. He does not allow his mind to dwell on the possibility that his present cruise may be his last. He must be a man of balanced judgment, neither too foolhardy nor, on the other hand, too prudent. The nature of his work demands that he should take risks, but never

recklessly. A perfect example of a born submarine skipper
was Malcolm David Wanklyn, V.C., D.S.O. Wanklyn commanded the submarine *Upholder* when he was awarded
the Victoria Cross for "outstanding valor, determination,
and leadership." This description fitted well the tall, keen-
eyed, thirty-year-old officer with the pointed black beard
and the quiet manner of a man born to command. In
September 1941 he was awarded the D.S.O., and in December the King added to it the crimson ribbon of the
Victoria Cross, thus making him the first submarine commander in the war to win the supreme award of valor.

Before the episode which won him the prize for outstanding courage and leadership Wanklyn had already distinguished himself in the Mediterranean as an ace submarine commander, with over 140,000 tons of enemy
shipping sunk. The attack that won him the V.C. occurred
while *Upholder* was on patrol off the south coast of Sicily.
For days nothing had been seen, but at dusk on May 24 a
south-bound Italian convoy escorted by destroyers was
sighted on the horizon. The failing light made it difficult
to observe the enemy by periscope, but a surface attack
would have been detected at once. Since the submarine's
listening apparatus was temporarily out of action Wanklyn
was without this aid to navigation and, rather than lose
the opportunity, decided to go in and attack at short
range. Approaching to within what he believed to be the
correct range, he raised the periscope and received a
shock. One of the enemy destroyers was rushing towards
him at high speed, forcing him to crash-dive to avoid being rammed. A few minutes later he cautiously came up
again to periscope-depth and took a quick look around.
Right on the cross wires of the glass was a large enemy
troopship, and the order was given to fire three torpedoes
one after another. Submarine crews say that the most try-

ing moment in a submarine man's life is the suspense of waiting to hear if the torpedo hits the target, and *Upholder's* crew now listened in grim silence for—success or failure. It seemed that the torpedoes had missed; then came the distinct *ping* of metal striking metal, and two dull booms, like thunder at the bottom of a long tunnel, and the violent agitation of the sea, causing the boat to shudder. Then the inevitable depth-charges from the destroyers racing overhead. For twenty minutes they tore back and forth trying to destroy the unseen enemy, and in their anxiety to make sure of him dropped no less than thirty-seven of these deadly canisters. While the boat lay deep below the surface with engines stopped so that the noise of her propellers should not be picked up by enemy hydrophones, a petty-officer telegraphist, with the logbook on his knee, sat with a pencil calmly putting down a stroke for each explosion, while the perfectly trained crew stood at their stations awaiting the next order from the commander.

Some of the explosions were close enough to derange certain delicate instruments in the submarine and to start small leaks, but when the enemy finally departed Commander Wanklyn found that his boat, though damaged, was navigable, and after dark he came to the surface to charge his batteries. By nursing his craft he was able to reach his base without further adventure. As the rusty, salt-caked boat quietly slipped into harbor her unshaven crew lined the deck and stood to attention, while above them flew the Jolly Roger from the stump mast—the ensign of free sea rovers.

Before Wanklyn received the V.C. he had already won the D.S.O. for resourcefulness and daring in sinking for certain one destroyer, one U-boat, two 19,500-ton transports, an oil-tanker, and several freighters. Other probable victims (but not verified) were a cruiser and a destroyer.

Another submarine ace was thirty-two-year-old Lieutenant-Commander M. Willmott, of *Talisman,* one of the Triton class boats, the same class to which belonged *Thetis,* the boat which sank off the Mersey just before the war and after being raised was renamed *Thunderbolt.* *Talisman,* a big boat of just over 1000 tons carrying fifty-three men, was armed with one 4-inch and two smaller guns, and no less than ten 21-inch torpedo-tubes, a formidable craft embodying all the lastest developments in submarine design. In the winter of 1941–42 *Talisman* was one of the First Submarine Flotilla operating in the Eastern Mediterranean from Alexandria. One dark night in January when *Talisman* came to the surface to charge the batteries and compressed-air flasks the Commander saw, to his great surprise, the black shape of a large enemy submarine not more than seventy yards away. The U-boat commander saw *Talisman* at about the same moment as he had been seen, and went into action before the British boat could get into position for firing. Swinging the long craft round, he discharged two torpedoes which could be seen coming by the wake of air bubbles. Putting his helm hard over, Commander Willmott managed to avoid both of the 'tin fish,' and they rushed harmlessly past him. While the two submarines maneuvered for favorable positions to attack, *Talisman*'s gunners had swung the 4-inch deck-gun round and fired at what they thought to be the U-boat's conning-tower, though they could not be sure, so dark was the night. The gun-layer, peering into the blackness, suggested that the trainer of the gun should try a little more to the right, and the second shell tore through the conning-tower, probably killing the men there, for the U-boat now behaved in such an erratic manner as to suggest that there was no one in control. She was moving on

the surface towards *Talisman,* but obviously not for the
purpose of ramming her, as the U-boat was approaching
on a course oblique to the British boat and one that would
put the enemy in a dangerous position. She swept past
only five yards away, and as she did so the astonished
crew of *Talisman* saw a bright light shining through the
open hatches of her conning-tower and lighting up the
surrounding water. Then a terrible thing happened, for
with the hatches wide open the bows went down and the
U-boat dived, drowning the unfortunate men in her like
rats. The action from the time *Talisman* surfaced to the
time the U-boat sank had lasted only eight minutes. The
British sailors returned to their duties in silence, for they
knew that but for the grace of God this terrible fate might
have been theirs.

The success of a submarine's career necessarily depends
mainly on the quality of her commander, and if he is re-
sourceful and clever as well as daring his craft, which cost
the government, say, $1,500,000 may pay the country good
dividends. *Talisman,* handled by Commander Willmott,
earned her cost many times over in the mounting toll of
enemy craft in the Eastern Mediterranean. On another
occasion while cruising on the surface in rough weather
Willmott sighted a craft which in the bad light he mis-
took for an enemy submarine. Quickly taking a bearing, he
let loose three torpedoes at the supposed U-boat, only to
see all three pass under her. His smart gunners then opened
fire and pumped four shots into the enemy before it was
seen that it was a destroyer they had so audaciously challenged. Far from being awed by the discovery, *Talisman's*
men went in close enough to spray the destroyer's deck
with machine-gun fire. The destroyer put the helm hard
down in an effort to ram the submarine, but missed her
by fifteen yards, and before she could renew the attack

Talisman had crash-dived and escaped. A few nights later while the boat was on the surface Willmott sighted a large enemy troopship which he judged to be a vessel of 15,000 tons. Approaching within range, he fired five torpedoes at her and heard four explosions. A few minutes later the transport rolled over and sank. *Talisman* was piling up the dividends.

Though it was not the government's policy to announce U-boat sinkings, as we have already pointed out, there were occasions when, for special reasons, the loss of a U-boat or her commander was given full publicity. Such an occasion was the destruction of the U100, commanded by the redoubtable Kapitan Schepke, one of Germany's cleverest and most daring submarine commanders, a man who had for a long time been a menace to Atlantic shipping. He set forth on his last cruise from Kiel in March 1941, bound for his favorite haunts, the Western Ocean shipping lane, where there were always plenty of richly laden convoys to be found. A few days later he sighted a convoy and remained submerged till nightfall, when he surfaced for an attack. Raising the periscope to take a precautionary look round, he saw a destroyer too close to risk giving his presence away. He pulled down his periscope to wait until the warship had got out of range, but when he looked again half an hour later the destroyer was still in the neighborhood, and, though the periscope was again hauled down, the U-boat must have been seen, or its presence revealed by the destroyer's hydrophones, for depth-charges were dropped and Schepke was forced to withdraw to a safer position. Trusting to the dark night for concealment, he followed the convoy from astern and on the surface, but three destroyers sighted him and he was forced to make a crash-dive when they closed in on him to attack. This daring commander had miscalculated the strength of the escort, and two minutes later a pattern of depth-charges put out all the lights in the boat and forced him to dive deep for safety. Overhead the destroyers were rushing about dropping charges, which could be heard exploding under the sea, some close enough to rock the U-boat and put the pumps out of action. In total darkness the crew remained for three hours listening to the terrible explosions, but Schepke was a brave man, and although air was escaping from damaged valves, and water squirting into the boat through the sprung plates, he grimly hung on until it became obvious that unless he came to the surface at once it would be too late. He reluctantly gave the order to take the boat up.

As the conning-tower broke surface Schepke and some of his men flung open the upper-hatch cover and sprang on deck. But they were too late to save the boat, for an alert destroyer was waiting for them and was approaching at full speed to ram. As Schepke saw the knife-edged bows racing towards the U100 he shouted a warning down the open hatch, but even as the men began to scramble up the ladder the steel forefoot of the destroyer ripped through the U100's plating and she rolled over as the sea rushed into her interior. Owing to the suddenness of the attack it was not possible to rescue more than six of her crew.

Another famous U-boat commander to pay the price of over-confidence was Otto Kretschmer, a wearer of the Grand Cross (a class of the Iron Cross order) and a national hero. He was a skilful and brave sailor but a ruthless enemy, who earned a dread reputation for machine-gunning people forced to take to the boats. He himself had had several narrow escapes from destruction, and it was said that he bore a charmed life, for his crew would relate, on their return to base, hair-raising stories of how he had defied British warships to sail right among a convoy like a fox among a flock of chickens. His speciality was hunting convoys, a work at which he was extremely successful.

One dark night when he had torpedoed a tanker one of the escorting ships caught sight of the U-boat's conning-tower and forced Kretschmer to dive, but depth-charges so damaged the boat he was forced to come to the surface. In the light of the burning tanker, victim of the U-boat's torpedoes, the escort vessel's crew could see little figures on the U-boat jumping into the sea. Some were rescued, and among them was Otto Kretschmer.

An account of a single day and night's happenings to H.M. submarine *Spearfish* off the German coast in September 1939,[3] shortly after the beginning of the war, brings home to the landsman the anxieties, the vicissitudes, and strain of life in a submarine in war-time. The *Spearfish,* a 640-ton boat carrying a crew of forty under Lieutenant-Commander J. H. Forbes, arrived off the German coast at night without being seen by the enemy patrols. Before dawn she submerged and lay on the bottom till the boat's chronometer told her captain that it was daylight on the surface. During this wait the crew were mystified at hearing the sound of depth-charge explosions, one of which was sufficiently close to do some slight damage inside the boat. It was impossible to tell whether the enemy was attacking another British craft or whether his patrols had picked up the sound of *Spearfish's* propellers.

While the enemy could be heard overhead through the submarine's listening devices Commander Forbes ordered everyone to remain quiet and not to walk about or make any noise. Speaking above a whisper was forbidden lest even the sound of the men's voices might give the boat's position away. During the morning the sounds of more

---

[3] In August 1940 *Spearfish* left her base on patrol and was not heard of again.

than forty explosions were counted, but to the crew's great relief the sounds got farther away and presently ceased altogether. Commander Forbes was too experienced a submarine skipper to conclude from this that the enemy had given up the hunt, for it might be a trick to lure him to the surface. He knew too the Teutonic reputation for thoroughness, and his guess that the enemy might return proved to be correct. *Spearfish's* hydrophones picked up the sound of a wire sweep being dragged over the sea-bed. To these sweeps are attached electrically fired charges which can be set off from the surface, so one can understand the feelings of the British crew when early in the afternoon they heard a wire cable scrape over *Spearfish* in a series of jerks and muffled thuds.

The imprisoned men were listening to this new menace when they were temporarily stunned by a heavy explosion. One of the electric charges had been set off, putting out every light in the boat and doing severe damage to the hull and machinery. In the darkness water could be heard coming through the cracks in started plates, and the hiss of compressed air told them that some part of the high-pressure air system was damaged, allowing the air to escape into the boat. This raised the pressure uncomfortably, and the remedy was to release some of the air into the sea through an outlet valve, but to do this would have advertised the position of the boat to the surface watchers. Meanwhile the electricians worked frantically to restore the lights, and when at last they were able to switch on the emergency lighting system and make a survey of the damage it was found that both Diesel engines and the main electric motor were out of action. The first and most pressing necessity was to stop the worst of the air leaks, and in the dim light the men worked with grim urgency and were at last rewarded by partial success, but not before the pressure inside the boat had mounted far higher than the human lungs had ever been meant to bear.

As soon as the time showed that it must be dark on the surface preparations were made to bring the boat up. In enemy waters the correct procedure is first to take a precautionary look round through the periscope, but as this useful instrument had been smashed by the explosion Commander Forbes had no alternative but to take the risk of coming to the surface and possibly being discovered. As the boat slowly rose through the water with her positive buoyancy, Forbes stood inside the conning-tower ready instantly to open the hatch when the boat broke surface. But since he was a small man and the high pressure of air in the boat's interior might blow him through the open hatch like a shell out of a cannon he took the precaution of ordering one of the ratings, a heavy man, to hold on to his ankles. Forbes got out without accident, and close behind him came some of the crew, ready to man the deck-gun and fight if necessary, but to their enormous relief the enemy was nowhere to be seen. *Spearfish* crawled away from this unhealthy area on one motor while her engineers struggled to get the Diesel engines working.

A submarine's two sets of engines—oil and electric—are interdependent in the sense that the Diesels are necessary to turn the dynamos, which in turn charge the batteries that feed energy to run the electric motors when the boat is submerged. Thus it follows that *Spearfish* could not submerge because, until the Diesel engines were repaired, the dynamo could not be driven to supply the batteries with energy for the motors, which, as we have seen, are used for driving the boat when submerged. Slowly, on one motor, which would soon exhaust the batteries if they were not recharged by the dynamos, the submarine crawled westward under the protecting cover of darkness while her men fought to get her crippled machinery going. Just before the huge batteries were completely exhausted the engine-room staff got one Diesel engine started, and two hours later the chief engineer reported to the Commander that the second engine was working. The wireless transmitter had been put out of order by the explosion, but during the night the electricians rigged up a makeshift transmitter, and a request was sent to the base for an escort to come to the submarine's assistance. All day *Spearfish* traveled on the surface, fortunately without being seen by an enemy patrol, and at midnight she was met by British destroyers and safely escorted back to the base. Repairs were put in hand at once, and within a remarkably short time she was back in service. Later her name was mentioned in an Admiralty communiqué for torpedoing a pocket-battleship. As already noted, she was lost in August the following year.

The adventure of *Spearfish* was by no means unique; it was, in fact, a common enough sight at submarine flotilla bases to see a boat return after a cruise with her periscopes bent and battered like lead piping and her upper structure holed with shell-fire. The story of H.M.S. *Sealion* should be included in this record of some of the vicissitudes of British submarines.

Sealion, skippered by Commander Bryant, R.N., was on a cruise in German and Norwegian waters in the summer of 1940 when she sighted through the periscope an enemy supply vessel of some 3000 tons steaming alone just off the Norwegian coast. Commander Bryant surfaced and signaled the steamer to stop, at the same time ordering the crew to abandon ship. The steamer was then sunk by gunfire. Later that same day while submerged *Sealion* sighted a U-boat traveling on the surface, and Commander Bryant began stalking her to get into position for firing a torpedo, but the U-boat, apparently unaware of *Sealion*'s presence, leisurely dived and was not seen again.

A few days later during the same cruise *Sealion* sighted an enemy convoy and at once dived to attack. Approaching the convoy submerged for five minutes before raising the periscope, Bryant took a quick look around and saw that the convoy was escorted by at least ten E-boats. With great daring he dived beneath this dangerous escort and came up to periscope-depth right in the middle of the convoy. While he was still studying the ships to pick out a big one the entire convoy altered course several points, and he had to lower periscope and make a quick dive to avoid being run down. A little later he again rose to periscope-depth to maneuver for position, but was again forced to submerge when the convoy altered course. But this time he was so close that one of the ships smashed both periscopes and the wireless mast before he could get out of the way. To make matters worse the enemy began dropping depth-charges, and for an hour *Sealion*'s crew had an anxious time, though none of the charges exploded close enough to do any damage.

The submarine stayed down all day, and when she came to the surface after dark there was no sign of the convoy. The weather was so bad that it took all night to clear the wreckage of the wireless gear and broken periscopes. Fortunately the engines were unharmed, and at dawn *Sealion* was able to submerge. She stayed down all day without once coming up to periscope-depth, for the enemy, who must have suspected her presence, returned to the area and dropped more depth-charges, but none exploded near. As soon as it was dark the boat came to the surface and steered for home as fast as the heavy seas would permit. So rough was the sea that the crew, rigging up a temporary wireless aerial, had to be lashed to lifelines to save them from being swept overboard. At dawn, when *Sealion* was at least fifty miles west of the danger area, Commander Bryant deemed it possible to radio the base without revealing his position to enemy patrols. Thirty-six hours later the battered submarine slowly entered harbor and moored alongside the depot ship, another patrol ended. Her crew, unshaven and haggard with loss of sleep, made her fast to the parent ship and then went aboard the latter to live the lives of civilized men until the time came for them to go forth again.

Let us end this record of grim submarine warfare with a little comic relief in the story, from the London *Daily Telegraph*, of a Jugoslav submarine which escaped from an enemy-occupied port. When the Germans overran Jugoslavia a number of Jugoslav patriots found themselves trapped in the naval base of Kotor, on the Adriatic. Escaping before the advancing German armies, they reached the port a few hours ahead of an enemy Panzer division. Though not yet occupied, it was impossible to escape by steamer as Italian patrols were off the coast, and any ship attempting to get away would be caught at once. Lying alongside the dock was an old and obsolete submarine which had been employed as a training vessel, and it occurred to someone that here at hand was the means of getting away. He had no difficulty in collecting a group of patriots willing to make the attempt, despite the fact that hardly any of them knew anything about submarines, and the boat itself was dangerously unseaworthy. The batteries were liable to get hot when charged, and the shell of the boat was so thin from corrosion that it would not stand the pressure of deep diving. Apparently the worn bearings of the machinery made a noise that could be heard a mile away. In spite of these dangers and the presence of Italian destroyers outside the harbor there was no lack of volunteers to make the perilous attempt. For engineers two young army sergeants were chosen, though they had never been in a submarine in their lives. Among the crew was a Cabinet Minister, some army, air force, and naval officers, and finally a general of the Jugoslav army.

Manned by this Gilbertian crew, the submarine set out from Kotor on the surface at 1 A.M., and at 5 A.M. was forced to submerge to avoid enemy patrol ships. The harbor was well guarded with surface patrols and a minefield, but the boat slipped through both without disaster. Every man had to learn his job, and it is not surprising that the boat dived with a heavy list and moved through the rough sea like a gamboling porpoise. Like children with a new toy, the amateur engineers and navigators sang old Serbian ballads for sheer pleasure in their achievement. In spite of the thin shell of the boat, they took her down to sixty feet entirely confident that she would see them through. Only when the air of the crowded boat became too thick for comfort did they return to the surface. And only just in time, for then it was found that the ancient batteries were exhausted and must be recharged before the boat could submerge again. It was evening when they surfaced, and about a mile distant they saw some Italian warships; and as the bright moon would sooner or later give their position away they were forced to submerge before the batteries were fully charged.

Running the gauntlet of the Strait of Otranto, which was bristling with mines and enemy patrols, was a nerve-racking experience; but fortune continued to favor the reckless adventurers, and on Easter Sunday they sighted the Greek island of Cephalonia. After leaving the Strait of Otranto they learned that they had traveled underneath a minefield, unaware of the fact. Off Cephalonia they saw British ships in the distance, and a little later sighted a Jugoslav torpedo-boat and went alongside for news. Happy to see one of their own ships and their own flag, these gay adventurers wanted to tarry awhile, but they were warned that it was too dangerous to remain and so, reluctantly, got under way again, and made for the island's chief port, Lixuri, where they were cordially received by the Greeks. Obviously the amateur crew of the submarine failed to appreciate the quality of their feat, for they had spent much of their time singing roisterous songs and laughing over the erratic behavior of the boat. They had brought the ancient craft safely through incredible dangers largely by trial and error, or, as it would have been expressed in the British submarine service, "by guess and by God," an allusion to the difficulties of accurate navigation in a vessel that must spend most of its time under the sea, and can only safely come to the surface at night, when a solar observation is not possible.

CHAPTER VI

E-Boat Alley and the Channel

In the First World War the Strait of Dover, the narrow twenty-one-mile channel between Dover and Calais, was closed to enemy warships and U-boats by booms, nets, and mines, as well as a force of destroyers and auxiliaries known as the Dover Patrol. Closing the narrows was possible only because the opposite coast was in friendly hands. After the collapse of France in June 1940 it was no longer possible to prevent enemy craft passing through the narrows into the North Sea and *vice versa.*

The Germans mounted guns of the heaviest caliber at Cap Griz Nez, firing shells that could reach Dover. Also the northern French airfields were in their hands. Thus the enemy could not only use the Channel for his own ships, but could interfere with British shipping at his pleasure. Though for a while this resulted in the partial paralysis of the great Port of London, it did not entirely stop sea trade, for small convoys continued to pass through the Channel to and from the Thames.

Experience showed that, with the British on one side of the Channel and the Germans on the other, it was impossible to prevent an opponent from passing his ships through those waters, though the passage could not, of course, be made with the ease and freedom of peacetime. The Germans had lurking in French harbors scores of the small torpedo-carrying torpedo-boats called E-boats by the British, and their main hunting ground was known as 'E-boat Alley.' Hundreds of minor sea actions took place in E-boat Alley, in which these mosquito craft would dash out to attack a convoy or an individual ship and then dash back to shelter before they were caught. Occasionally a major action would develop when E-boats were assisted by dive-bombers flying out from northern French airfields. A sea and air action between enemy aircraft on one hand and British naval forces on the other which took place early in February 1942 illustrates the difficulties and perils that beset convoys passing up the Channel.

The action lasted seven hours in the teeth of a winter gale and under extremely bad conditions of visibility. The convoy, escorted by the ex-American destroyer *Leeds* and the 510-ton escort corvette *Puffin,* was rolling in heavy seas and proceeding northward after having passed through the narrows without incident when just after breakfast a German Dornier, flying only 150 feet above the sea, appeared, and after taking a look at the convoy flew off to report its position. It was sped on its way by a violent fusillade from every gun in the convoy. During the night a snowstorm had covered the ships' decks with snow. At dawn the weather had improved, but the sky had remained leaden gray with banks of low cloud which had made perfect cover for the Dornier. Half an hour after it had disappeared the drone of aircraft could be heard, and the escorts' gunners followed the sound with the muzzles of the guns, for the enemy as yet could not be seen. Then out of a cloud so low that its fringe almost touched the sea roared a Dornier, making straight for one of the merchantmen. A hundred guns spat tracer bullets and shells at the plane, forcing it to take cover in a cloud-bank.

Now came another bomber, firing its machine-guns as it

dived at a large merchant ship. After raking the decks with fire it zoomed into the cloud before any guns could be trained on it, and out of the cloud four heavy bombs whistled down and exploded in the sea so near the ship as to hide her in fountains of spray but without causing any serious damage. In a break in the clouds several German planes were seen twisting and turning to dodge the shell-bursts which filled the sky around them. The destroyer *Leeds* was persistently bombed, but her guns so upset the enemy's aim that his bombs fell wide. The ships rocked and shuddered with the blast of exploding bombs, but none of the vessels was hit, so fierce was the defence barrage. At the height of the battle three R.A.F. Hurricanes from a land station came roaring up to the ships' assistance, and there followed a series of aerial dog-fights which lasted till four in the afternoon, seven hours after the battle had begun.

Here are excerpts from a joint Admiralty and Air Ministry communiqué concerning an attack by E-boats and aircraft on a convoy off the East Coast. Watchers on the coast saw the first phase of the action. On Thursday evening, February 19, 1942, a convoy escorted by three small 900-ton "Hunt" class destroyers, *Pytcheley*, *Mendip*, and *Holderness*, was entering the North Sea when the enemy attacked it with a mixed force of dive-bombers and E-boats. The main action was fought in the teeth of a howling gale with visibility of only a few hundred yards. It began on Thursday night and continued until Friday morning. R.A.F. Fighter Command aircraft, under Squadron Leader I. F. Smith, were engaged in shipping-protection duties when six enemy planes were sighted approaching the convoy. Three R.A.F. Defiants went into action at once and engaged two Dorniers while flying two hundred feet above the sea. Forcing the enemy down almost to sea-level, Squadron Leader Smith's machine opened fire directly into the cockpit of the leading Dornier, one of the latest long-range bombers, and forced it to crash into the sea. The Defiant's gunner, Flight Sergeant A. G. Beale, now opened fire on a Junkers 88, which dived on his tail from a cloud two hundred yards away. As the bullets ripped into the Junkers it turned away and escaped in the cloud from which it had come. The Defiant patrol in a few minutes destroyed one machine, damaged four out of the remaining five, and drove them all off.

Just before midnight the enemy made his first surface attack. E-boats were sighted by the destroyer *Holderness* (Lieutenant A. J. R. White, R.N.), which immediately engaged, but the enemy turned away and withdrew under cover of a smoke-screen. *Holderness*, in company with *Pytcheley* (Lieutenant-Commander H. Unwin, D.S.C.) and *Mendip* (Lieutenant-Commander G. N. Rolfe, D.S.C.), gave chase and managed to damage the enemy before contact was lost. When the warships returned to their stations on the edge of the convoy H.M.S. *Mendip* sighted two more E-boats, and engaged and drove them off.

Two hours later H.M.S. *Holderness* engaged what were probably the same two boats which had been following the convoy. The destroyer hit one with her first salvo, and the enemy blew up and immediately sank. As more E-boats were seen scurrying about in the darkness the destroyers dashed after them, and in the action which followed another E-boat was sunk. Eighteen survivors were picked up and made prisoners of war. Meanwhile H.M. trawler *Turquoise* was engaged with further E-boats, which were driven off. None of the ships of the convoy or the escort suffered any loss. The action was an excellent example of perfect co-operation between sea and air forces and was correctly described as a decisive success.

The episodes just related were mere skirmishes compared with the running battle which took place in the Channel when the 26,000-ton German battleships *Scharnhorst* and *Gneisenau* and the heavy 10,000-ton cruiser *Prinz Eugen* were attacked by British surface and air craft when the enemy warships were making their daring escape from Brest to their home bases. It will be remembered that *Prinz Eugen* had taken refuge in the enemy-occupied naval base of Brest after the *Bismarck* battle, and with *Scharnhorst* and *Gneisenau,* also at Brest, was persistently bombed night after night by R.A.F. Bomber Command, and it was said that four thousand tons of bombs had been dropped on that unfortunate port. The escape of these ships, two of which had been imprisoned in Brest for ten months by air raids, aroused a storm of bitter criticism in the country, which demanded to know why, if the British Intelligence Services knew that the ships were seaworthy and preparing to leave Brest, adequate forces had not been sent to intercept them. And how did they come to reach the Strait of Dover before discovery? American critics suggested that gallant British sailors had been let down by the Admiralty, which was caught napping, unorganized and unready. To the question of why no British battleship was in the action the answer was quite simply that the battleships of the fleet were elsewhere.

The night of Wednesday, February 11, 1942, was black and stormy with visibility at zero, an ideal night for the German ships to put to sea unobserved. At 10.42 the next morning two Spitfire pilots on patrol sighted the two battleships and a cruiser escorted by a fleet of E-boats proceeding up the Channel on the French side and almost abreast of Boulogne, three hundred miles from Brest. The discovery was radioed to a British base, and planes and warships were sent out to try to intercept them. That the enemy had been able to steam up the Channel, the last three hours in daylight, may be partly explained by the very poor visibility caused by cloud and rain. At 12.25 P.M. a number of fast M.T.B.'s (motor torpedo-boats) set out from Dover at full speed in a very rough sea to find the enemy. Meanwhile destroyers were steaming to intercept the enemy in the North Sea, and torpedo-carrying Swordfish planes from land bases had begun the attack.

In mid-Channel the M.T.B.'s saw a long, low bank of smoke which the wind presently dispersed to uncover a strong force of E-boats. Beyond them were the gray shapes of three big warships moving in line astern and screened by flanking destroyers. It was a suicidal risk, but the M.T.B.'s drove on through the rough seas to approach within torpedo range, in spite of the hail of shells hitting the sea all around them. Overhead Messerschmitt fighters joined the E-boats in an attack on the British craft. While the Messerschmitts were harassing the torpedo-boats a squadron of Hurricanes arrived and attacked the enemy planes, which had been reinforced by Focke-Wulf bombers. Avoiding the torpedoes of the E-boats, the British craft slipped through the defence and raced towards the battleships, all the while exposed to a murderous fire from every enemy vessel. The fire was too heavy to allow them to approach very near to the battleships, but the leading torpedo-boat got within five thousand yards and released a torpedo at *Prinz Eugen,* which was leading the line. A huge fountain of water rose amidships on the cruiser's port side, which gave the British good reason to think the torpedo had found its mark. Several torpedoes were fired at the two battleships, but the rough seas and low visibility made it impossible to observe the results. After releasing all their torpedoes the M.T.B.'s turned and ran the gauntlet of fire from everything the enemy had. Torpedoes, bombs, shells from light and heavy guns, were loosed at them. A German destroyer chased them, but they escaped under cover of a smoke-screen.

As the M.T.B.'s sped back towards England their crews saw the heroic self-sacrifice of the pilots of six Swordfish torpedo-planes which, without any escort, went in to attack with their torpedoes and were all shot down into the sea. The planes were, of course, lost, but five out of the eighteen making up the crews of these aircraft were picked up at great risk by the Navy. The pilots had pressed home their attack in the face of a fire so heavy that their planes began to disintegrate in the air almost before they were within torpedo range. As for the torpedo-boats, it was not so much a question of whether their torpedoes had hit, but whether they had even had the chance to fire them.

The little M.T.B.'s were first of the surface craft to reach the enemy, but the destroyers were close behind them. Like the torpedo-boats, the destroyers were sent into battle with the dice loaded against them. They were asked to carry out the impossible task of stopping a formidable enemy squadron of two big ships, a large cruiser, a destroyer flotilla, E-boats, and a protecting 'umbrella' of several hundred airplanes. It was 3.40 P.M. before the enemy were sighted at a range of four miles—a short range for the heavy guns of the battleships. The destroyers thus had to face not only an overwhelming superiority of guns and armor, but hundreds of German aircraft which from the start of the action did their best to sink the destroyers with a deluge of bombs of all sizes. Nevertheless the destroyers went in at full speed, their only hope to discharge their torpedoes and escape if possible. Driving head on towards the enemy, they managed to get within 3500 yards without being sunk. At this dangerously close range all but one of the destroyers turned and, running on a parallel course to the enemy, loosed their torpedoes. The exception was the 1100-ton H.M.S. *Worcester* (Lieutenant-Commander E. C. Coats), which held her course until within a little over 2000 yards from the nearest battleship. Turning, she fired her torpedoes, and a moment later was hit twice and set badly on fire forward. It had been impossible to ascertain whether any of the torpedoes had hit because of the heavy seas and enemy interference which made an accurate observation impossible. Between *Worcester* and the target was an opaque curtain of water thrown up by shells and bombs, but her crew believed that two hits had been made on the leading battle-cruiser. Farther to the east another destroyer attack, led by the 1500-ton *Mackay* (Captain J. P. Wright), was being made on *Prinz Eugen,* and at a range of under 3500 yards torpedoes were fired. Here again one destroyer went in closer, and almost certainly made one hit, as an orange flash was observed coming from the cruiser. After the destroyers retired they were attacked on the way back to their base by enemy bombers but without success. *Worcester,* although badly damaged in the bows, got safely home without assistance.

The destroyer flotilla commanded by Captain Mark Pizey in H.M.S. *Campbell* was engaged in gunnery practice in the North Sea when it received the message to intercept the German ships. Under forced draught it smashed through rough seas to get to the reported position in time. The destroyers constantly yawed off their course owing to the buffeting they were receiving, and most of the time the officers on the bridge could not see ahead for flying spray. When the enemy was sighted their line-ahead positions had changed, *Gneisenau* leading and *Prinz Eugen* in the rear. The presence of the enemy was revealed by gun-flashes before the ships were seen. His A.A. guns were firing at two Beaufort fighters who were attacking him. A few moments later the long gray shapes of the German destroyers were seen and faintly in the mist behind them the big ships. The British destroyers, with no battleships behind them to cover their approach, boldly dashed in close enough to fire their torpedoes. The heavy seas made accurate aiming difficult, for one moment the outboard ends of the torpedo-tubes were pointing into the sea and the next they were directed at the sky. In such seas a torpedo would porpoise, leap and dive, and yaw from its course, making the chance of a hit at extreme range problematical. The crews on the wet, rolling decks had the greatest difficulty in swinging the heavy tubes around without themselves being washed overboard by waves breaking as high as the bridge. When the torpedoes were fired the destroyers were dangerously close to the enemy, and to have approached any nearer would literally have been suicide. It was now that *Worcester*, which was a little closer to the enemy than the other destroyers, received direct hits with 11-inch and 5.9-inch shells. The destroyer crew's statement that they had made three hits seemed to have been borne out by the reduction in speed of the enemy after the attack from twenty-eight to eighteen knots. Again and again the British destroyers pressed home their torpedo attacks, each time passing through a curtain of gunfire so heavy it seemed impossible that they could escape destruction. Before approaching the battleships they had to run a gauntlet of twenty-eight-knot Gelietboots (high-speed eight-hundred-ton patrol ships) and the dangerous

E-boats, which were capable of forty-five knots, a higher speed than that of the destroyers.

The engagement was finally broken off when the running fight had brought the ships to within approximately fourteen miles off the Dutch coast and opposite the estuary of the river Maas. Later the British destroyers put out again in search of the enemy, but were unable to find him.

The enemy, with characteristic thoroughness, had provided ample protection for his capital ships in the shape of destroyers, E-boats, and an air 'umbrella' of fighters and bombers. As the German squadron steamed up the Channel they were protected from air attack by hundreds of fighters and bombers flying out from a chain of airfields along the northern coast of France. In the air fight over the ships approximately six hundred aircraft were engaged, the biggest air fight since the Battle of Britain. The cloud ceiling was never higher than fifteen hundred feet, which severely restricted the room for air fighting and forced the R.A.F. and Coastal Command planes down to within machine-gun range from the ships, with the result that of the forty-two British planes lost most were brought down by the warships, not by enemy aircraft. Some of the pilots, on their return, said that at times the ceiling was so low it was hard to tell where the sky left off and the sea began. Enemy air opposition was so fierce and so persistent that the British bombers and torpedo-carrying planes were never able to get a steady sight on the target long enough to make certain of a hit. The German tactics were to lure the British within range of the A.A. batteries on the French coast, but in this they were not successful. The torpedo-carrying bombers sent out were mainly Beauforts, but there were also at least six of the old naval Swordfish biplanes, all of which were shot down. Practically every operational type of machine in the R.A.F. was sent out.

There were Wellingtons, Hampdens, Manchesters, Halifaxes, and Blenheims among the bombers and Spitfires and Hurricanes among the fighters. And though the pilots of this air armada showed the utmost disregard for danger in the way they pressed home their attacks, the whole action must be looked on as disappointing. The Beauforts carried torpedoes large enough to sink a battleship, yet the enemy was not prevented from getting home. The answer to critics who compared this action with that in which the Japanese sank *Prince of Wales* and *Repulse* with torpedo-carrying planes was simply that the Japanese pilots were able to approach the battleships in conditions of perfect visibility and with no fighter opposition.

No British warship was lost in the action, although forty-two planes were lost against eighteen of the enemy's. The balance of losses in the battle was difficult to assess. While the British lost more than twice as many planes as the enemy, the Royal Navy lost no ships, and even the Germans admitted the sinking of one of their patrol ships and damage to a torpedo-boat. On the other hand, they suffered no major set-back and their three big ships were able to reach home, later to become a menace to Allied shipping and sea supremacy. The British sailors and airmen had once again shown that they possessed courage of the very highest order, but the obvious lesson learned from this action was that courage is not enough for winning battles.

The honors of this battle in the Channel were shared by the Navy and Air Force, and we cannot end this brief record without paying homage to those men of the R.A.F. and the Fleet Air Arm who gave their lives in the action, especially those men in the six Swordfish planes which were shot down into the sea. On February 28 an Admiralty communiqué announced that the Victoria Cross had been awarded posthumously to Lieutenant-Commander Eugene Esmonde, D.S.O., the thirty-two-year-old leader of the squadron of the Fleet Air Arm which went to its doom in the attack on the German battleships. The official communiqué said:

> Lieutenant-Commander Esmonde knew well that his enterprise was desperate. . . . His high courage and splendid resolution will live in the traditions of the Royal Navy and remain for many generations a fine and stirring memory. . . . Soon after noon he and his squadron of six Swordfish set course for the enemy, and after ten minutes' flight were attacked by a strong force of enemy fighters. Touch was lost with his fighter escort, and in the action which followed all his aircraft were damaged. He flew on, cool and resolute, serenely challenging hopeless odds to encounter the deadly fire of the battle-cruisers and their escort, which shattered the port wing of his aircraft. Undismayed, he led his squadron on straight through this inferno of fire in a steady flight towards his target. Almost at once he was shot down, but his squadron went on to launch the gallant attack, in which at least one torpedo is believed to have struck the German battle-cruisers, and from which not one of the six aircraft returned.

In addition to the V.C. award to Lieutenant-Commander Esmonde, four other officers received the D.S.O. and an air gunner the Conspicuous Gallantry Medal. Reading the story of the desperate attack of the Swordfish pilots, flying straight into a wall of bullets and bursting shrapnel with the hope that they might do some damage to the enemy before they died, one inevitably compares it with the Charge of the Light Brigade—a winged Light Brigade—and sees these modern dragoons of the air no less brave than their forefathers who gave their lives at Balaclava.

CHAPTER VII

War in the Mediterranean

Up till June 1940, when Italy entered the war, patrolling the two-thousand-mile length of the Mediterranean was a relatively simple matter. The powerful French Navy, with its principal base at Toulon and another base at Oran, in Algeria, looked after Allied interests in the great inland sea, leaving the British Navy to take care of other waters. Those enemy U-boats that got into the Mediterranean had never more than a nuisance value until Italy's participation in the conflict not only opened her ports to German submarines, but reinforced the latter with her own considerable underwater fleet, believed to have totaled some hundred and thirty boats. Since Britain's Eastern colonies, her Asiatic and Pacific outposts, were manned and supplied via the Mediterranean, it was essential to keep open the doors of this sea-route, Gibraltar and Suez—all, be it noted, a long way from the Mother Country.

Until the opening of the Suez Canal in 1869 the sea-route from Britain to India and the East was by way of the Cape of Good Hope, and the shorter route thus opened up greatly simplified Britain's naval problems—so long as the Mediterranean countries were friendly. In anticipation of a time when those countries might not be so friendly, far-sighted British leaders fortified three strategic spots in the Mediterranean—Gibraltar, Malta, and Alexandria.

When Italy came into the war and France was out of it

the Navy's Mediterranean Fleet began to get its full share of action. Without the Navy, Egypt and the Suez would have been almost certainly lost. The successful Abyssinian campaign could not have been carried out. The defeat of the Italians in Libya would not have been possible, and Malta would have fallen into the hands of the Axis Powers. The Navy made it possible to transport and maintain 750,000 troops in the Middle East; it rescued nearly 17,000 troops from Crete after the defeat of Greece. It made the holding of Tobruk possible for many months against all assaults by supplying it from the sea and bombarding the enemy positions inland. It moved over 8000 prisoners and thousands of troops. And it seriously hampered Axis attempts to supply Graziani's and, later, Rommel's African forces by destroying supply transports crossing from Sicily to Tripoli. It blockaded the Levantine coast during the Syrian campaign and repeatedly attacked the Italian fleet, notably at Taranto and Cape Matapan, of which more later.

The first encounter with Italian forces took place early in July 1940, when a British force on patrol out of Gibraltar towards the Central Mediterranean was attacked by enemy aircraft, of which at least four were shot down. In November an Italian submarine flotilla met British surface ships south of the Balearic Isles and retired, leaving two submarines to run for the shelter of Tangier in a damaged condition.

In November Fleet Air Arm planes from *Ark Royal* discovered an Italian naval force proceeding on a westerly course south of Sardinia. The aircraft-carrier was in company with the battleship *Renown* and a small force of cruisers under Vice-Admiral Sir James Somerville when its planes sighted the enemy. The two forces came in contact off Cape Spartivento, the British putting on all speed to overtake the enemy. In a running fight one of the two Italian battleships and one cruiser were hit by torpedoes. Another cruiser was set on fire by shells, and two destroyers fell behind in a sinking condition. The only British casualties in this action were two hits on the 10,000-ton cruiser *Berwick*. One British and two Italian aircraft were shot down.

On February 8, 1941, Sir James Somerville's fleet was again in action, this time in an attack on Genoa. The force included the heavy ships *Renown* and *Malaya, Ark Royal*, and the 9000-ton cruiser *Sheffield*. Aircraft flown from *Ark Royal* directed the salvos, and over 300 tons of high-explosive shells were hurled into docks, oil installations, power stations, and factories on the sea front. During the bombardment several ships were sunk at their moorings, and the vast Ansaldo shipbuilding yards were wrecked. British people had always felt an affection for Italy and Italian cities, and it was a tragic necessity to have to shell the birthplace of Christopher Columbus.

Another tragic necessity was the British Fleet's shelling of the French warships at Oran, Algeria, after the surrender of France. Early in July it was known that a French fleet was at Oran, and another one at Dakar, and the Oran fleet was large enough to be dangerous if it surrendered to Germany. Therefore a strong British squadron was sent to offer the French Admiral a choice of four alternative decisions: (1) that his ships should steam to a British port, their crews then being repatriated if they chose to be; or (2) that they should proceed to the French West Indies and be demilitarized; or (3) that they should be demilitarized where they were within twelve hours; or (4) that they should be sunk.

A time-limit was set, although this was afterwards extended, but when the French Admiral refused to consider any of the four conditions the British had no alternative but to open fire. Fleet Air Arm planes hit *Dunkerque* with no less than six torpedoes. *Strasbourg* was also hit, but escaped to Toulon. One battleship, *Bretagne*, was sunk, and another, *Provence*, was badly damaged. This attack on their ships made many French people feel bitter towards Britain, especially as they did not know that the French Admiral could have saved his ships by accepting an alternative offer. But no one regretted the need to make the attack more than the British sailors and the British people.

Britain's old ally, France, seemed fated to cause the Royal Navy a great deal of embarrassment. The anomalous position of the French fleet in the Mediterranean while France was neither friend nor enemy itself created a delicate situation which sorely tried the patience of the bluff sea-dogs under Admiral Somerville. For example, in March 1941 a French convoy escorted by a destroyer, and suspected of carrying supplies of war materials for the Germans, was sighted by British forces as it entered the Straits of Gibraltar. Since the convoy kept well within Spanish territorial waters the British could not interfere, but when the convoy left territorial waters British destroyers signaled it to stop in order to submit to a perfectly legal search for contraband cargo. The convoy, which was then close to the Algerian coast, ran for the shelter of the nearest harbor while French shore batteries opened fire on the British ships. As the latter steamed away they were attacked by airplanes bearing French markings.

When France surrendered she had nine capital ships, including the two then unfinished battleships *Jean Bart* and *Richelieu.* In commission were the 13-inch-gun battleships *Dunkerque* and *Strasbourg,* the 13.4-inch-gun *Bretagne, Provence,* and *Lorraine,* and the 12-inch-gun

Paris and *Courbet*. She had twenty-two cruisers and about seventy destroyers—a fleet that would have changed the balance of power against the British had the enemy secured these ships. The French Navy also possessed about ninety submarines at the signing of the armistice. One of these, *Surcouf*, the largest in the world, was in a British port when France fell, and afterwards formed part of the Free French Navy under Vice-Admiral Muselier. With the enemy intriguing to get control of the formidable fleet, some French warships were at Alexandria, and these—the battleship *Lorraine*, four cruisers, three destroyers, and a submarine—were demilitarized and their crews guaranteed full pay and keep until the end of the war. Over a hundred French men-of-war of all types joined the Free French Naval Forces, and though most of them were small ships, the force included the battleships *Paris* and *Courbet*, each of which was armed with twelve 12-inch guns, and *Triomphant*, a destroyer as large as a light cruiser.

Of the nine battleships under the French flag *Courbet*, *Paris*, and *Lorraine* had passed into British control, *Bretagne* was sunk, the uncompleted *Jean Bart* was towed across to Casablanca, Morocco. The battleship *Richelieu* was lying at Dakar, West Africa, and as there was the same danger that the enemy might use this powerful ship against Britain the French Admiral at Dakar was offered similar terms to those sent to Oran, but he refused and consequently put the British Navy to the unpleasant task of attacking a former friend. Lieutenant-Commander R. H. Bristowe entered Dakar harbor in a motor-boat, managed to approach *Richelieu* undetected, and succeeded in placing depth-charges under the battleship's port quarter in order to wreck her rudder and propellers. When Bristowe withdrew the motor-boat's engine failed, and he was chased and fired at by French light craft, but they ran foul of the harbor boom, and Bristowe managed to escape. Meanwhile Fleet Air Arm planes attacked the battleship with torpedoes and left her with a heavy list to port and down by the stern. This incident did nothing to improve the relations between Britain and Vichy France, already severely strained by the tragic happenings at Oran.

The material result of all these incidents, however regrettable they may have been, was that France's potentially dangerous big ships had been reduced from nine to five, three of these severely damaged but not beyond repair. Apparently only *Strasbourg*, which had reached Toulon, was fit for action. But a year and a half later—that is, by January 1942—it was known that the battleship *Dunkerque* was repaired and had returned to Toulon. A veil of mystery concealed the movements of the four other capital ships.

When Italy entered the war her Navy was far larger than the forces the British could spare in the Mediterranean, but for reasons best known to themselves the Italians did not attempt to exploit this superiority to drive the British from those waters in a stand-up sea-fight. Failing the opportunity to meet the enemy, the British Mediterranean Fleet was left the alternative of wearing the Italian Navy down by a war of attrition, nibbling at their ships in surprise raids. The now famous attack on the harbor at Taranto was a successful example of war of attrition, and it incidentally showed friend and foe alike the value of torpedo attacks from the air, a lesson that later the Japanese, with their well-known faculty for imitation, were quick to profit by.

The attack at Taranto was carried out on the night of November 11, the Armistic Day of the First World War, and made by torpedo-carrying planes from the old 22,600-ton aircraft-carrier *Eagle*, which was completed in 1924, and the recently commissioned 23,000-ton carrier *Illustrious*. Taranto, an unusually strongly fortified naval base, lies inside the heel of Italy in the Gulf of Taranto, and could be reached only by planes taking off from aircraft-carriers. It was known that the main enemy fleet lay at Taranto, and Admiral Sir Andrew Cunningham, commander of the British Mediterranean Fleet, decided to attempt to destroy it in its base. At that time the Italian battle fleet consisted of six capital ships—the new *Littorio* and *Vittorio Veneto*, two of the largest battleships in the world, and four slightly smaller ones of the *Cavour* class. This fleet alone, without the cruisers and smaller craft in the harbor, was far more powerful than the British Mediterranean Fleet. The importance of the raid was not exaggerated, since it reduced the strength of the enemy battle fleet for some time to come by half, and thus removed a very serious handicap of the British Fleet—inferiority in numbers and armament. And it demonstrated for the first time the value of torpedo-carrying planes in the hands of skilled and resolute men.

The naval base, one of the best natural harbors in Europe, is divided into an inner and outer harbor, or, as the Italians named them, the Big and Little Sea—Mar Grande, Mar Piccolo. The outer harbor is used mainly for merchant vessels, and here are the commercial docks. The inner harbor, entered by a swing bridge, is the naval harbor, and here on the night of November 11 the Italian battle fleet lay at anchor, protected by hundreds of anti-aircraft guns and a balloon barrage.

With a screening force the carriers *Illustrious* and *Eagle* approached almost within sight of the outer harbor before sending off their planes—first Skua dive-bombers each carrying a 500-pound bomb, and then the Fairey Swordfish with 18-inch torpedoes slung beneath the fuselage. In bright moonlight the Skuas flew over the sleeping port and dropped their heavy bombs among the ships and on harbor installations. Following them came the Swordfish flying low over the water with their 'tin fish,' weighing nearly a ton apiece. Flying straight on in the face of every A.A. gun in the harbor the Swordfish dropped their torpedoes while skimming just over the water and then made rapid climbing turns to escape. In spite of the terrific barrage, only two planes failed to return. Rushing through the water at nearly fifty miles an hour, the torpedoes found their targets in a series of deafening explosions which added to the hell's inferno of noise over the harbor. The warships, immobile and at anchor, were unable to maneuver to avoid the torpedoes, and so every missile found its target. The pilots reported that a *Littorio* class and two *Cavour* class battleships and four cruisers had been hit, though naturally it could not be stated positively that they had been sunk.

The next day a British reconnaissance plane flew over the harbor and brought back photographs that told the story, and an Admiralty communiqué dated November 16 read, in part, as follows:

A further reconnaissance of the Italian naval base at Taranto has established with certainty that three battleships were crippled during an attack by the Fleet Air Arm on the night of November 11–12. Efforts are being made to salve the battleship of the *Littorio* class which was previously seen to have her fo'c'sle under water and a heavy list to starboard. Auxiliary and salvage vessels are lying alongside on both sides of the ship and nets have been laid all round for her protection. Pumping is in progress. The bows of the ship have been raised, and she now has a list to port. The reconnaissance has confirmed that two battleships of the *Cavour* class are aground. One of these is beached and an auxiliary vessel is alongside her. Nets have been laid all round for the protection of the ship. The second *Cavour* class battleship appears to have been abandoned. She is lying heeled over to starboard with only the forward part of her upperworks out of water. The pilot of the reconnaissance aircraft has reported that four shapes can be seen under water off the entrance to the graving dock in the inner harbor.

This report may seem to all but experts an unexciting and even disappointing document, but to the naval strategist it is highly satisfactory, for he sees in the results achieved the removal of a grave threat to Egypt and British forces in Africa and the Near East. The Italian fleet lay athwart Mediterranean convoys supplying the British armies. Even though the enemy repaired his ships within a few months those months were precious in a war where time meant so much to the democracies, who were desperately building up their armed forces to match an enemy greatly superior in numbers and equipment. When the passing of time permits a true perspective of the war, and the value of isolated battles is assessed, it may be found that the Taranto exploit had repercussions that permanently influenced the fortunes of war in the Mediterranean. To say that it turned the tide of the whole war might be a too optimistic guess, but even that would be possible.

During the month following the Taranto raid the Italians retaliated by attacking the British naval base at Alexandria. In an air raid the enemy claimed to have crippled the French battleship *Lorraine*, which, it will be remembered, was interned there. Meanwhile British submarines were not idle. H.M.S. *Thunderbolt* (formerly the *Thetis*, which sank on her trials in 1939) and H.M.S. *Parthian* sent to the bottom enemy supply ships, some transports, and an unknown number of submarines. H.M.S. *Pandora* destroyed two large transports proceeding to Libya. H.M.S. *Osiris* sank the Italian destroyer *Palestro*. H. M. S. *Regent, Upholder, Utmost,* and *Triton* all sank supply ships and tankers sailing in convoys, and materially held up the enemy attacks on Egypt. Later the submarines *Unique, Tetrarch,* and *Triumph* caused heavy losses to Italian supply convoys, and about this time the Free French submarine, operating with British forces, was sunk by the Italians, who lost two submarines, one of which was identified as *Anfitrite*. In March a British submarine torpedoed and sank one of the *Condottieri* class cruisers. A cruiser of the same class, *Bartolomeo Colleoni,* had been sunk in the previous July by the cruiser *Sydney.* In May (1941) a British submarine sank the 18,000-ton liner *Conte Rosso,* which was carrying three thousand troops to Libya. In October the cruiser *Ajax,* which had been one of the ships in the action against *Graf Spee* off the river Plate, met an Italian squadron southeast of Sicily, and sank two torpedo-boats and the destroyer *Artigliere.* The British then sent a radio message to Italy on a commercial wave-length giving the position of the survivors, who were in rafts and boats. By doing this the British were taking a serious risk, for it gave their position away, and since they were close to Sicily and the weather was clear they might have been attacked.

So the doleful toll of sinkings mounted, not without losses to the British Navy. Among these was the destroyer *Mohawk,* one of the famous "Tribal" class destroyers, which are almost as big as light cruisers. She was lost during an attack on an enemy convoy off Sicily in April. The cruiser *Southampton* was lost while attempting to defend the carrier *Illustrious* in January.

From the British point of view the most successful naval action in the Mediterranean was the action that came to be known as the Battle of Matapan. The most costly and tragic action was that during the withdrawal of troops from Crete when the Royal Navy suffered losses heavier than those at Dunkirk. The Battle of Matapan, a perfect example of co-ordination between air and sea forces, was divided into two phases which lasted approximately fifteen hours. On March 27 (1941) the Commander-in-Chief of the Mediterranean Fleet, Sir Andrew Cunningham, received a radio message in code that an Italian battle squadron had been sighted steaming eastward south of Cape Matapan, and early in the afternoon of the same day he put out of Alexandria with the battleships *Warspite*, *Valiant*, and *Barham* and the aircraft-carrier *Formidable*. The battleships were all old ships of 35,000 tons built before the First World War, but the carrier was one of the most recent additions to the Navy and of the same class as *Illustrious*, whose story was told in Chapter II.

Already at sea under Vice-Admiral Pridham-Wippell was a strong cruiser force consisting of *Orion, Perth, Gloucester*, and *Ajax*, and these ships established contact with the enemy at 8 A.M. on March 28 about a hundred miles south-west of Crete. Smoke was sighted ahead and to the west, and half an hour later three large enemy cruisers with a destroyer were clearly made out. Admiral Pridham-Wippell, in *Orion*, turned his squadron to the south-east to draw the Italian warships towards the main British battle squadron coming up from the south-west and still far away. The two opposing forces began firing salvos at each other, but without apparent damage to either side. The British cruisers altered course several times to put off the enemy's aim, and slowly drew out of range until, unexpectedly, the Italians swung on their tracks and steamed in the opposite direction. The British, so as not to lose touch, also turned and had worked round astern of the enemy when it became apparent that he had turned to have the support of a huge *Littorio* class battleship which suddenly appeared on the horizon steaming at high speed towards the British cruisers. The latter at once turned away, but even while they were turning, the battleship opened fire at a range of 30,000 yards, or nearly eleven miles. The cruisers produced a smoke-screen, and some shells fell close to *Gloucester*, the weather ship,[1] but none hit her. British destroyers tried to get in between the enemy and the cruisers, but the latter were steaming at over thirty knots and the destroyers were some time before they could work round to lay their bank of smoke; and before they were able to do this the battleship's attention was diverted by a torpedo attack from planes which had taken off from H.M.S. *Formidable*.

The enemy ceased fire as he turned to avoid the torpedoes, and the cruisers were able to draw out of range. When the smoke-screen cleared, the battleship and cruisers were not in sight, but coming up from the south were seen the main British battleships, and the cruisers now took their stations ahead of the fleet, which pressed on in pursuit of the enemy. A radio message had come through from a reconnaissance plane that the Italian battleship had been damaged and slowed up by a torpedo. About sunset a striking force of torpedo-carrying planes from *Formidable* flew over on its way to attack the enemy, and the sailors cheered wildly. At dusk the enemy cruisers could just be made out, but in the growing darkness they were lost sight of. A little later the night sky to the north was lit up by searchlights, A.A. shells, and explosions as the torpedo-bombers went into action.[2]

The two forces had lost touch in the darkness. The

[1] The weather ship is the ship farthest to windward.

[2] The Italian force consisted of one battleship, seven cruisers, and about ten destroyers.

skirmishing stage had ended and soon the second phase was about to open. At 10.20 P.M. the battleships *Warspite* (flagship), *Barham,* and *Valiant* were steaming in line-ahead formation when a searchlight from *Greyhound,* one of the screening destroyers, flashed on and disclosed three enemy cruisers—*Zara, Fiume,* and *Polo*—at almost point-blank range. Before the Italians could recover from their surprise, for they were unaware of the presence of the British battle squadron, a broadside from *Warspite* ripped through *Zara,* knocking overboard a rear turret and creating fearful havoc fore and aft. A thousand-foot column of smoke rolled upward from the stricken ship, which listed over and began to sink immediately. *Pola* and *Fiume* were simultaneously engaged by *Barham* and *Valiant,* whose broadsides turned the two cruisers into blazing wrecks. A few wild shots were fired from the enemy, but without doing any damage or causing any casualties whatever to the British forces. When the destroyer *Havoc* went in to finish the burning cruisers her captain sent the following message to the Commander-in-Chief: "I am hanging on to the stern of *Pola.* Shall I board her or finish her off with depth-bombs?" He did not board.

The remaining enemy forces in the vicinity scattered, but not before the Italian destroyers *Vincenzo, Gioberti,* and *Maestrale* were sunk. The searchlights from the British ships disclosed hundreds of men swimming in the sea or clinging to rafts, and British and Greek destroyers which had joined Cunningham's forces worked all night picking up survivors. Nearly a thousand men, including about three hundred Germans, were rescued, and three hundred more might have been saved had not Axis planes come over and bombed the rescue boats, so forcing the ships to withdraw and leave these unfortunate creatures struggling in the sea. But Cunningham sent a wireless message to the Italian Naval Staff giving the position of the men left behind and suggesting that a hospital ship be sent.

At dawn on March 29 a diligent air search was made for the *Littorio* class battleship which had been crippled by Fleet Arm aircraft, but as she was not seen, in spite of a wide survey over hundreds of square miles of sea, it was concluded that she must have sank, as her speed, which had been slowed down to fifteen knots, would scarcely allow her to reach port in time to avoid discovery. But, omitting 'probables' and counting only 'certains,' the enemy had lost three cruisers and two destroyers while the British ships had not had a scratch. Of airplanes each side had lost two. The Battle of Matapan was one of those flawlessly executed actions which war seldom provides an opportunity to carry out, and the news of the battle's successful conclusion greatly heartened the British people, who were enduring all the horrors of air raids at that time.

The work of the Fleet Air Arm in aiding the Navy in the Mediterranean was of immense value. For example, one squadron of naval torpedo-bombers in seven months attacked and damaged or sank 500,000 tons of enemy merchant shipping besides many warships. An idea of what this means may be gathered by comparing it with the depredations of the famous German cruiser *Emden* in 1915, which destroyed 70,000 tons of Allied shipping. And when it is remembered that this small force of torpedo-bombers was operating in one area of the Mediterranean only the value of these naval aircraft is strikingly driven home. The types used were mainly the famous Swordfish and the Albacore.

A successful attack made on a big Italian liner in January 1941 was typical of the work of the Fleet Air Arm.

The 14,000-ton liner *Victoria*, loaded with stores and arms for Tripoli, was sighted traveling in a convoy at sunset. The convoy, consisting of three freighters and the liner, which was strongly protected by a battleship and several destroyers, was 180 miles north of Benghazi when sighted, but the pilot who made the attack, Lieutenant H. M. Ellis, waited until dusk before approaching, in order to lessen the chance of being seen. He kept only twenty feet above the sea, as two Junkers 88's were flying at fifteen hundred feet above. Getting into a position so that the last light of the sunset was behind him, and skimming only a few feet above the sea, he approached to within about six hundred yards of the liner before releasing the torpedo. At that range it could not miss, and the torpedo sped straight for the doomed ship. The people on board did not fire their A.A. guns until the plane had dropped the torpedo, and then the guns blazed away furiously, but without seriously damaging the aircraft, which zigzagged away until it was out of range. The pilot saw a gigantic column of water spout up amidships as the torpedo struck the liner, and she had already begun to settle before he got out of range. The plane had been hit in the engine, and it looked as though it might not bring the air-crew back to land, especially as the Junkers now began attacking it with cannon-shells. But by superb piloting Lieutenant Ellis, dodging the enemy and flying so low the Junkers could not get beneath him, managed to avoid disaster and escape in the darkness and return to the base without further adventures. For his successful attack on the convoy Lieutenant Ellis was awarded the Distinguished Flying Cross.

The evacuation of Crete was in some ways a repetition of Dunkirk except that the Navy's losses were higher. The moment that it became obvious that Hitler's armies in-

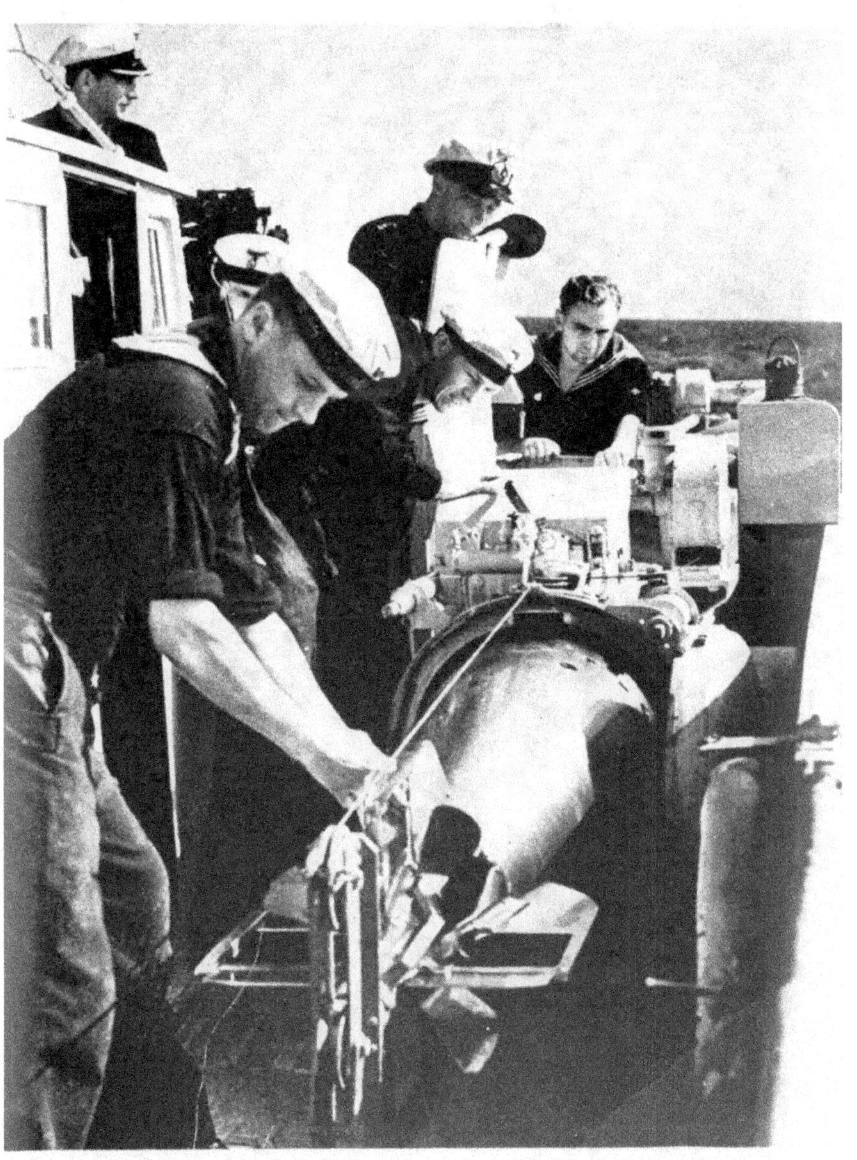

The crew of a German E-boat load a torpedo into the tube. *British Combine Photos.*

A Nazi floating casualty station that drifted ashore at a British coast town. These refuges are moored off the French coast for Nazi airmen shot down over the Channel. *British Combine Photos.*

tended to invade Crete the Commander-in-Chief of the Mediterranean fleet, Sir Andrew Cunningham, ordered warships available to steam at full speed to that area to prevent at all cost a sea-borne invasion of the island. In this the Navy succeeded, for every enemy attempt to get ships across from the mainland was frustrated, but the Navy was impotent to prevent an air-borne invasion, and so within a few days Nazi paratroops turned the lovely island into a modern Golgotha. There was plenty of criticism by the British people over the loss of Crete but it is not our purpose here to offer any explanation or excuse other than to point out that the British Army, still handicapped by the stupendous loss of equipment at Dunkirk, could not be in superior numbers everywhere at once. So it fell to the Navy to come to the defense of the island, and here let us summarize briefly the doleful but stirring story of the Navy's sacrifice.

The ships had a clear duty to perform, that is, to prevent the enemy's bringing tanks, ammunition, troops or supplies by sea, and this order was faithfully carried out. Since this task kept the ships within easy range of enemy airfields on the mainland, and since the Navy had no air protection worth mentioning, it meant that the ships would be exposed to the full fury of the Luftwaffe, and this is precisely what happened. On May 21, the destroyer *Juno* was bombed and sunk. That night a British naval force headed by the cruiser *Dido* intercepted an enemy invasion fleet and, in spite of the darkness, succeeded in sinking every one of the troop transports and scattering their escort. The enemy was taken by surprise; and, though Italian destroyers loosed several torpedoes, they all went wild and no harm was done. The transports, mostly commandeered Greek wooden schooners and caïques, were crowded with German troops who leaped overboard with their full equipment on when the British ships opened fire.

At daylight the next morning the enemy, always reckless with human life in battle, made another attempt to get his armored forces across the stretch of water between the mainland and Crete. A reconnaissance plane reported a big troop convoy south of Milo Island. Rear Admiral King in the cruiser *Naiad* at the head of a force of cruisers and destroyers sailed out to intercept the enemy and succeeded in sinking or dispersing all the ships but not without suffering heavy casualties, for throughout the day swarms of Nazi bombers attacked the British ships. Early in the afternoon a direct hit sank the destroyer *Greyhound* within a few minutes. The cruisers *Gloucester* and *Fiji* and two destroyers closed in to take off the crew of the stricken *Greyhound,* and at once were attacked by the bombers, which concentrated their fury mainly on the *Gloucester* until a direct hit amidships put an end to her career. The next victim was the *Fiji* which, after several hits from heavy bombs, went down, her A.A. guns firing to the end. But the Luftwaffe had not gained these victories without loss, for the guns of the warships shot down German planes like pigeons until the sea was littered with the wreckage of burning planes.

The next morning the enemy made his third and last attempt to invade Crete by sea but this too was scotched, the Fifth Destroyer Flotilla intercepting the ships and sending them to the bottom of the Cythera Channel, that seventy-mile-wide strip of water between Crete and the mainland. This impudent interference with his plans infuriated the enemy, who, in revenge, set out to destroy every British ship in Cretan waters. At dawn the Luftwaffe came until the sky thundered with the roar of airplane motors. The planes were flying high, and of the hundreds of bombs dropped none actually hit any of the ships. After three hours of this, low dive-bombers arrived and this time were more successful. The first victim was the destroyer *Kashmir,* which split in two and sank in a few minutes from a direct hit by a half-ton bomb.

The next victim was the famous destroyer *Kelly,* commanded by Lord Louis Mountbatten. Another half-ton bomb burst her sides open and she sank in less than a minute. Her captain was washed off the bridge and was among those who were picked up later. The *Kelly,* a large single-funnel destroyer, had come to the public's notice when in May, 1940, she figured on one of the most remarkable salvage feats carried out during the war. While leading a flotilla of destroyers in search of German minelayers off the Belgian coast, she was hit by a torpedo from an unseen U-boat. The explosion killed every man in the forward boiler room and tore a gaping hole in her side from keel to deck. So much water entered the ship that she settled till her decks were awash. But her bulkheads held, and it was decided to make an attempt to tow her into an English port.

This seemingly impossible feat was accomplished in spite of a determined effort by the Luftwaffe to sink her and the escorting destroyers. Slowly the stricken destroyer was towed toward the English coast. Fortunately the sea remained calm and after a tow lasting ninety-one hours the *Kelly* was brought to safety. One night enemy torpedo boats tried to give her the *coup de grâce,* but her time had not yet come, and, as we have seen, she lived to take part in the operations off Crete. This heroic epic of the sea was not immediately made known by the Admiralty, and not till three months later did the bald statement appear in an official communiqué that H.M.S. *Kelly* had been torpedoed and seriously damaged by enemy forces but was now repaired and back in active service. This stark announcement covered one of the most determined fights against adversity in all the long history of the Royal Navy.

To return to the operations off Crete. The survivors of *Kelly* and *Kashmir* were picked up three hours later by the destroyer *Kipling* who, though pursued by the fury of the Luftwaffe, for several hours carried on with her errand of mercy. While the Navy's efforts to prevent a sea-borne invasion of Crete only delayed the inevitable fall of that inadequately defended island, the sacrifice had not been in vain, for thousands of British and Colonial troops were taken off and brought to safety. The rescuing cruisers and destroyers entered the gates of Hell when they coolly steamed into the narrow Cretan bays to save what they could of the Imperial forces.

In one night nearly 14,000 men were taken off while death rained from the skies. The second night the Navy saved another 5,500 troops under conditions of appalling difficulty and risk. On the third night another 16,000 men were withdrawn. During this dreadful night a transport packed with troops was bombed and sunk, but the destroyer *Diamond* went in and managed to rescue from the sea 600 men. *Wryneck*, another destroyer, picked up a further 100 men. The next morning both these destroyers were sunk by German dive-bombers, and only 50 men were saved. The survivors said that they had been ruthlessly machine-gunned by Nazi pilots as they swam in the sea.

On the fourth night over 4000 men were taken off and on the fifth night the Navy made a determined effort to bring away 12,000 troops as well as 750 R.A.F. personnel; but, owing to ceaseless bombing, the ships were able to take off only some four thousand-odd troops besides the R.A.F. people.

After this, one would have thought the Navy had had enough, but on the night of May 1 the ships went in and found on the beaches a few hundred men, who were taken on board. Altogether about 45,000 men were safely brought away from Greece, but at a heavy cost in ships. Among other Naval losses not hitherto mentioned were the cruisers *Calcutta* and *York*, the latter being bombed to destruction while she was at anchor undergoing repairs at Suda Bay, Crete. Altogether the Navy lost in the Greek operations three cruisers and six destroyers as well as a number of Army troop-ships. A sad disaster for British arms, but the Prime Minister silenced the critics by pointing out that Britain had promised Greece all assistance possible and she had kept her promise.

The famous aircraft-carrier *Ark Royal,* which over a period of two years the enemy claimed to have sunk, was finally torpedoed in the Western Mediterranean on November 14, 1941. As she went down one of her officers was heard to remark, "That is damned hard luck on the old lady." For two years she had been the phantom ship of the Navy. The Nazis would, from time to time, derisively ask over their radio "Where is the *Ark Royal?*" and the Admiralty's natural reticence over the ship's whereabouts did nothing to dispel the mystery. Credulous people influenced by plausible enemy propaganda began to believe that the *Ark Royal* had been sunk. But when the Admiralty communiqués describing the chase of the *Bismarck* appeared it was noticed that the *Ark Royal* was mentioned as one of the ships which took part in the hunt. She had been in action off Norway, in the hunt for the *Graf Spee* in the South Atlantic, and in more than one Mediterranean action. In over two years of operational service her Skua dive-bombers and Fairey Swordfish torpedo-carrying biplanes had sunk many enemy ships and shot down over one hundred enemy planes. But at four o'clock on that November afternoon while the great *Ark* was steaming through a calm sea almost within sight of Gibraltar an unseen torpedo struck her on the starboard side amidships and below the water line. All the loud speakers below decks were put out of action and orders had to be passed verbally throughout the ship. All lights went out and the vast floating aerodrome listed ominously and began to spill black oil over the surrounding water. She did not sink at once but the single torpedo had torn such a large hole in the hull that although the men in the boiler room kept the pumps going for eleven hours they were unable to check the rising water and early the next morning the great ship went down when within 25 miles of Gibraltar. She had cost three and a quarter million pounds.[3] Out of a complement of 1545 officers and men only one rating was lost.

After the torpedo had struck, all those who had nothing to do with the working of the ship such as hundreds of air personnel were mustered at their stations and remained there quietly awaiting orders. As the heavy list made it impossible to launch the boats one of the escorting destroyers came right alongside the sinking carrier and took off hundreds of men who slid down ropes onto the destroyer's fore deck. A seaman and a stoker each brought down one of the ship's cats in their arms. The paymaster lowered on the end of a line two suitcases stuffed with £20,000 in notes taken from the ship's safe. But they could not save the half-dozen Swordfish planes standing forlornly on the fore flight deck, or the scores of others in the hangar deck, or the boats or guns or a million pounds'

[3] Built at Cammell Lairds, Birkenhead, she was the latest thing in aircraft carriers. Her hangar could house 72 planes, she had three lifts for hoisting planes to the flight deck. Her wardroom was the largest in the Navy. Electric welding in the hull had saved 500 tons in rivets.

worth of precious equipment which Britain needed so badly.

There were plenty of episodes of heroism, particularly in the boiler room where a volunteer party remained for eleven hours fighting the rising flood without heeding their own safety. The chief petty officer in charge of the attempt to save the ship watched the water gaining but he did not abandon hope till about three in the morning when the vast hull lurched over to 24 degrees. Water spilled out of the tanks and the boilers had to be shut down. Oil ran from the furnaces and caught fire as it spread over the boiler room floor. The chief P.O. was forced to order the men to abandon the boiler room and save themselves while there was still time. As the list made the ladders unclimbable the men hauled themselves up hand over hand by ropes, and then crawled up the steeply sloping flight deck in the darkness to lower themselves down to the tug waiting alongside. In the offing the escorting destroyers stood by like faithful watchdogs to prevent a U-boat attempting to interfere with salvage efforts. But all efforts were in vain for at 6.20 A.M. the *Ark Royal* rolled over and sank. The enemy could at last announce with truth that Britain's famous aircraft carrier was sunk.

Part Two

CHAPTER VIII

The Merchant Navy

AT THE beginning of hostilities the British Empire possessed about 9000 merchant ships of over 100 tons, with a total tonnage of approximately 20,000,000 tons. At once two important things happened to this vast armada. Most of the bigger vessels immediately became part of the Royal Navy, to be employed as transports or armed liners, and the rest were no longer permitted to sail their own independent ways as free ships, as in peace-time. For their own protection they were obliged to sail in convoys, protected by armed escorts. For the duration of the war the tramp steamer had disappeared from all Empire sea-routes. Nevertheless during the war there were never fewer than 2000 British merchant ships at sea apart from those loading and discharging at ports. By February 1942, after two-and-a-half years of war, the Merchant Marine had been armed with no less than 13,000 anti-aircraft guns and thousands of other devices, such as degaussing apparatus, anti-submarine detection instruments, searchlights, depth-charges, and even barrage balloons to discourage low dive-bombing attacks. Thousand of gunners and technicians had to be hastily trained to man and work these protective devices. The enemy made strenuous attempts to checkmate these measures by a colossal programme of U-boat construction and new tactics in submarine warfare, assisted by long-range bombers flying far

130

out over the Atlantic from French airfields in Brittany.

Until Japan entered the war in December 1941 most of the losses in the Merchant Marine occurred in the Atlantic (hence the name the Battle of the Atlantic), but when attacks started on Allied shipping in the Pacific after Japan's entry into the war the Battle of the Atlantic became the Battle of the Seven Seas. Since Britain possessed the largest merchant fleet in the world it was inevitable that the enemy should concentrate his attacks on British ships, his main purpose being to starve the people of Great Britain into submission. The Battle of the Atlantic resulted in the loss of scores of valuable ships and their precious cargoes. The bed of the Atlantic was strewn with wrecked ships, most of them merchantmen, but also a number of men-of-war. Down there in the utter darkness of the Atlantic deeps, beyond any hope of salving, lay the crushed and rusting hulls of ships spilling their cargoes of foodstuffs, tanks, airplanes, trucks, and guns into the black ooze of the ocean floor. Down there lay the wrecks of two giant battleships (*Hood* and *Bismarck*), a famous luxury liner (the 42,000-ton *Empress of Britain*), the 15,000-ton Blue Star liner *Arandora Star*, which took down with her 610 enemy aliens en route to Canada, the 20,000-ton Cunarder *Carinthia*, the giant 28,000-ton French liner *Champlain*, the 14,000-ton P. and O. liner *Sussex*, the 15,000-ton Union Castle liner *Dunvegan Castle*, the 19,000-ton Anchor liner *Caledonia*, the 11,000-ton Ellerman liner *City of Benares*, in which 77 children were drowned, the 13,000-ton Donaldson liner *Athenia*, the first merchant ship in the war to be lost. Among the armed merchant cruisers in this vase submarine graveyard are the 19,000-ton Cunard White Star liner *Laurentic*, the two 16,000-ton P. and O. liners *Rawalpindi* and *Rajputana*, the 14,000-ton Aberdeen and Commonwealth liner *Jervis Bay*, and a host of others of lesser fame. They lie crumpled wrecks covered with barnacles, their rotting and rusting cargoes representing millions in money and lost man-hours, a horrible indictment of the folly and the wastage of war.

At the outbreak of war the government took over these and other merchant vessels, thus following a time-honored custom in war-time. The big passenger liners became temporary warships armed with medium-caliber guns and other offensive armament. Their chief use is to harry enemy trade and escort convoys. Because of their complete lack of armor-plating they are very vulnerable to any form of attack, and the percentage of losses is inevitably high. They are very useful in helping the Navy, though outmatched by any ship except small destroyers and patrol craft. Stripped of all their luxury fittings, they are also employed as troop transports. As armed merchant cruisers they are invariably manned by R.N.R. and R.N.V.R. officers and crew.

The modern convoy system has been developed into a routine procedure. The ships' captains assemble together at the port of departure and receive their instructions from a naval officer, who gives each ship a number and explains the course to be followed and other matters for their safety. They have positive orders which must be obeyed. They must keep in formation, but if one of the ships lags behind through engine or other trouble the convoy continues on its voyage. A lame duck must take its chance alone, for the safety of the convoy must not be jeopardized. Likewise if one of the ships is attacked by the enemy the convoy must leave it to its fate. Convoys are made up of from twenty to two hundred ships steaming in lanes through which rush the fussy little destroyers and corvettes watching their charges like hens watching their chicks. One of the obvious disadvantages of the convoy system is that all ships must travel at the speed of the slowest vessel, and speed is an important safety factor in waters patrolled by submarines. All ships in the convoy must keep in their station, and this is a difficult maneuver when the convoy is ordered to steam on a zigzag course if U-boats are about. The orders are passed to the ships through loud-speakers from the escorting destroyers. The senior captain in the convoy is usually appointed commodore for the voyage. While opinions differ as to the relative advantages of sailing alone or in convoy, experience has taught that the convoy system is undoubtedly the better. Lone ships scattered all over the ocean without a protecting escort are sitting targets to prowling submarines, whereas a large convoy, while more easily seen, is so jealously guarded that a submarine is exposed to a grave risk in attacking it.

The Merchant Navy has been called upon to carry out strange tasks in war-time, but none more bizarre than when it went to the aid of the British Army stranded on the beaches around Dunkirk. This was the work mostly of the small ships, and no less than 700 of these small craft took part in that tremendous affair. Besides this there were 57 passenger steamers of the type that cross the Channel in peace-time and carry tourists on the Clyde. There were also 91 freight steamers. Included in this mixed armada were tugboats, motor-launches, fire-boats, sailing barges, fishing ketches, and ships' lifeboats. The Port of London Authority alone sent 880 lifeboats and 34 motor-lifeboats. The Royal National Lifeboat Institution when asked for help managed within twenty-four hours to send to Dover seventeen lifeboats from various stations on the South and East Coasts. Incidentally, this giant fleet was nobly assisted by the Navy, which sent across 222 naval vessels of all kinds from destroyers to motor-boats.

In the seven days of the evacuation the naval and merchant vessels lifted a total of 334,000 troops. The Merchant Navy's sacrifices at Dunkirk included many pleasure steamers well known to British people. Among these were the former cross-Channel packets *Engadine* and the ultra-modern *Royal Daffodil*. The latter was built to replace the old *Daffodil* that had made the name famous for the part that vessel took in the heroic Zeebrugge raid in the First World War. The masters of fifty-seven passenger ships, ninety-one merchant ships, and fifty-four tugboats were officially thanked by the government for their part in the affair. The ships' lifeboats alone saved more than 100,000 men. At the call for small craft to go and bring back the beleaguered troops London did its part—and more. Scores of small pleasure craft, motor-boats, yachts, and launches from as far up the Thames as Teddington put down the river and went to sea for the first time since they were built. Pleasure craft designed for gentle cruising up the quiet reaches of the river and never meant for deep water crossed the Channel and returned, some of them many times, facing Nazi shell-fire, mines, and dive-bombers on their errand of mercy. Also from the London River went the fire-boat *Massey Shaw* with its crew of firemen to face the inferno of the Dunkirk beaches and bring back sixty men, some of whom were badly wounded. She made a second trip to the beaches, where she acted as a tender and brought out to bigger ships waiting in deep water hundreds more soldiers, and then, when her work was done, returned to her berth near Blackfriars Bridge, her decks red with the blood of wounded men.

In the Dunkirk evacuation 125 merchant sailors gave their lives and another 81 were wounded. Many of the smaller craft had neither chart nor compass and found Dunkirk by the smoke from the burning town. Many were lost on the treacherous Goodwin Sands. Others were sunk by mines or bombs, and altogether 171 British ships were damaged by enemy attacks.

Trawlers, minesweepers, tugs, ferry-boats, river-steamers, wherries, barges, lifeboats, and motor-launches lay off the beaches under a rain of bombs and machine-gun fire so persistent that it is a miracle that any escaped. The Thames tug *Nicholas Drew* crossed to Dunkirk towing a dozen lifeboats, and a 30-foot motor-launch went through the surf to ferry out to waiting ships 600 men, and in several trips herself carried 420 men safely to England. The last ship to leave Dunkirk jetty was the pleasure steamer *Princess Maud,* and as she pulled away from the quay a shell fell at the very spot she had just occupied.

The experience of the General Steam Navigation Company's *Royal Daffodil* was typical of the risks all vessels took when they went to Dunkirk during that nightmare week at the end of May 1940. *Royal Daffodil* was a 2060-ton, 20-knot ship, 313 feet long and with accommodation for 2000 passengers on short runs. In peace-time she was on the regular Dover-Ostend service. On her first trip back from Dunkirk she brought 950 soldiers, who were landed safely at Dover. On her second trip she brought 1800, and on the third 1700 soldiers. On the fourth trip she rescued 2500 French troops, and on the sixth 1900 mixed French and British. On the seventh and last trip an aerial torpedo put an end to this wonderful little steamer's rescue efforts, but by the heroic work of her officers and crew she was brought, battered but safe, back to England. She had saved altogether 8850 troops. She had escaped from all previous bombing attempts to sink her, but on the last trip the enemy did his best to destroy her. Six aerial torpedoes were dropped by Junkers bombers, but the first five missed. The sixth, however, passed through three decks and the engine-room and out at the starboard side, exploding in the sea. The force of the explosion burst in the plating on the water-line and started small fires in various parts of the ship. Water pouring in through the hole in her side caused her to list to starboard, and to bring the ship upright the captain ordered all lifeboats to be hung over the port side and filled with water. This operation was successfully carried out, in spite of repeated machine-gun attacks from enemy planes, and the ship heeled sufficiently to port to lift the hole above the surface of the water. The chief engineer and the second then, by hard work and up to their necks in water, managed to plug the hole with bedding rammed tightly into it. This done, *Royal Daffodil* steamed slowly home.

The only pier where ships could be berthed to take off troops along the nine miles of coast where the British and French soldiers waited was the East Pier at Dunkirk, the much-bombed Jetée de l'Est which thrusts out seaward at the end of the 900-yard-long stone causeway known as the Promenade de la Digue. The whole structure is nearly a mile in length, and along that narrow causeway thousands of British and French soldiers waited in patient queues for days to be taken off. Thousands more stood massed on the low sandy beaches without cover against the incessant air attacks, waiting their turn while a fleet of small boats carried them out to the waiting ships. Many boats were sunk, but others took their place and the work of rescue was never interrupted for long. Since the five-foot-wide East Pier at Dunkirk could not suffice to embark the thousands of waiting men before the enemy arrived, military policemen outside the town diverted long columns of tired men to the beaches. The army authorities did not expect to save more than 10 per cent of the British Expeditionary Force, but by the efforts of the British sailors, and the heroic rearguard actions of certain units of the Army, over 90 per cent of the troops were lifted from Dunkirk and the beaches. Critics have suggested that the Merchant Marine had done work properly the function of the Navy, and the answer to this is that the Navy was there and lost six destroyers during the operations. It is also of interest to note that three destroyers, *Codrington*, *Shikari*, and *Vanquisher*, made seven trips, *Malcolm* eight trips, and *Sabre* nine trips. Six British destroyers lifted from Boulogne in seven-and-a-half hours 4600 troops. The French admiral Abrial distinguished himself for the great part he took. Seven French destroyers were sunk during the operation, making a total of thirteen destroyers lost.

To return to the merchant ships, the exploit of the drab little freighter *Benlawers* was as inspiring as anything that happened during those tragic days, and had it been an isolated episode instead of one of a hundred similar ones it would have become the theme of maritime sagas comparable to that of Grenville's *Revenge* or *The Loss of the "Royal George."* *Benlawers*, a single-funneled, three-island [1] cargo ship of 5800 tons and with a crew of forty-eight, left Dover on May 23 loaded down above the Plimsoll marks with army trucks and ammunition for the British troops defending Boulogne. The German Army had broken through the French northern wing and were advancing on Calais, and it was essential that Boulogne should be held as long as possible to assist the Dunkirk withdrawal by relieving some of the pressure on that besieged town.

Benlawers was escorted across the Channel by a destroyer from whose captain she took orders. The little

---

[1] 'Three-island type' refers to steamers with raised poop, fo'c'sle, and central superstructure.

steamer could not make better than twelve knots, and the trip across took over two hours, but was accomplished without enemy interference until the two ships came within half a mile of the Boulogne breakwater. Here they were met by such fierce artillery fire from German guns along the coast that it looked as if *Benlawers* would be sunk before the cargo could be unloaded. The destroyer's captain therefore ordered the freighter to follow him to Calais, but when the latter arrived opposite the two pier-heads which are the entrance to the harbor an Aldis lamp from the shore blinked the signal "Keep out." However, her captain went in, but took the precaution of turning round in the harbor so that the ship's head pointed seaward in order that he could get away quickly if necessary. The town was being heavily shelled by enemy howitzers, and German troops were already in the suburbs. The British C.O. at the dock called out that he could hold off the enemy if the cargo was landed at once, but unfortunately the French stevedores, quite naturally not wishing to be killed, had left, and the Royal Engineers who would have normally done the job were too exhausted after working three days without sleep or rest to unload the cargo; so *Benlawers'* crew started getting the trucks off, though they were frequently interrupted by shrapnel and high-explosive shells bursting on the dock or in the harbor. To make matters worse a stream of wounded men was being brought on board, and as there was no accommodation or facilities for giving them proper attention they had to be laid in the alleyways and in the cleared spaces in the hold.

As the afternoon wore on the shelling got worse, and it was obvious that the Germans were directing their heaviest fire on the ship in an effort to sink her. *Benlawers* was still tied up alongside the quay, but her position was

Battle in the Mediterranean. One British cruiser throws out a smoke screen to shield the convoy, while another elevates her forward guns for action. *British Combine Photos.*

The Battle of the Atlantic is directed from headquarters in secret underground warrens. The captains of merchant ships are receiving instructions on their next convoy. *British Official Photograph.*

growing hourly more perilous. Huge lumps of stone torn from the quay by bursting shells were hurled among the crew and the lorries they were heroically getting ashore. Late that night, when still half the cargo remained in the holds, the captain of *Benlawers* told his crew that he would have to leave the port or lose his ship as bombs and shells were bursting all round and making the position one of the gravest danger, but before the lines were cast off Army officers rushed on board and begged for more ammunition to be unloaded as the gunners were short of shells and the enemy were in the town. This plea could not be ignored, and *Benlawers'* crew went back to their unloading.

By 2.30 in the morning the shelling had got so much worse (a shell had hit the ship) that the captain ordered the lines cast off. With 700 wounded troops packed in every available bit of space below and the decks crowded with civilians, unwounded soldiers, and some prisoners, the drab little steamer drew away from the quay and with increasing speed began to move towards the harbor entrance. At first she was protected from direct observation by the buildings round the dock, but as soon as she passed the end of the piers the enemy coastal batteries directed a steady fire at her. To clear the sandbanks offshore, ships passed through a channel running parallel with the coast, but to do this now would have exposed *Benlawers* to the concentrated fire of the batteries at point-blank range and almost certainly have sunk her, so her captain decided to risk taking his deeply laden ship over the sandbanks. A worse time could not have been chosen, for the tide was low, but the steamer just scraped over the shoal, and although the enemy continued to shell the ship until she was several miles out he did not hit her. She crossed the Channel without further interference, arriving at Dover at breakfast-time after a series of escapes that were barely short of miraculous.

The principal railway companies of Great Britain are also steamship owners, and their ships took a noble part in the Great Exodus. A number of steamers from the famous cross-Channel fleet of the Southern Railway, well known to hundreds of thousands of British travelers to the Continent in the forgotten peace-time days, and other equally famous railway steamers from the Clyde and the Irish Channel, all did fine work in lifting the troops from the beaches. The Southern Railway sent *St. Helier, Paris, Engadine,* and *Maid of Orleans,* and the Isle of Wight-Portsmouth ferry-boat *Fishbourne.* The London and Northwestern sent their 4200-ton steamer *Prague,* which was severely damaged and nearly lost. The London, Midland, and Scottish sent their *Princess Maud,* straight from the Irish Sea service.

Princess Maud, a fine modern steamer of 2900 tons, had accommodation for 1250 passengers and a crew of seventy. This ship's experience well illustrated the hazards of all vessels approaching the French coast during that tragic week. In a haze that reduced visibility to a mile and a half *Princess Maud* sighted the Dunkirk pier and prepared to enter the harbor when she was struck by several shells from a shore-battery. Shells began to fall like hailstones, and the captain hurriedly turned his ship round so that its stern faced the land and so presented a smaller target, but in spite of this precaution a shell tore a large hole in the plating on the water-line and injured a number of the crew. Nevertheless, her captain doggedly put his ship about and made another effort to get into the harbor. Water was now pouring into the ship, and the boats were swung out in an effort to list her over, but the bombing and shelling were getting so bad that to have remained would have meant losing the ship, so the plucky captain was forced to return to Dover. After two days' and nights' hard work dockyard hands had put a temporary steel plate over the hole, and the steamer once again set out on her dangerous mission. Guided to Dunkirk by the light of fires from the burning town, she ran the gauntlet of heavy shelling from German batteries, scattered wrecks, and minefields to pass at last through the entrance between the twin jetties. The confusion in the harbor was so great that *Princess Maud* had to wait outside patiently enduring the shelling and bombing until a berth could be found for her. And even then she was rammed more than once by other ships trying to leave the narrow harbor. At last, along the jetty, the waiting troops who had stood in a mile-long queue for hours scrambled aboard, and *Princess Maud* cast off just as a shell hit the quay. The only light was from the fires in the town, and in semi-blackness she maneuvered past the dark wrecks in the fairway and put to sea, reaching Dover at dawn without further adventures.

Among the oddly assorted armada that went to the rescue of the harried army on the beaches was a number of seagoing tugs sent by the famous Sun Tugs Company, of London. These sturdy little vessels towed barges and smaller craft across the narrow seas and faced the hell of shells and bombs in Dunkirk roads, never leaving until the job was done. London also sent over the famous fleet of paddlewheelers which sailed in the summer-time taking their daily load of Cockneys to Southend and Margate. The favorite of Londoners, *Crested Eagle*, received a direct hit by a bomb and instantly burst into flames. Her captain ran her on the beach, where she was left blazing from stem to stern. From her burst oil-tanks blazing oil spread over the sea, burning to death the soldiers who had leaped overboard. The Llandudno pleasure steamer *St. Seiriol*, which happened to be near by, approached as close to the blazing ship as possible and managed with her one undamaged boat to save about 150 men, most of them wounded, many seriously. This little steamer made seven trips across, in spite of severe bombing, and brought back a grand total of over 6000 men. Though she seemed to bear a charmed life, she did not escape untouched, and when she tied up at Dover Quay for the last time she bore plenty of evidence of the hell she had been through. Her funnel and deck-houses were perforated with shell and bomb fragments, her woodwork torn and splintered by machine gun bullets, her windows and ports broken, and her four boats smashed to matchwood. Half-way through the evacuation her crew were forcibly replaced by fresh men as the army doctors at Dover considered that those who had endured so much were unfit for further service until they had had a rest. Protesting, this brave little group of men was sent home, and when they returned to report for duty the Dunkirk affair was over.

Every Londoner is familiar with the slow, cumbersome red-sailed sailing barges that go down the Thames loaded to within a few inches of the water and managed by a crew of three. Not the sort of craft to go to war in, since their slowness and lack of maneuverability made them easy targets for the German coast batteries and bombers. Yet no less than sixteen of these ungainly barges went across. Their crews (all volunteers) received five pounds danger money and extra for expenses. The barges, with their flat bottoms, proved ideal for running up on the beaches and after taking on a load of soldiers floating off again at high tide. Perhaps the oddest craft to take part in the evacuation, if we except the London fire-boat *Massey Shaw*, was a Thames sludge-hopper (a barge receiving mud brought up by dredgers) which brought back half a thousand men.

This motley fleet that shuttled back and forth across the Channel for seven days, bringing to home shores the British Army and over a hundred thousand of its allies, was a triumph of improvisation. The disaster had taught the British people the first big lesson of the war—that courage is not enough. The old chivalrous days when valor surmounted mountains had gone, and the cry went up from the nation, "Too little and too late." It was a colossal disaster. The British Expeditionary Force had lost all its transport trucks and motor-cycles, field kitchens and stores, all its tanks and artillery; but it had not lost its courage, and in that sense disaster was saved from tragedy. Once again the British had muddled through. The Merchant Navy in saving the Army had probably saved the country, for had the Army been captured the country would have been practically defenseless. When time permits a true perspective of the war it will certainly show that the lifting of the Army from Dunkirk was one of the most decisive factors influencing the outcome of the conflict.

While the little ships were lifting the troops at Dunkirk, and suffering heavy losses for their daring, bigger ships far out in the Atlantic were facing dangers no less deadly. Prowling enemy cruisers, at least one battleship, armed raiders, and U-boats were making the life of merchant seamen the most hazardous of all trades. For example, the so-called pocket-battleship *Graf Spee* destroyed at least ten large British merchantmen in the South Atlantic. Among these was the 10,000-ton Blue Star Line steamer *Doric Star*, bound for England with a cargo of Argentine frozen meat, with the result that hundreds of British butchers missed their meat quota for that period. *Graf Spee* was attended by various German ships, which kept her oil-tanks refueled and took over the prisoners. *Altmark*, which was afterwards known as the 'prison ship,' was taking over three hundred British merchant seamen prisoners to Germany when she was intercepted by the destroyer *Cossack* in a Norwegian fiord and the prisoners released and brought home in the destroyer which had rescued them. *Graf Spee* was known to have sunk nine other ships—the steamers *Clement, Africa Shell, Tairoa, Mapia, Ashlea, Streonshalh, Huntsman, Newton Beach,* and *Trevannion.* All these ships were missing for a long time before it was definitely known that *Graf Spee* had sunk them. The enemy battleship was chasing the French-owned passenger and cargo steamer *Formose* when the timely arrival of the three British cruisers, *Exeter, Ajax,* and *Achilles,* saved the steamer. *Formose* had all her lifeboats swung outboard and her passengers had put on their life-jackets ready to leave the ship when *Graf Spee* suddenly gave up the chase. *Formose* was steaming under forced draught in an endeavor to reach the sanctuary of Brazilian territorial waters, but it was evident that she could not escape and the unhappy passengers had abandoned hope when the three cruisers came in sight. They laid a smoke-screen between the steamer and her pursuer, which then turned to fight the newcomers. Captain Langsdorf, of *Graf Spee*, was a gallant officer and did not hesitate to accept battle with the three cruisers, but instead of destroying them one by one with his superior armament as he might have done he attempted to engage them all at once, with the result that his ship got such a hammering that he had to take refuge in the river Plate.

In the glorious annals of the Merchant Marine the names of certain former passenger liners which at the beginning of the war were armed and sent out as auxiliary warships will live so long as British history is remembered. Such ships were the P. and O. liner *Rawalpindi*, the Anchor liner *Scotstoun*, and the Aberdeen and Commonwealth liner *Jervis Bay*. *Rawalpindi*, a 16,697-ton ex-luxury liner taken over from the P. and O. Company and commanded by Captain E. C. Kennedy, who had served in the First World War, was on contraband patrol between Iceland and the Orkneys one cold, stormy afternoon late in November 1939 when she sighted the two sinister gray shapes of enemy warships. One of these was the battleship *Deutschland*. Although Captain Kennedy knew that he hadn't a chance against the warships, with their heavier guns and longer range, he refused to surrender when he found that he could not escape and chose to go down fighting rather than strike his flag. When the enemy signaled him to heave to and surrender he replied with a salvo from his 6-inch guns. But the range was too far, and with his 11-inch guns the enemy was able to batter *Rawalpindi* into a blazing derelict. Forty minutes after the opening of the action all her guns were knocked out and her decks were strewn with dead and wounded. Captain Kennedy remained on the bridge to the last, when the ship rolled over and went down four and a half hours after the action began. The White Ensign, shot to tatters, still flew gallantly from her masthead and was the last thing to disappear beneath the sea. The three boats which had not been destroyed were launched, but the heavy seas smashed one like an eggshell. The two remaining boats, which got away, were afterwards picked up by the enemy. The German High Command let it be known that they had rescued twenty-six men from *Rawalpindi*. The majority of the crew had died with their ship, preferring death to surrender.

The 17,000-ton Anchor liner *Caledonia*, which in peacetime carried passengers between Glasgow and New York, was at the outbreak of war taken over by the government and renamed *Scotstoun*. In June 1940 this liner, now an armed merchant cruiser, was in the North Atlantic on lone patrol when she was shaken by a tremendous explosion under the stern. In the poor light of early morning her look-out had not seen the torpedo which had been fired from an unseen submarine, which in any case had probably raised its periscope only long enough to take aim. The sea was rough, and the prospect of having to take to the boats not an attractive one. The explosion had wrecked the rudder and torn open several plates, and the ship at once began to settle by the stern. It was the practice of the Admiralty to fill the empty holds of these armed merchant cruisers with sealed barrels to give the ship buoyancy in just such an emergency as this, but unfortunately the barrels began to float out of the hole in the ship's stern, and soon she was surrounded with these bobbing casks, which under less serious circumstances would have seemed a comic sight.

After the torpedo had hit the ship two U-boats were seen through a veil of driving rain less than half a mile away. In a desperate attempt to confuse the enemy's aim the gunners of *Scotstoun* opened fire on the two U-boats and continued to fire until the breeches of the guns were almost level with the sea and the gun-crew had to hold the shells above their heads to keep them dry. Several more torpedoes were fired, and two struck the ship, hastening her end. The heroic crew worked the guns for an hour before they were compelled by the rising sea to give up. They had fought to the last, and *Scotstoun* went down with the flag still flying. Captain O. K. Smyth, the grayhaired commander of the ship, refused to leave after he had ordered the crew to launch the boats, and his officers, for once ignoring discipline, took him by the arms and pushed him overboard. Before they so unceremoniously pushed the old sea-dog overboard to save his life he was heard to say,"We've not done badly, gentlemen. All flags flying and the guns firing to the end." It is pleasant to relate that the gallant commander and over three hundred officers and men were shortly afterwards picked up by British destroyers.

No record of the work of the armed merchant cruisers would be complete without some reference to the heroic fight of *Jervis Bay*, which was deliberately sacrificed by her skipper, Captain Fogarty Fegen, in order that the convoy he was escorting could get away. *Jervis Bay* was a 1400-ton passenger and cargo steamer owned by the Aberdeen Commonwealth Line, converted on the outbreak of war into an armed cruiser. She was escorting a convoy of thirty-eight ships across the North Atlantic when she took part in the action which made her name immortal in the history of the British Merchant Marine. At five o'clock in the evening of November 5, 1940, at the end of a calm autumn day, a large warship was sighted on the horizon about twelve miles distant. The warship was first sighted by the look-out of a Swedish ship in the convoy, and three minutes later flashes were seen from the stranger's guns and a salvo of high-explosive shells burst in the middle of the convoy. The enemy was believed to be one of the German pocket-battleships against whose 11-inch guns the smaller guns of *Jervis Bay* were hopelessly outranged. It soon became obvious that the enemy fire was directed against the largest steamer in the convoy, the 16,700-ton New Zealand Steamship Company's *Rangitiki*, and shortly afterwards shells began to fall round *Jervis Bay*. Captain Fegen, the senior commander, in charge of the convoy, ordered all ships to scatter and take avoiding action under cover of smoke. He then turned his ship and steered straight towards the battleship with the two-fold object of closing the range sufficiently to bring his 6-inch guns into action, and to draw the enemy's fire away from the convoy. In doing so he knew, of course, that he could not himself escape destruction, but the sacrifice would enable at least most of the ships to escape under cover of the fast-approaching darkness. *Jervis Bay* was hit forward by 11-inch shells early in the action, her steering-gear was wrecked, and she was on fire amidships, but she continued on her course towards the enemy, her guns firing all the time. She was receiving fearful punishment, and her superstructure was soon reduced to a twisted mass of metal. On the bridge Captain Fegen, with one arm smashed by a shell fragment, stood grimly directing his ship, which was hopelessly on fire and rapidly sinking. So he and his ship went to their doom, the guns firing to the last and the White Ensign defiantly waving from the mast-head. The sacrifice was not in vain, for his heroic action had held off the enemy long enough to permit most of the ships to escape. Out of thirty-eight ships, thirty-four got clear away. Captain Fegen was posthumously awarded the Victoria Cross for his gallant and selfless devotion to duty and for upholding the finest traditions of the Royal Navy.

In *Jervis Bay* convoy was a tanker named *San Demetrio*, which after being shelled and set on fire by the enemy and given up for lost by the crew, who took to the boats, was sighted two days later by her own crew. They boarded her with much difficulty, and after superhuman efforts put out the fires and brought her back to port, thus saving the ship and 10,000 tons of petroleum. By a strange coincidence another tanker some months later was set on fire and salvaged in a similar way. This ship, *Franche-Comte*, was torpedoed in the night without warning and immediately caught fire. Her commander, Captain Church, believing the ship would blow up at any moment, ordered the boats lowered, and officers and crew got away safely and were picked up by an escorting destroyer. Captain Church requested the destroyer's commander to stand by until the tanker went down, but the request was refused as the naval officer's duty was to search for the U-boat, which was probably still in the neighborhood. Captain Church and several volunteers from his crew therefore elected to take a boat across and try to board the burning ship. A heavy sea prevented them from getting on board in the darkness, but in the morning they succeeded and to their great joy found that the high waves, washing over the vessel, had put out the fires. Two hours later the engineer had got steam up, and, though the ship was badly damaged and low in the water, the sea had flooded only one compartment and she was sufficiently seaworthy to steam at slow speed through the rough seas and so crawl home with her skeleton crew of volunteers. Her steering-gear had been so damaged by the heat of the fire as to be useless, but a jury gear was rigged, and in this way she was nursed through an Atlantic gale without an escort, ultimately to reach port with her precious cargo.

Rajputana, a sister-ship to *Rawalpindi* and herself an armed merchant cruiser, also met her fate while on patrol protecting convoys bringing munitions and food to Britain. She was torpedoed in the North Atlantic by an unseen U-boat, and sank after four hours, during which time her gunners remained at their guns keeping up a continuous fire to prevent the U-boat coming closer. A second torpedo, however, created such havoc that the great liner rapidly began to settle, and the captain was forced to give the order to abandon ship. The men in the boats were sighted by a Coastal Command flying-boat which reported their position to British destroyers and guided the warships to the men's rescue. An interesting point about *Rajputana* was that as a liner she had two funnels, but one of these was a dummy to impress passengers, who prefer ships with twin funnels on the assumption that two-funnel ships are larger and more important. The P. and O. Line in fitting *Rajputana* with two funnels was only following the practice of most big steamship companies. But when the government took over *Rajputana* the dummy funnel was removed, as were all unessential fittings, and the ship was stripped for the grim business of war.

In March 1942 the Shaw, Savill liner *Ceramic*, an 18,000-ton vessel, crawled into Rio de Janeiro after an exciting passage from Liverpool. *Ceramic* seemed to bear a charmed life, for she had several times been unsuccessfully attacked by U-boats. She landed at Rio 365 passengers, most of them women and children evacuated from the war zone, as well as a valuable cargo of British goods. In peace-time she regularly made the passage from Liverpool to South America in two weeks, but an encounter with a U-boat in the South Atlantic had drawn the passage out to forty-five days, and she arrived with her food stores and fuel oil exhausted. She had had a narrow escape from being sunk and owed her survival to seamanship and the aggressive spirit of her gunners, who fought a running battle with a U-boat for several hours and almost certainly sank it, but not without receiving a severe battering from the enemy's guns—so severe, indeed, that after discharging her passengers and cargo she had to go into dock at Rio for repairs before she was fit to go to sea again.

CHAPTER IX

Torpedoed and Bombed

STATISTICS have shown that the submarine is the greatest enemy of merchant shipping, and after the submarine, in the order of importance, the airplane and the warship. Torpedoes and bombs, then, are the merchant sailor's greatest hazard, and the episodes related in this chapter are of ships that have been sunk by one or the other of this form of attack. The most dangerous periods of the day at sea are at dawn and at dusk, when it is impossible to detect a submarine's periscope, although the victim can himself be seen, since the dark mass of the ship, unless perfectly camouflaged, stands out unmistakably in the gloom.

The Asdic, or anti-submarine detecting device, sensitive as it is to the peculiar sound-waves made by U-boats, is not infallible, and cannot function with 100 per cent accuracy in bad weather. Moreover, this excellent instrument is not usually fitted to merchant ships, and the only warning of the proximity of a prowling submarine is then the look-out's alertness. However keen a watch is kept, the slender tube of a periscope is literally invisible in certain lights, and the first warning the unlucky ship has of the danger is the explosion of the first torpedo against her side. Moonlight is the ideal time for the submarine, for a moonless night makes a ship difficult to see and daylight is dangerous for the attacker. More merchant ships were sunk during moonlight hours than at any other period of the day, and the story which follows illustrates how dangerous the moon can be to men who go to sea in war-time.

The victim was a tanker and the season midwinter; the place, the North Atlantic, graveyard of so many tankers. The usual look-outs were stationed all over the ship—men at the mast-heads, on the bridge, and in the bows—and certainly no laxity was responsible for the loss of the ship. A heavy sea was running before a howling gale, which whistled mournfully in the wire rigging—a bad night for launching the boats should it be necessary. The watch, with sou'westers jammed down on their heads and kapok life-jackets over their oilskins, peered across the tumbling waters, but saw nothing suspicious. A submarine would scarcely be about on such a night. But as it happened there were two U-boats in the vicinity, and both had seen the tanker. At half-past seven a terrific explosion shook the long steel hull of the ship, knocking men off their feet and putting out most of the lights. The tanker was armed with two guns in charge of one of the officers, and the first men to recover from the shock of the explosion were the gunners, who trained their guns in the direction in which they thought the submarine to be and began pumping shells at the unseen foe in the desperate hope of driving him off. A few minutes later the moon disclosed the conning-towers of two submarines, and at the moment of discovery the tanker was rocked with a second explosion. She almost jumped out of the water, and when she settled it was obvious by the unnatural twist in her long main deck that she had been nearly torn apart. By all the laws of gravity she should have sunk like a stone, but the stricken ship continued to float, and her gunners continued to fire at the barely visible superstructures of the U-boats.

Down in the engine-room heroic men fought to keep their engines going, while the firemen, wading knee-deep

in water, struggled to prevent the rising flood from quench-
ing the furnaces. These are the men who share all the
dangers without the stimulus of being able to fight back.
Imprisoned among their boilers and machinery, they have
little chance of escape when their ship goes down. Although it was plain that the ship might go without warning, every one of that heroic company stayed at his post
with no thought of leaving until the order to do so came
from the bridge. Meanwhile the gunners had their hands
full, for overhead an enemy plane had appeared and was
trying to get in position to bomb the crippled ship. A properly placed bomb would have sent the tanker up in one
roar of flame that would have incinerated every man
aboard her, but the gunners gave the ominous visitor from
the air such a fierce reception that he prudently flew away
and was not seen again. Down in the engine-room the
toilers there knew nothing of this. They had their hands
full trying to stem the flood that poured through the
cracked plating. Somehow the engines were kept going,
but the reading on the revolution counter did not tally with
the ship's speed, which had dropped almost to zero. The
racing screws could no longer drive the broken, water-
logged hull through the heavy seas, and the way she yawed
told only too plainly that the steering-geer had broken
down. As the weakened hull fell into the trough of the
seas she rolled violently, and the added strain opened the
gaps in the plating still wider. As it was clear that the ship
could not float much longer the order came down to abandon her. The tired men climbed the steel ladders through
the gratings and reached the deck just as the sea began
to pour down the open engine-room hatch. The main deck
was already awash and the lifeboats afloat. The guns,
which had been fired until no ammunition was left, stuck
up at crazy angles, their work done. The captain, the last

man to leave the bridge, looked at the ship's chronometer and noted that it was half an hour after midnight.

The men were forced to take to the boats in the mountainous seas that immediately filled one of them. The men in this boat sat all night up to their waists in icy water, and by dawn nine of them had died. When the boats pulled away one of the submarines approached closer and shelled the sinking ship. Above the thunder of crashing seas and the howling of the wind the voices of men singing could be heard, singing to keep up their spirits and forget their suffering. When the first torpedo had hit the ship the explosion had destroyed one of the lifeboats, which was, of course, swung outboard in accordance with the regulations for ships sailing in danger zones, and as there were now not enough boats to hold everyone a number of men had to be left behind. Shortly after the boats had got away a horrible thing happened. Some of the crew had managed to climb on board a raft, and these men all lost their lives through a device which was intended to save life. This was nothing more than a small electric lamp with a red globe fixed to their life-jackets. The red lights, designed to guide rescuers to men in the water, were seen by one of the U-boats, which immediately fired a torpedo at the raft, blowing everyone on it to pieces.

All night the boats tried to keep together, but in the darkness they drifted apart as they dared not show a light. At daylight one of the boats sighted a ship, and a blanket was hoisted on an oar to attract attention. Two hours later the castaways were safely on board, and the captain of the ship which picked them up returned to the spot where the tanker was believed to have gone down, on the faint chance that some more men might be rescued. As the ship approached the spot the look-outs noticed a dark cone-shaped mass sticking out of the water, and on drawing closer were astonished to discover that it was the bow of the tanker sticking vertically twenty feet above the sea. The ship was standing on end like some grotesque buoy. To add wonder to wonder, two shivering men were seen clinging to the railing round the bows, swaying precariously twenty feet above the sea. With the greatest difficulty these two half-frozen men were got down from their insecure perch and hoisted on board the ship, which then turned towards the land and so brought the survivors safely home. The second lifeboat, in command of the second mate, George Taylor, was picked up the same day and brought to port. Taylor was awarded the George Medal for his part in saving the men, and Third Engineer Grinstead, who had charge of the first boat, received the M.B.E. First Mate Stanley Miller was given the O.B.E. He had remained on the bridge directing the guns throughout the five-hour fight with the U-boats. All of these men, after a brief stay ashore to recuperate from their ordeal, returned to sea to resume their dangerous trade.

Another tanker story came to light when Sir Sydney Jones, the Lord Mayor of Liverpool, at a public ceremony presented eighteen-year-old Leslie Pye, second radio officer of a tanker, with the Royal Humane Society's certificate for valor in saving life at sea. In a little speech of eulogy, when he presented the embarrassed youth with the society's certificate, the Lord Mayor said, "It was one of the bravest of the countless brave deeds which the men of our Merchant Navy have done during this war." Pye's ship was in mid-Atlantic when a torpedo struck her and instantly set the inflammable cargo on fire. Fire at sea is always bad, but the worst of all is fire in a tanker, and so rapidly did the flames spread that some of the crew were caught by the fire before they could launch the boats. The deed of Leslie Pye to which the Lord Mayor referred took place after he and others had got away from the ship. The captain, the third officer, and two other radio operators were lost, but Pye managed to get on to a raft with eleven other men. This raft had been tied by a line to the bows of the tanker to prevent it drifting away until the men had got on to it. But this line now proved a deadly peril to the twelve men, for before it could be cast off the raft was threatened by the burning oil which spread round the ship. Coal-black clouds with a center of orange-colored flame rolled up hundreds of feet from the red-hot tanker, and from the rents in her torn plates oil poured over the sea and burst into flames. The flames ran over the oily surface like a forest fire towards the raft, still fast to the bows of the blazing ship. The oil which covered both the raft and the men made it difficult to maintain a hold on the slippery platform, and a young Scottish seaman lost his hold and slipped into the sea. The swell immediately swept him towards the edge of the spreading patch of blazing oil. The man struggled to swim away from the danger, but the sea was stronger, and in despair he shouted for help. There was no rope to throw to him, and, seeing the man's peril, Pye, who had not had time to get his life-jacket when the ship was torpedoed, dived into the sea and swam boldly towards the sailor, who had reached the edge of the blazing oil. Almost unable to see through the blinding smoke, Pye was guided by the man's cries and, seizing him by the webbing of his life-jacket, slowly dragged him towards the raft. Pye himself was so spent that he had to be lifted on to the raft by his shipmates.

Meanwhile the edge of the burning sea had crept up to one side of the raft, and the men made frantic efforts to paddle the cumbersome craft clear with their hands; but the sea of blazing oil spread round them and the unfortunate men were forced to jump overboard and swim for their lives. All hope seemed lost, for they could not continue swimming in mid-Atlantic indefinitely. Very soon four of the twelve men became exhausted and died, but the others continued paddling about and treading water for an hour and a half, by which time a ship hove in sight and picked them up. Young Leslie Pye, of course, returned to the sea as they all do. Sailors are fond of saying that the fool of the family goes to sea, but the landsman islander whose very existence depends on the crews who man the ships looks upon the sailor not as a fool but as a hero, since in wartime the normal hazards of the sea are increased a hundredfold.

Among the names on Lloyd's list of the world's merchant vessels prior to the year 1942 appeared this entry: "*Svend Foyn,* 1931, 15,000 tons—whale oil factory—St. Helier Shipowners Ltd., London." To amplify this bald description, it may be added that the whale factory is an invention of the enterprising Norwegian whalemen, who designed a ship that could take on board the largest whales and render the blubber into oil while at sea, thus saving time, labor, and money. The whale is hauled on board up a ramp in the stern, and once on deck the giant carcass is stripped of its blanket of blubber by the crew, who feed the blubber into machines with revolving knives, which chop it up and shoot it into the rendering boilers. When cool the clear oil is barreled and carried to market. The whale factory ship is a big, ugly vessel designed solely for utility, and she has completely revolutionized the old picturesque form of whaling. Modern whaling is done by a fleet of small sturdy steamers resembling trawlers with a harpoon gun in the bows. The whales are killed from these small vessels and afterwards collected by the factory ship.

Such a ship was *Svend Foyn,* which had the misfortune

to encounter a U-boat in the Atlantic in the winter of 1941. A fierce gale blowing at the time made it out of the question to launch the boats, which would have been swamped immediately they touched the sea. The long, box-like hull was rolling and pitching so violently it was impossible to stand on deck without hanging on to something. The crew of 235 men in all their experience at sea had never seen worse weather, and when the torpedo blasted a ragged hole in the ship's plating 40 feet wide by 70 feet long it seemed that nothing could save her. *Svend Foyn* was bringing home 20,000 barrels of whale oil, but fortunately it did not catch fire or this tale would not be told. Had that happened every man on board would have died in the holocaust, and *Svend Foyn* would have joined the long list of missing ships—*spurlos versenkt,* as the U-boat captains had said.

That the ship with a seventy-foot-long hole in her starboard side did not sink at once was simply because part of the damage was above the water-line, and though she began to list on the damaged side, she showed no signs of foundering immediately. After studying the situation and surveying the damage as far as possible, the captain came to the conclusion that there was a faint hope that the ship might be kept afloat until the weather moderated sufficiently to permit the launching of the boats. *Svend Foyn* was an oil-burning ship, and the fuel oil was stored in big steel tanks along either side of the hull amidships and below the water-line. If the tanks on the damaged side could be emptied the resulting lightening of that side might bring the ship back on a level keel and keep her afloat indefinitely. The tanks could be emptied by valves, but unfortunately the valve wheels were by now under twelve feet of water, and it seemed impossible to get at them.

Among the sturdy Norsemen in the crew was a quiet

young man who volunteered to try to reach those valves. The difficulties and dangers of the task were increased by the rolling of the ship, which had torn loose four of the sixty-ton blubber tanks which were now charging about the interior of the vessel and smashing everything in their way. Undaunted by the almost insuperable difficulties, the young Norwegian seaman went down to the deck nearest the submerged valves, and, waiting for one of the periods when the ship was not rolling so violently, he took a long breath, dropped into the oily water, and disappeared. Helpers stood by ready to lift him out when he came up, and they counted the seconds anxiously. The lives of every man in the ship depended upon his succeeding. There were many valves to open, and it would be necessary to make several dives to do this. Down in utter darkness in the ice-cold water the Norwegian youth found one of the valve wheels and turned it till he knew the valve must be open. Mingled with the roaring noise of the sea in his ears he could hear the dull booms of heavy objects colliding as they rolled together somewhere in the ship. In later dives to open the valves he knew that these ominous noises were from the huge oil boilers which had broken loose and were charging madly about the ship. Once he narrowly escaped being crushed to death by one of these sixty-ton monsters as it plunged past him. Nor was this the only danger. The violent motion of the vessel had torn loose iron stanchions, steel gratings, and other fittings, any of which could have killed a man as they washed about the interior of the ship. But the young seaman stuck to his job and made several dives until exhaustion and cold forced him to stop. Each time he was hauled out of the water after a dive he vomited oil and water swallowed while struggling with the valves, and his limbs had to be massaged to drive out the numbness and cold.

Meanwhile the gale, which showed no signs of abating, was battering the ship into a sad wreck. Two of the four lifeboats were crushed like eggshells, and the two patent rafts were swept away. Some of the rendering boilers which had broken loose crashed through the ragged hole made by the torpedo and disappeared into the sea, a welcome riddance. In spite of the heroic struggle to open the valves and lighten the ship, the position looked so grave that the captain had the remaining lifeboats made ready for instant launching, though he well knew that they could hardly escape destruction if that last resort became necessary. All of the crew who were not occupied with immediately vital work were ordered to stand by the boats all day, ready to cut them adrift if the ship foundered suddenly. The hole in her starboard side had gravely weakened the hull, and a violent twisting motion as she rolled in the beam sea might break her back, in which event the handful of men working below would be doomed.

The difficulties of the work of opening the valves so that the pumps could empty the oil into the sea and lighten the ship cannot be appreciated by anyone not familiar with the complicated system of valves in a tank ship, for it was not merely a matter of turning a lot of wheels under ten or fifteen feet of oily water at freezing temperature. Only a little at a time could be accomplished, and it took four days of heroic effort to open all the valves and get the pumps working. On the fourth day the pumps discharged enough oil overboard to bring up the starboard side and trim the ship on an even keel. By this time the force of the gale had moderated sufficiently for *Svend Foyn* to steam slowly ahead, and in this way the crippled ship was permitted to reach a British port without further interference from the enemy or the elements. The saving of the ship and the greater part of her valuable cargo was undoubtedly due to the superhuman courage of that nameless young Norseman who for four days repeatedly risked his life in circumstances that would have justifiably dismayed the stoutest heart.

The worst of all marine hazards is fire at sea, particularly fire in a munition ship. The mind can imagine no experience more appalling than to be aboard a burning ship loaded with explosives. During the First World War a munition ship caught fire and blew up while lying at anchor in the harbor at Halifax, Nova Scotia. The force of the explosion spread destruction not only in the big harbor but for miles inland. Dozens of vessels were sunk or damaged, and a large part of the town was wrecked.

In January 1942 the crew of a ship carrying explosives to Britain were landed at a Canadian port after their ship had caught fire in mid-Atlantic. There were fifteen British and forty-four Chinese members of the crew, and all these men had remained on board fighting the fire until there was no hope left. Not till then, and only just in time, did they launch the boats and get away. The ship was on her way to Britain, steaming in a convoy, when one of the officers noticed a wisp of white smoke issuing from one of the cargo hatches. Thousands of tons of shells and high explosives were beneath those hatches, and at any moment, with the suddenness of a flash of lightning, that mass of compressed energy might explode and blow ship and men to pieces. The captain, however, did not hesitate in his duty, which was first to try to save the ship. A signal was sent to the convoy to draw away to a safe distance as quickly as possible, and meanwhile hoses were run along the deck to the hatch from which the smoke was coming. Generally speaking, fire on board a ship will smoulder indefinitely for want of air if the hatches are kept battened down, but here was an emergency in which the risk of opening a hatch must be taken. The entrance of fresh air might cause the fire to burst into flames; but it was the only chance of flooding the hold, and it was done without loss of time. Thousands of gallons of water were pumped into the hold where the powder was stored, but the volume of smoke increased in spite of the water, and after more than two hours the captain decided that there was no hope of saving the ship and reluctantly ordered the men to get the boats over. The deck plating where the crew had been manning the hoses was already too hot for comfort, and in the heart of the smoke could be seen an ever-widening red glow as the fire spread. Even had it been safe to continue fighting the fire for a while longer there was the very real danger that the tall column of smoke might advertise the ship's presence, and that of the convoy, to a U-boat. It was nearly dark when the crew got into the boats, and in the bad light the captain slipped and fell, injuring his back and shoulder. He slipped between the heaving lifeboat and the ship's side, and would have been fatally crushed but for the quick action of an able seaman who, with great presence of mind, dragged his chief from what would have been certain death.

As the two boats' crews pulled away from the burning ship they watched the glow of the fire in the darkness and realized that a prowling U-boat would see that fire twenty miles away. The convoy was now hull down to the eastward, but one ship, a tanker, had remained all afternoon in the offing to pick up the munition ship's crew if they should abandon her. The captain of the tanker was taking a grave risk in doing this, but his merciful act was rewarded and with no evil consequences. The men in the boats bent their backs to the long oars, pulling with all their strength to put as much distance as possible between themselves and the blazing ship before the cargo exploded.

The sea was rough, and those who were not at the oars baled out the water with caps and buckets, fighting to keep the boats from filling and sinking before they could reach the distant tanker. As no lights were permitted there was a risk of the boats being lost in the darkness, but a lookout in the bow of each never took his eyes off the dim, blurred shape of the waiting ship, and an hour later all were safely alongside and scrambling up the ladders. Far astern the blazing munition ship rendered those waters exceedingly unhealthy, and the rescue ship made all speed to get away. As her engines gathered speed under the forced draught of her boilers a great flash astern illuminated the ocean, and a few seconds later there rolled across the water a roar like a thousand guns. Even at that distance the blast was felt in the tanker, bursting open doors and sweeping the decks with a small gale of wind. The light died out of the sky, and the tanker proceeded on its way in the total darkness imposed by the exigencies of war.

One bleak autumn day in 1941 three American naval planes on patrol over the North Atlantic, three hundred miles from the Canadian mainland, sighted a lifeboat tossing on the gray stormy ocean two thousand feet below, and the radio operators at once sent out a call to all ships in those waters, giving the latitude and longitude of the boat. The planes flew over it for four hours, flashing down signals by the Aldis lamp, which, however, the castaways were unable to read. Before the planes flew away they dropped by parachutes two big packages which fell near the boat and were picked up. Each package contained condensed milk, canned meat, and a four-gallon drum of water. As the boat's stores already comprised some twenty gallons of water, a large tin of biscuits, chocolate, and milk tablets, the additional food and water greatly heartened the men, coupled with the very reasonable belief that a rescue ship would find them within a few hours. They celebrated their imminent deliverance by having a good feed all round. They had been in the boat for three days and were all soaking wet and suffering from exposure, but the airplanes had so raised their hopes they spent that night in cheerful expectation that their miseries would soon be over. But the day did not bring the anticipated relief, and all hands keenly felt the depressing reaction of disappointment. Strict rationing, which had been enforced at the outset, was resumed when help did not come immediately, and every one was allowed half a cupful of water, ten biscuits, half a dozen chocolate squares, and a few milk tablets per day. This, of course, was a comparatively generous amount compared with the starvation rations of some castaways, but the beggarly water allowance—a mere mouthful a day—made it difficult to swallow the dry biscuits however hungry the men became.

The unrelenting bad weather which kept the men constantly wet with rain and spray, as though they were sitting under a cold shower-bath that could never be turned off, brought grievous misery and suffering, causing everyone's hands and feet to swell, and in attempts to restore the circulation each man took it in turn to massage the limbs of his neighbor. Some had no boots, but they were no worse off than those with boots, for their feet were always in the water that washed in the bottom of the boat, and everything was soaking wet except the contents of the sealed provision tins. In spite of suffering that sometimes forced a moan from a man, the castaways did not give way to despair, and to keep up their spirits made gallant efforts to sing as they pulled at the oars. They revived all the ancient jokes they could remember and kept up this pretence of cheerfulness for the first week in the boat; but after that the effort was too much for their failing strength, and the subsequent days were passed mostly in silence, each man alone with his thoughts and his suffering.

On the ninth day a young apprentice died and was silently lowered into the sea. He was sixteen years old, and this was his first trip. Then two seamen died, and the day the men were rescued the twenty-one-year-old wireless operator died after an airplane had flown over the boat and sent a wireless request to a Canadian corvette thirty miles away. An hour later the corvette came racing towards the boat, throwing up a curling bow wave as she sped to the rescue. On board the corvette the eleven survivors were too weak to stand, and after their clothes and boots were cut off they were wrapped in warm blankets and given their first hot food for a fortnight. All recovered. Eleven men had survived after thirteen days in the boat.

Two months later another boat from a torpedoed ship was picked up in the North Atlantic, and this boat also contained eleven men. They had been thirteen days adrift. These men had endured terrible sufferings, and three of them, after rescue, had to have their legs amputated. Another lost one leg. The weather was stormy throughout the whole time they were in the boat, and twice the frail craft was capsized and all hands thrown into the sea. But the will to live gave them the strength to turn the boat over although it was half full of water and most of its gear was lost. Baler, boat-hooks, oars and other gear disappeared in the double catastrophe, and they had to bale for their lives with their caps and a biscuit tin which had been kept in the stern locker. With ample food, but short of water, they stopped eating their rations after five days for lack of liquid to relieve their swollen throats. Most of the thirteen days they spent in silent misery huddled together under a patch of tarpaulin which served as a partial shield against the bitter cold wind. But forced to crouch in the icy water, which could not be entirely baled out, their feet and legs became swollen, and salt-water sores produced the deadly gangrene which afterwards brought four of these unfortunate men to the operating table for leg amputations.

The London steamship owners, France, Fenwick and Company, Ltd., had a fleet of small steamers carrying freight between London, the East Coast ports, and the Continent. The names of all their steamers had the suffix 'wood' —*Dashwood, Sheerwood,* and so on. One of the company's steamers, *Goodwood,* commanded by Captain H. S. Hewson, had the ill-luck to stop a torpedo fired from a predatory U-boat, and the subsequent conduct of the captain and one of his officers, Second Mate Black, is worthy of the finest traditions of the Merchant Marine. *Goodwood* was not armed, for the limited supply of guns had to be allotted to larger ships, and the little ship, steaming along the East Coast, the favorite haunt of U-boats, had no means of defense against attack even if forewarned of danger. In this case, however, the unseen torpedo from an invisible enemy struck the vessel amidships with the suddenness of a thunderclap, and the orderly routine of the little steamer was thrown into instant confusion. In the darkness, for it happened before dawn, orders were passed to get a lifeboat over as it was obvious that the ship had been severely hit and would not float for long. On the bridge Captain Hewson lay helpless with both legs broken, and his chief officer, Mr. Wolfe, though severely injured, managed to crawl to a locker and pass down a number of life-jackets to men on the main deck standing by the boat-falls. The stokers and engineers had scrambled up from below as the water poured into the ship, but the engines had not stopped and the ship was still moving through the sea.

Now the captain was heard shouting to the men to get the boat launched at once and leave him. They must save themselves before it was too late. Mr. Black, the second mate, obeyed the order and superintended the delicate operation of launching the boat in the darkness since he dared not show a light lest they were shelled or machine-gunned by the enemy. Once the loaded boat was in the water it had to be cast off to avoid being swamped, but Black had no intention of abandoning his skipper, and as now the boat was safely waterborne he directed the men to pull up alongside the sinking steamer to take off the wounded captain. But the forward way on *Goodwood* made it impossible to come alongside, and Black, stripping off his jacket, dived overboard and struck out for the ship. But his strength gave out before he could cross the intervening water, and he was hauled back exhausted into the boat. Undaunted by the failure, he put on a life-jacket, and, with two seamen volunteers accompanying him, made another attempt and this time succeeded. *Goodwood* was now so low in the water the three men got on board without difficulty. Without a moment to lose they gently lifted the injured captain down the ladder to the main deck and swam back with him to the lifeboat. Just as they hauled him on board *Goodwood* sank. This story was only revealed when the laconic report of the loss of the ship was duly recorded.

The historian of gallantry at sea suffers not from a paucity but rather from an embarrassment of choice. We cannot include the experiences of all the ships' crews who had the misadventure to lose their ship, so we choose at random the first to hand. We were at one of the famous Foyle's Literary Luncheons in London during the third year of the war when Admiral of the Fleet Lord Chatfield related the story of seventeen sailors who drifted on a raft for a week in the shark-infested waters of the South Atlantic. This ship was torpedoed by a U-boat a hundred miles off the coast of

Brazil, and when the men got on to rafts the submarine approached close enough for the German commander to question the survivors while one of the Nazi sailors took photos of them. There were six white men and eleven Negroes on two rafts, and after the rafts had been lashed together to make a more stable platform the rations were equally apportioned to last for a month. The water ration, for example, was apportioned at one pint per week, and their food four ship's biscuits per day. The Admiral took occasion on giving these facts to chide those pampered landsmen who, in war-time, complain about having to forgo certain peace-time luxuries. Since necessity is frequently the mother of invention hunger soon spurred these starving men to make ingenious attempts to supplement their larder. There were plenty of sharks, perpetually swimming alongside the raft watching the men with their horrible eyes, and it occurred to one of the seamen that a shark would make a good meal for all hands if they could catch one. They had no pole with which to make the shaft of a harpoon, but a large hook was lashed firmly to the handle of a water-dipper, and with this clumsy instrument they managed to hook a small shark and lift the wriggling creature on board. The shark, which was four feet long, was cut into strips and half-grilled over a fire made in a tin cooking-pot lid. The starving men enjoyed the shark, comparing its flavor to that of cod, and speaking of it as a change from dry biscuits. In this way the men kept themselves occupied, for they had nothing else to do all day since they had neither sail nor oars, and after a week, when they were sighted and rescued by a Spanish steamer near the island of St. Vincent, they had drifted three hundred miles. After the gallant Admiral had recounted this story he informed his listeners that during the first twenty-eight months of the war the Merchant Marine had lost between six and ten thousand officers and other ranks through enemy action.

Commander A. B. Campbell, who is well known for his books on the sea and also as a prominent member of the B.B.C. Brains Trust, also told a story at this luncheon. It concerned an eighteen-year-old boy whom he had just visited in a London hospital. This boy's ship had been torpedoed by a U-boat, and he had been a week adrift before being picked up. An injury to his right arm necessitated its amputation. When the surgeon told him that he would have to lose his arm he made no fuss at all, and refused the hospital's suggestion that they should send for his mother. When Commander Campbell visited the boy the day after the operation he noticed that the arm still appeared to be there, but the plucky boy confessed that he had stuffed the empty sleeve with newspapers as his mother was coming to see him that afternoon and he did not want her to know about the loss of his arm until he was better. And as the commander left him the boy reminded him that he would still be able to swab decks with one hand, and not to forget this when he was discharged from hospital. And this little story might well serve as an epitome of the gallant spirit of that body of men who kept Britain's life-lines open during the most critical period of her history.

During Christmas week 1941 many Londoners saw a somewhat battered ship's lifeboat on show in the main booking hall at Charing Cross Underground Station. The boat formed part of an exhibition of life-saving equipment, and with it was a short account of its recent history. It belonged to the freighter *Lapwing*, a small 1300-ton single-decked coaster owned by the General Steam Navigation Company of London. *Lapwing* was steaming in a convoy when two ships of her company were torpedoed during a heavy gale. In spite of the poor visibility and with very high seas running, a number of men from *Lapwing* under the chief officer volunteered to go and look for survivors. After several attempts the boat was got safely away, and the men were last seen pulling hard towards the point where the two ships had gone down. It was late afternoon, and they spent the whole night searching for survivors. Utterly exhausted by their exertions, and drenched with rain and spray, they returned towards *Lapwing* at daylight, but when the boat was within a few hundred yards of the freighter she was struck by an unseen torpedo, and within two minutes she was gone.

Lapwing was torpedoed only a few miles from the north coast of Brittany, and it would have been a comparatively simple matter to reach the shore, but to have landed there would mean a German prison camp for the survivors, and they unanimously decided to attempt, in the face of the gale, to reach the distant British coast. Provided that they made a landfall within three or four days at the most, they believed they could last the journey. There was not sufficient food in the boat for more than a day or two and there were twenty-two men, but as the risk was preferable to a prison camp a big sail was hoisted and a course laid for the coast of Cornwall. Eleven days later nineteen exhausted men staggered ashore at Slyne Bay, in Southern Ireland, and told the first people who met them that they were the survivors of *Lapwing*. Three of their shipmates, a wounded seaman and two Asiatic deck-hands, had died from exposure a few days previously. There was no drinking water in the boat, and the survivors had partially slaked their thirst by catching rainwater. The first officer of *Lapwing*, Mr. Woodhouse, kept a daily log of the voyage with the stub of a pencil and the back of one of the seamen's discharge papers. One man had a pipe and some tobacco, and this was passed round as long as the tobacco lasted. They began their voyage at the western entrance of the Channel, but were carried out into the Atlantic before they were able to regain a northward course; thus they missed Cornwall and landed in Ireland. The decision to attempt to reach England and face the perils of a long open-boat voyage was agreed upon by all hands, and the nineteen survivors looking back upon those terrible eleven days decided that the risk and hardships had been well worth it, for they were still free men, and within a fortnight some of them were at sea again.

What attraction has the sea which draws men back to it after the most appalling experiences? Once a sailor always a sailor. And yet on a long voyage your deep-water sailor invariably looks forward to the arrival in port and the pleasures of life ashore. He often despises the landsman, and is fond of repeating that only fools choose a seafaring career. As he grows older he talks about the little garden he is going to cultivate when he has swallowed the anchor. But he continues to go to sea and often dies at sea without ever having realized his dream of a garden ashore. After a spell in port he grows restless and is glad to be off to sea again, only to repeat the process of nostalgic reactions. In war-time his life at sea is made doubly arduous and infinitely more dangerous, but he remains under the spell that first attracted him, and when he returns home after distinguishing himself for some act of self-sacrifice that brings him a medal and temporary fame he is seldom spoiled by the lion-hunters. The austerity of his life has taught him to judge things at their true value, and instead of succumbing to the temptations of a safe life ashore he returns to his dangerous job without regret. Many listeners to the B.B.C. talks during the war heard an anonymous sailor describe the hardships and dangers of a merchant seaman's life and tell of his own experience after his ship was torpedoed and he was severely wounded. The name of this quiet-voiced man was later revealed as Frank Laskier, a Liverpool seaman, and his talk had proved so successful with its homely truths and inspiring message that he was invited to give more talks, and it looked as though this plain sailor would grow spoiled with his sudden fame and the soft life ashore. And who could blame him if he did not return to the sea, for his last adventure had cost him one of his feet and he had surely done enough? He was interviewed, and articles about him appeared in the papers, and even a book was published about his experiences.[1] This book consisted of his recorded talks for the B.B.C., and it may be said to his great credit that he did not wish his name to be revealed; but the Press would have it otherwise. But, in spite of having lost a foot and in spite of all the blandishments of his admirers, Laskier went back to sea.

Frank Laskier was born in Wallasey, a suburb of Liverpool, and came from a seafaring family, and, like thousands of boys before him, ran away from home to go to sea. For the next few years he served in many ships and never regretted his chosen career. He said that he had no ambitions to rise to officer's rank, and was quite content to remain a deck-hand. Then the war came, and a series of experiences that might have sickened most men forever of the sea began to happen to Laskier. One bitter winter's day, in mid-Atlantic, he and some of his shipmates found a ship's lifeboat adrift with sixteen dead children in it. This shocking experience left its mark on his soul and filled him with a hatred for the folly and cruelty of war. He had other experiences so macabre that nothing would induce him to talk about them.

[1] *My Name Is Frank*, by Frank Laskier (George Allen and Unwin, Ltd.).

Then one day he went to sea in the freighter *Eurylochus,* a 5700-ton ship owned by the Blue Funnel Line of Liverpool, and it was on this voyage that he had the misfortune to lose his right foot. *Eurylochus* was traveling in a large convoy for three weeks during which it was repeatedly attacked by Focke-Wulf dive-bombers. At the end of the three weeks the convoy split up, most of the ships steaming independently to the various ports to which they were destined. They were beyond the U-boat and airplane cruising area, and in consequence were reasonably safe from attack. *Eurylochus* was steaming alone with all lights out one dark night eight hundred miles from the nearest land when, without warning, from out of the darkness came flashes of flame followed by the roar of guns. At once shells began to burst with deafening explosions on and around the steamer. She had been caught by the German pocket-battleship *Von Scheer* and was being shelled by the warship's 11- and 5.9-inch guns, a whole broadside in each salvo. Laskier was on watch by the small 4-inch defense gun of *Eurylochus* and without hesitation trained the weapon at the battleship and fired again and again. But it was like using an airgun against a rhinoceros, and the unequal duel was ended almost as soon as it began. While Laskier was trying to train the gun on the battleship's searchlight, which lighted up the steamer with its maddening beam, a shell burst close to the gun, wrecking it, but by one of those freaks of fortune not killing the gunner. But shell-splinters had mangled Laskier's foot, though at the time he scarcely felt it.

The battleship, which had attacked without warning at point-blank range, shelled the freighter for twenty minutes and then ceased firing, but kept her searchlight on the doomed ship. In the glaring beam of the searchlight the fourth mate signaled that the crew were abandoning the ship, with the hope no doubt that they would be spared further slaughter, but if so he hoped in vain, for the battleship opened fire again, and under this hell of bursting steel ten survivors somehow managed to get on a raft. Three of these ten men were wounded, and as they lay sprawled on the 10-by-8-foot float the Germans swept them with machine-gun fire. The raft was still fast to the ship by a line, and suddenly the distraught men noticed that *Eurylochus* was going down, and someone slashed the painter with a knife just in time. The whirlpool caused by the ship as she went down capsized the raft and threw everyone into the sea. Somehow they helped one another back on the unsteady platform, and after a while the battleship's searchlight was switched off and the enemy left them. All that night and throughout the next day the survivors lay on the raft, the unhurt men holding the wounded on the crowded platform to prevent them from sliding overboard, while the second engineer kept the sharks at a distance with the only paddle on board. Laskier said that as he lay there half conscious he remembered the rasping sound of the sharks scraping the bottom of the raft which sank gradually lower in the sea as the water entered its punctured floats.

At dusk when they had almost abandoned hope they saw the wisp of smoke from a distant ship, and a little midshipman fixed his coat to the paddle and stood up and waved it violently while some of the men held him steady. The signal was seen, and the steamer, which turned out to be a Spanish ship, altered course and bore down to them. Laskier remembered being hoisted on board the steamer in a large fish-basket and being put into a bunk, but receiving no medical attention as there was no doctor in the little tramp steamer. He was three-and-a-half days without medical aid, but his life was saved by the fortunate appearance of a

British armed cruiser, which took off the survivors of *Eurylochus* and put them in her own sick-bay. Laskier had developed pneumonia, but he recovered from this and the amputation, and in the course of time learned to walk with an artificial leg almost as well as normal men. The experience had not embittered him, but it did fill him with a fierce desire to wake up his apathetic and unimaginative countrymen to their danger. He did not seek publicity, but when a B.B.C. scout found him in Liverpool he was perfectly willing to broadcast the story of the merchant sailor's part in the war effort. There were people who criticized his talks, saying that he piled on the agony. Such people plainly feared to know the truth. There were others who wondered if he might not be spoiled by the sudden lifting from obscurity to fame. Laskier answered this question after his last broadcast by going back to sea as a gunner. With him he carried a letter of appreciation from the Minister of Information, who had heard his talks on the wireless.

On November 18, 1941 the *London Gazette* announced that Richard Hamilton Ayres, Second Officer of a freighter torpedoed in the Atlantic, had been awarded the M.B.E. The citation included these words: "Undismayed by suffering and death, he had kept a stout heart and done all a man could to comfort his shipmates and bring them to safety."

Aged thirty-one, Ayres was the son of a retired sea-captain living at Birchington, in Kent, and by a remarkable coincidence the son was serving in the same ship which his father had commanded twenty years previously. In April 1941, the younger Ayres sailed as second officer in his father's old ship, which was engaged in bringing "Lease-Lend" supplies from America. During the spring and summer the ship made several voyages in convoy. Some of these voyages were interrupted by enemy attacks, but the old steamer seemed to bear a charmed life, for many ships in the convoys were sunk during those spring and summer months. Then, in October, during one of those heavy equinoctial gales so familiar to Western Ocean sailors, Ayres's ship was hit fatally by a torpedo, and three boats were safely launched before the ship went under. Two of the boats were never heard from again.

The third boat, only twenty-three feet long, and into which were crowded eight Europeans and twenty-three Lascars, thirty-one men altogether, was in charge of Second Officer Ayres, the only one among them who understood navigation. At the outset the gale all but swamped the overloaded craft, but Ayres by personally taking charge of the tiller kept the boat's head to the seas and saved it from disaster. By his example he greatly encouraged the others during the bitter cold night when their morale was at its lowest. Realizing that the Lascars were less fitted to endure the cold than the Europeans, he had them all moved to the forward end of the boat, where they could find some shelter from the wind and spray under a tarpaulin. They were also given all the blankets. Some of the sailors even gave their jackets to the shivering Lascars, but in spite of this they grumbled and quarreled over the meager rations Ayres wisely doled out to all hands. Anticipating two or three weeks at sea, he divided the food stores to last for the maximum period, but, like Columbus, Ayres kept this to himself and let the men think that land would be sighted within a day or two. By one of those cruel turns of fate, half the boat's stores, which were normally sufficient for three weeks, were lost overboard when the boat was launched. Two cupfuls of water daily was the drinking allowance, and soon some of the Lascars began to drink sea-water, with the inevitable tragic consequences. When a man died his clothes were stripped off him before he was put overboard and the clothes shared out among the survivors.

The men died off so rapidly that at the end of the first week only seven out of the thirty-one remained alive. They all died, not from hunger, but from exposure or from drinking sea-water. Everyone had suffered severely from frostbitten hands and feet, and had they lived many would have lost one or more of their limbs. On the eighth day the water-beaker was found to be empty, but the survivors managed to keep alive by catching rainwater in the tarpaulin spread over the thwarts. The water dissolved the salt crystals caked on the tarpaulin and in consequence was brackish and unpalatable.

The first man to die was one of the engineers, the biggest man in the boat. He died on the fourth day, and during the next three days twenty-three died—an average of more than seven every day. Each day Ayres would say "Land tomorrow!" but he did not tell them that contrary winds had forced him to abandon his course, which had been due east, and forced the boat to make a wide circle to edge towards the distant land. But the men still alive had grown too apathetic to be stirred by promises, and most of the time they sat crouched on the thwarts, silent and huddled together for the sake of animal warmth. Sometimes a comic gibe from Ayres would rouse them to half-hysterical laughter, but they quickly subsided into the silence of men who had nothing more to ask from life. Then one evening, the thirteenth day—the lucky thirteenth—Ayres pointed to the east and called out "Land!" and there, sure enough, on the distant horizon was the faint bluish shape of low hills. This was Cornwall, though the survivors did not know it then. Trimming the ragged lugsail, Ayres sailed the boat towards the nearest headland, which happened to be The

Lizard, on whose craggy shore so many fine ships have left their bones.

Two small girls living in Helston were on the cliffs when they saw a sailing-boat pitching in the big Atlantic rollers about half a mile off shore. They watched the boat coming in at a good speed until it was close to the beach, when suddenly it rolled over and threw a number of men into the water. Then the boat appeared floating right side up, and they saw a man haul himself up into and begin to help other men into the boat.

As they watched, fascinated, the boat swung round into the deep trough and a curling wave again turned it over. As the foam subsided they saw the boat floating bottom up and three figures clinging to the keel. A moment later one of the figures had slipped back into the breakers, but the remaining two men fought to reach the shore. One of them was seen to crawl on to a wave-swept rock, but was washed away and disappeared. The other staggered on to the beach and fell down exhausted at the water's edge. The little girls ran home and notified the coastguard. Then they returned to the man with some hot milk and remained with him until the local ambulance arrived. And so Richard Ayres had come home, the sole survivor out of the thirty-two men who had left their sinking ship thirteen days previously.

One of the most appalling ordeals to befall British seamen during the war fell to the survivors of the torpedoed British tramp *Anglo-Saxon*. The survival of the two men, Bob Tapscott and Roy Widdicombe, is possibly the most remarkable instance ever recorded of the tenacity of the human spirit. Tapscott and Widdicombe were both West Country youths, as their names suggest, and both were seamen on *Anglo-Saxon*, a 5000-ton single-screw cargo steamer with a normal crew of forty-nine officers and men and accommodation for twelve passengers. These two remarkable young men were the only survivors from their ship. They drifted three thousand miles in an eighteen-foot open boat for seventy days, a world's record utterly eclipsing the famous forty-eight-day boat journey made by Captain Bligh and the men of the *Bounty*. *Anglo-Saxon*, owned by Lawther, Latta and Company, of London, was on a voyage to South America with a cargo of Welsh coal when, on the night of August 1, 1940, she was attacked and sunk by shell-fire from the German armed merchant cruiser *Weser*. The attack was so sudden that most of the crew were killed at once by the exploding shells, which wrecked the bridge, deck-houses, and boats.

The captain was killed with the first salvo, and the chief officer, C. B. Denny, took charge of the only boat not smashed by shell-fire. Seven survivors, four of them wounded, got away in this boat, a small eighteen-foot jolly-boat used by the captain when in port. It contained a keg with three gallons of water, three tins of mutton, a few cans of condensed milk, and a tin of ship's biscuits. The nearest land was Cape Verde Island, about a thousand miles to the east. To the west, 2800 miles away, were the Leeward Islands, and the mate decided to sail westward because he would have the trade winds with him.

The systematic way in which the raider shelled *Anglo-Saxon* left no doubt that the enemy deliberately meant to destroy all the lifeboats, so that the ship would disappear —*spurlos versenkt*—and no witnesses would survive to tell how she had been attacked. A few of the crew had got away on a raft, but these men were unlucky enough to be seen in the raider's searchlight, and they were quickly "liquidated" by machine-guns. The seven men in the jolly-boat expected the same fate, and, in view of their subsequent sufferings, it might have been better if they had been put out of their misery there and then. In the boat were Chief Officer Denny, Third Engineer Leslie Hawkes, Radio Operator R. H. Pilcher, Gunner Richard Penny, Assistant Cook Leslie Morgan, and Seamen Robert Tapscott and Roy Widdicombe. Pilcher's leg and foot were badly wounded; Penny had a bad hip wound and a bullet in his arm; Morgan had a leg wound, and Tapscott shrapnel in the back, hand, and buttock. Only two men were not wounded. Without medical attention the badly wounded men were doomed unless rescued within a week, for gangrene would inevitably set in and nothing could be done to stop the poison spreading.

Until he died the mate had charge of the boat, and by his fortitude set an example to the rest. Notches were cut in the gunwale to keep track of the days, and the mate, and later the third engineer, kept a log on pages torn from a book of quotations which someone possessed. They had left the ship in such a hurry there had been no time to bring warm clothing, extra food, or other necessities, and the men soon began to suffer for want of them, especially medical supplies. They had dressed one another's wounds as well as possible, but since it was impossible to clean and sterilize the wounds they soon began to fester. On the tenth day Pilcher died of gangrene, and his body was lowered into the sea. On the thirteenth day Penny, the gunner, deliberately jumped overboard. Two days later the mate, who was dying, agreed to go over with the third engineer. So they died together, after saying good-bye to the three remaining men.

At first the mate had been a tower of strength to the others. He maintained discipline when the men's overwrought nerves made them quarrelsome and mutinous. He dressed the festering wounds of the injured ones and kept up their spirits by his own refusal to dwell on the somber prospect before them. He devised simple games to pass the time away and encouraged them to believe that every new day would raise the land. When the birds known to seamen as flying bosuns flew over he refused to admit that these creatures are birds of evil omen, an ancient superstition among sailors. His last thoughts were concerned with the welfare of those left behind, and his last words sailing instructions to find the nearest land. Morgan, the assistant cook, went mad and jumped overboard on the eighteenth day.

Tapscott and Widdicombe, aged nineteen and twenty-two, were destined to survive, though they did not expect to then, and had they known that they would be another fifty-two days in the boat their hearts would surely have failed them. The food and water were gone, and the blue tropical skies showed no promise of rain, but somehow they managed to survive by eating minute crabs and molluscs from floating kelp, but only just survived, for when they finally sighted the palm-fringed West Indian island called Eleuthera they were as much like dead men as living ones, and their appearance at first frightened the colored people of the island who discovered them.

They had managed to crawl ashore, but the effort exhausted them, and the kindly Negroes who found them thought that they were dead. A colored farmer and his wife were combing the beach for flotsam, a recognized occupation on that outpost in the Atlantic, where the fortunes of war cast up all manner of wreckage and cargoes from torpedoed ships. The farmer and his wife first saw the jolly-boat on the beach and were hurrying to examine this valuable find when they saw two human beings lying on the sand, so emaciated that they resembled mummies, their dried skin, darkened by the sun, stretched over their almost fleshless bones. The first reaction of primitive fear at the sight of these living specters quickly changed to pity, a pity that might have been the death of the two castaways, for the colored people fed them with reckless and unwise liberality, feeding them with coconuts, meat, bread, and other foods; and consequently they were sick, and were only saved from being killed with kindness by the arrival of the British Commissioner of the island, who had them at once carried to the local hospital.

The two young men had been starving too long and had suffered too much for a miraculous recovery, and for many days they were desperately ill, and at first it seemed they would not survive their terrible ordeal. The Duke of Windsor, Governor of the Bahamas, heard of their remarkable voyage, and with the Duchess visited them in hospital. Careful nursing gradually restored them to life, and a few months later Widdicombe returned to his old calling, signing on *Siamese Prince*, a 6600-ton motor vessel owned by the Prince Line, of London. This ship was torpedoed by a U-boat in the Atlantic early in 1941, and Widdicombe went down with her.

These two young sailors had survived mental and physical hardships that had killed or driven mad their five companions. They were plain, ordinary young men without the heroic qualities of the mate and the third engineer who committed suicide. They did not want to die. Twice they jumped overboard, but climbed back into the boat frightened by the thought of plunging into eternity. Yet to have survived that fearful ordeal they must have possessed some extraordinary quality lacking in most men. It certainly was not superhuman physical stamina, for they were not particularly strong, nor were their spirits kept alive by any burning ideal. But they had some inner quality—the will to live, perhaps—that brought them through when greater men had failed. The third engineer, for instance, had died gallantly with a jest, but Tapscott and Widdicombe were too miserable to joke about their fate. By surviving they were able to give to the world a story of human endurance and suffering unexcelled in the annals of the sea.

This claim may well be challenged by those familiar with the amazing experience of three United States naval airmen in the Pacific who were adrift for over a month in one of those collapsible rubber rafts carried by seaplanes. While on patrol in mid-Pacific their plane crashed into the sea, and the three occupants of the machine had barely sufficient time to inflate and launch the rubber raft before the plane sank. The three men found themselves crowded into a space 96 by 48 inches, without food, water, sail, or navigating instruments. Theoretically, in such a plight they should not have survived more than a day or two under the scorching topical sun without water, and the incredible thing is that they survived for thirty-four days. On the thirty-second day they lost all their clothes overboard while collecting rainwater in them during a storm, and for the last two days they were completely naked! They kept alive by catching an occasional fish, including a small shark, which they, of course, had to eat raw. In the shark's stomach they found a delicacy in the shape of two herrings. The pilot had a revolver and managed to shoot an albatross, which was also eaten. At one period they were without food of any kind for a week. When the raft was becalmed they paddled it with shoes tied to their hands. Sharks frequently snapped at their hands and the radio operator was severely bitten. On the twentieth day they picked up a coconut floating in the sea. The jerky motion of the tiny raft made sleep almost impossible, and the strain began to tell on their tempers. The pilot, a Californian named Harold Dixon, steered by the sun and the stars, setting a course in the direction where he believed the nearest islands to be. A squall brought them the welcome rain, but upset the raft. However, they managed to right the frail craft. It was in this storm that they lost all their clothes. The tropical sun on their naked bodies was unendurable, and for some protection they tore the fabric covering from the rubber tube which formed the raft, but this cover was lost the next day when the raft was again capsized.

The sharks never left them, and they had to be careful when paddling to see that these creatures did not take their hands off. Dixon estimated that they were making thirty-five miles a day, but he had no idea how far off the nearest islands were. Huddled together in the cramped space, they were unable to move without jolting each other, and as they were unable to lie down they got no rest and their morale slowly deteriorated. On the thirty-fourth day, when they had lost hope, the palm-trees of an atoll were sighted, and with their remaining strength they paddled against a contrary tide to reach the land before dark. They crawled ashore in the last stages of exhaustion and entirely naked, after having covered a thousand miles from the point where their plane had come down. But within a month Pilot Dixon was back at his station again, carrying out patrols over the sea which had so nearly cost him his life and the lives of his two companions.

CHAPTER X

Escape from France

Escapes from France by sea began at Dunkirk and continued to the end of the war. The first escapes were a mass exodus which later became a trickle, sometimes ceasing altogether. We have seen in an earlier chapter how the British Navy and Merchant Marine helped that great exodus, how a thousand vessels, from liners to river-skiffs, lifted 334,000 men off in seven days. Then, when the last ship left the blazing port, the enemy occupied the coast and France was cut off from all communication with her neighbor across the Channel. One could only surmise what the people of Picardy, Normandy, and Brittany were doing and how they were living under the foreign yoke. The sturdy people along the coast were not resigned to their fate, and everywhere they were plotting and scheming to escape. But escape by sea required boats, and the German guards and the coast patrols watched every mile of the shore, and to be caught attempting to escape would be to risk severe punishment. Nevertheless many dauntless spirits tried, and a few succeeded.

No stories of adventure are more thrilling than those narrating escapes, especially escapes by sea. Some of the most diverting stories in annals of the sea concern the escape of white captives from the Barbary Coast in the seventeenth century. The two stories in this chapter concern the successful escape of young Frenchmen who preferred risking being caught and shot rather than accepting safety at the price of freedom.

One warm, sunny morning in the middle of September 1941 a Scots soldier doing guard duty on the coast of Cornwall saw five youths scrambling over a tongue of rock that jutted out half a mile to seaward from the shore. The soldier waited till they had got within hailing distance, then challenged them. He noticed that the youths seemed very unsteady on their feet as though they were drunk or exhausted, but, being a good soldier, he did not take any chances. At his shout of "Halt!" the five youths stood still and stared at him. Three of them wore shorts, one wore plus-fours, and the tallest wore long trousers. All were bareheaded and seemed very young. The soldier then noticed that one of them was holding a small flag which he recognized as the French colors. Now, by one of those curious chances usually met with only in works of fiction, this Scots soldier spoke fluent French and was soon engaged in questioning the youths in their own language. Quickly convinced of their harmless intent—indeed, that they were friends—the soldier took them to the nearest cottage, where they were given cups of strong brown tea, a beverage strange to coffee-drinking French, but none the less welcome after thirty hours in the Channel, which they had so recently crossed in two *canoes*.

The youngest of these plucky boys was sixteen and the eldest nineteen. Their true names were never divulged for fear of reprisals against their relatives in France, but let us call them Janot, Charles, Pierre, Louis and Georges. Charles was the eldest and Janot the youngest. When France fell they shared the bewilderment and unhappiness of their families, but in spite of the threatened death penalty for listening to British broadcasts they learned, via the wireless news, of General de Gaulle and the formation of the body of Frenchmen who were banded together to continue the fight under the title of the Free French Forces, or, as it was known to the French, the F.F.L., or Forces Françaises Libres. Frequently they heard the voices of Frenchmen over the radio urging the people of France to continue the fight. This was difficult and dangerous in their own country, but if one could only escape! If it were possible, for example, to get to England, one could enlist under the banner of Lorraine, the flag adopted by De Gaulle. The idea burned itself into the hearts of these five youths, and they resolved upon escape to England whatever the difficulties and the risks. Imprudently perhaps, they confided their intentions to their families, but they were young and hot-headed, and the plan palpably was so impossible that the parents did not take the idea seriously. They believed that when the boys realized the difficulties and dangers, what with lack of money and a seaworthy boat, they would be sensible and abandon the project.

Charles as the senior boy organized the project, with the other four as his assistants, each having his particular work to do. These five youths set an example in organization that would have put the muddling methods of some government offices to shame. One made it his business to get all the charts of the Channel and maps of the South Coast of England that he could beg or borrow. All five agreed to save up and pool their money to buy a canoe and eventually secured a small one-man craft for three hundred francs because it was damaged. It had a large hole in the bottom, but such a trifling matter did not discourage the young conspirators. Georges became friendly with the crew of a Nazi motor patrol-boat, and as the Germans were at that time at pains to be amiable with the French people, the motor-boat crew willingly assisted the French boy to repair his canoe. In the summer weather lots of young Frenchmen along the coast paddled about in canoes for pleasure, and the Nazis had no suspicion that they were helping to further the plans of five young men whose one desire was to join General de Gaulle. Charles and Janot were the joint-owners of another canoe—a large American type which would hold four. The boys planned to escape in these two frail craft which were not meant for anything but pleasure in calm waters. But, like so many French boys living on the coast, they were experts at handling canoes in the surf and had no qualms about facing a voyage which would take them out of sight of land. They expected to cross in fifteen or sixteen hours, given favorable weather.

Most of the summer was spent in repairing and strengthening the two canoes to make them more seaworthy, and when this job was finished they were tried out off the coast, and timed over a measured kilometer so that their crews might work out the approximate number of hours for crossing the Channel. All this was done openly in full view of the Nazi coastguards, who got so accustomed to seeing the boys playing with their canoes that they took no notice of them. The boys acted their part with Latin verve, gaily sporting with their canoes off shore, laughing and shouting to each other as they went ahead with their plan. Hidden under a sand-dune were their patiently accumulated stores and gear, awaiting the propitious moment— a fine night and a calm sea. There were six dozen hard biscuits, twenty pounds of bread, and an army rifle with forty rounds of ammunition stolen from German military stores. There was a home-made tricolor flag, a Bible, a cheap alarm clock, a pocket-torch, some charts of the Channel, and a small pocket-compass.

The summer had nearly gone when the boys were ready to start, but they had to wait a little longer until conditions of sea and weather were favorable. At last, on the night of

September 16, they agreed to start. They slipped quietly out of their homes after leaving a note to their parents that they had gone to join General de Gaulle. Each boy left one of these notes pinned to his pillow. To reach the beach meant passing through the town after curfew, when all French people were supposed to be indoors, but the boys managed to reach the beach undiscovered, although they had one bad moment when a Nazi night patrol passed close to them. They avoided discovery by lying flat in the sand. They knew that the patrol passed the spot where the canoes were kept once every hour, so that they had a clear hour to drag the canoes into the water, load the stores, and get away from the coast. Working speedily and silently, they pulled the two canoes down to the water, loaded the gear and stores, and pushed off. Georges was alone in the small canoe, and the others got into the big one.

For the first twenty minutes they paddled as hard as they could to put as much water as possible between themselves and the coast before the patrol returned, and, a south wind behind them, they made good progress with the aid of a small sail bent to a short pole. Using a coat to hide the light, they flashed the pocket-torch from time to time on to the compass to check the course, which was due north. There is something appealing about the faith these boys had in Britain even after listening for more than a year to anti-British propaganda. The conquerors of their country had tried to teach their people to hate the British by suggestions that Britain had deserted France, but in spite of all propaganda these five youths set out on a dangerous journey to a foreign land with touching faith in the welcome they would receive.

Once the course was set they steered by the stars, but in the early hours of the morning to their horror they found themselves sailing parallel to the French coast, and hastily took a fresh bearing. A little later they heard the noise of a Nazi motor patrol-boat approaching; Charles pulled down the sail in the big canoe, and they all lay down to make themselves as inconspicuous as possible. As the patrol launch rushed past a few hundred yards away its search-light swept across the canoes and for the next few seconds the boys feared the worst, but the launch did not stop, and after it had disappeared the fugitives continued their voyage. At dawn the French coast was nearly out of sight, and the boys, hungry and thirsty from the night's exertions, had their breakfast—that is to say, they ate some of the bread and drank some water. During the night a strong breeze had raised quite a choppy sea, and the canoes, with their low freeboard, shipped so much water that the boys had to bale all that day to keep it from sinking. Georges, alone in the smaller canoe, had been paddling nearly all night, and now the need to bale as well as paddle began to tell on him, and his little craft was lashed alongside the other canoe while he gave all his time to baling out the water. In this way the two canoes under the power of the sail and paddles crawled slowly northward towards the English coast. They were now in mid-Channel, out of sight of land, tired and seasick with the constant jerkings of the light craft in the short, choppy seas; but their spirits were high, and they looked forward to making a landfall before dark. In spite of vigorous baling, water continued to slop into the canoes, and to lighten them everything that could possibly be spared was dropped overboard. The heaviest objects, apart from the precious can of water, were the army rifle and the ammunition, and regretfully this was thrown over. Several inches of water washed about in the bottom of the canoes, and the boys, of course, had to sit in this water, since to have sat higher would have risked cap-sizing the canoes. Had the seas grown any larger the young adventurers would never have reached land, but with the magnificent confidence of youth they never gave a thought to such a possibility.

Late in the afternoon, with no sign of land ahead, they did begin to think that they would have to spend another night at sea, but there was ample water and bread, and the prospect did not trouble them. Fortunately the weather was warm, and, apart from the discomfort of having to sit in water and the occasional spells of seasickness, the boys remained in good spirits.

About tea-time one of them pointed out what appeared to be land on the northern horizon, and after they had watched it for some time there was no doubt at all—it was the cliffs of England. They gave a cheer and redoubled their efforts with the paddles, only to stop a few minutes later to watch, not without apprehension, an approaching airplane which was diving straight at them. Their relief was unspeakable when the plane proved to be a Hurricane. It swooped down and roared close over their heads, then flew away. They afterwards learned that the pilot had gone off to send an R.A.F. launch to pick them up, but when it arrived on the spot the canoes were miles away.

At sunset the boys resigned themselves to another night afloat, for the coast was rocky and too dangerous for a landing in the dark. They spent a cold night taking spells at the paddles, and in the intervals tried to get a little sleep. The sea had risen, the boys got very wet, and it was necessary to paddle hard to keep from being swamped. Before dawn they nearly crashed into a rock which loomed black and forbidding out of the darkness, but they managed to paddle into the lee of this rock and climb on to it. There they stayed huddled together for mutual warmth till daylight.

When it grew fully light they found that they were out

on a rocky promontory which curved into the sea for nearly a mile. They were scrambling over the slippery rocks shoreward when they were challenged by the Scots soldier, and soon their trials were at an end.

After being taken to the cottage where they were given food and hot tea they were whisked off by the local police, who gave them hot baths and clean clothes and sent them on to London to report to General de Gaulle's headquarters. In London they met the Prime Minister and Mrs. Churchill at 10 Downing Street, and had their picture taken many times by Press photographers. Their one regret was that they could not write their parents, telling of their safe arrival in England. The exploit of these five boys is particularly noteworthy because of their youth and the fact that they dared the crossing in canoes.

Our second narrative also concerns the adventures of five Frenchmen who escaped from France to join the Free French Forces in Britain. The eldest and leader, Pierre, was thirty-five. François, an ex-sailor of the French Navy, was twenty-five. Claude, a student, was twenty, and Jean and René, students in a naval academy, were aged twenty-one and nineteen respectively. All were Bretons, the men who make the best sailors in France. Pierre had won the Croix de Guerre on the Somme for bravery in remaining behind during the retreat to destroy defense works before the arrival of the Germans. After the surrender of the French government he found his way to a port in Brittany, where he fell in with the four young men who were ready to listen to any plans for escape. They met surreptitiously at night and discussed various schemes. The first necessity was a boat, and this was obtained honestly. The escapers paid for it, though to avoid suspicion they pretended that it was for someone else that they were buying it. In effect

Pierre told a story about a friend of his in Paris, who had asked him to purchase a boat in order that he could go fishing and send the fish home to his family as food was very short in Paris. Living on a small island near the coast was a man who came into the port every day in a thirty-foot motor-boat to sell fish and take back provisions. This man was willing to sell, at a price, his motor-boat to the mythical monsieur in Paris who wanted to go fishing to feed his family, and so the boat changed hands. Now the advantage in owning this particular motor-boat lay in the fact that it was well known to the German sentries, who had seen it daily for months, so that when it put out of the port on its eventful journey they thought that it was merely going out to the island.

As soon as the boat was secured the five men began planning their departure. Food, in a country where food was scarce, was not easy to obtain, and petrol for the motor was even more difficult to get, but by patience and judicious bribery they collected enough food to suffice for the journey barring any unforeseen delay on the way across. Like true Frenchmen, they laid in a stock of wine, Bordeaux being chosen as it was not rationed. They also managed to obtain several tins of sardines and a cooked chicken. In trying to obtain gasoline they eventually made friends with a Nazi non-commissioned officer, the equivalent to a British R.A.S.C. sergeant. This man had access to army gasoline stores. He owned a garage in Germany which had been wrecked by R.A.F. bombs, and the loss of his business at home had so embittered him that he was ready to make money selling army gasoline. Through this sergeant the Frenchmen obtained a hundred liters (equivalent to twenty-two gallons) of gasoline, which was secretly carried on board.

The time of year, February, was not ideal for crossing

the widest part of the Channel, but the five men had no desire to wait till summer before they ventured. François was a sailor, and the prospect of making the crossing presented no difficulties whatever to him. And the others were all impatient to get away. So one evening at dusk they embarked and set out under the very nose of the Nazi sentinel, who merely thought they were departing for the island off shore. It was already growing dark as the motor-boat left the quay, and before they reached the island night had fallen and the boat was then headed out to sea. Close to the land the water was comparatively calm, but once outside the sea became very rough, with waves fifteen feet high. To make matters worse the motor was not covered over with a casing, and the seas blowing into the boat drenched the motor, short-circuiting the ignition, with the result that it stopped. This was a serious matter, for the boat had no sails to keep its head to the seas, and François, who was a clever mechanic, worked frantically to get the dead motor going again. In spite of the bitter cold, he did not hesitate to tear up his shirt for rags with which to wipe dry the sparking-plugs and terminals. Presently he got the motor going, but shortly afterwards it stopped, and he again dried the plugs and terminals, and again got the motor going. Pierre, at the tiller, meanwhile fought to keep the boat from broaching to and capsizing. The bottom of the boat was ten inches deep in water, and Jean, René, and Claude spent the whole of the night baling out the rising water.

Everything seemed to go wrong, in spite of the care with which every detail of the trip had been planned. Now, when they needed it most, when they had lost all sense of direction in the darkness, they discovered that the compass had been left behind. Of all things they had forgotten to bring the compass! This indispensable instrument was the first part of the equipment they had secured, and they were stunned to find it missing. Nor were the stars of any assistance, for they were hidden by the heavy clouds. In the darkness it was almost impossible to judge the breaking direction of the huge seas, and a hundred times the boat was saved from swinging broadside on to the sea by Pierre's quick action at the tiller. Had that happened nothing could have saved the five men. There was no time now to think of seasickness or the bitter cold. They were fighting for their lives, and the night seemed as though it would never come to an end.

The dawn, when it came, brought but little relief. As for the sun, it was not seen during the voyage, and its position had to be guessed at by the lightest part of the overcast sky. But dawn brought some relief inasmuch as it permitted Pierre to see the direction of the waves and avoid broaching to. To add to the men's anxieties there was the ever-present danger of being discovered by enemy coastal patrols, and when during the morning three Nazi planes were sighted the fugitives scarcely breathed until the enemy had passed. The fact that they were flying high probably explained their failure to see the boat, which would be lost in the gray waste of sea flecked with white caps. While the planes were in sight the occupants of the boat remained quite still lest their movements might be seen.

François still struggled to keep the motor going. Afterwards he said that during three-quarters of the journey the motor had been out of action, and since the boat had no sail for three-quarters of the journey it drifted at the mercy of the wind and sea, and at times was moving back towards France. This was discouraging, and they regretted that they had not brought some sort of sail. They had to bale continually or the boat would have filled and sunk. Sleep was impossible, and the icy wind blowing through their sodden clothes chilled them to the bone. Through standing in nearly a foot of water for the last twenty-four hours their feet had lost all feeling. The lack of a compass continued to be a serious problem, for they had no idea where they were. As there was no sun from which to take a rough bearing the drift back and forth in the Channel made it impossible to estimate how much northing they had made since leaving France. Two days and two nights had passed, and they were lost somewhere in the Channel, in peril of being blown out into the Atlantic; but without a sail and with the motor dead there was nothing they could do about it. François worked unceasingly over the motor, but its periods of activity were brief, for sooner or later the sea drenched the exposed sparking-plugs and it would splutter and stop.

The fugitives had no illusions as to their fate if they were discovered by Nazi surface or air patrols. They would be slaughtered with machine-guns, and no one would ever have known their fate. The sea they knew and did not fear, but this other peril gave them considerable anxiety. It was a bitter disappointment after two days to be still at sea when they should have been safely in England. The cold and wet and lack of sleep did not matter, but the failure of the motor and their own failure to provide against such a contingency by fitting a waterproof casing over the motor might have brought disaster. On the other hand, it would have been risky to make extensive alterations to the boat as it would almost certainly have roused the suspicions of the Nazi sentries. Therefore they had put off just as though they were making a trip out to the island and no farther. Although the five men were beginning to feel severely the strain of fighting the sea, of sleepless nights, and of wet and cold, they never lost hope of eventually reaching their goal. They joked grimly about their difficulties, their wet clothes, and the motor which would not go. They were Bretons, descendants of sailors, and good companions in a situation that brings out the worst or best in men. They were described by the reporter of the French newspaper *France*, published in London, as *"vraiment gentils et sympathiques, ces garçons qui viennent de risquer leur vie. Ils répondent aux questions avec simplicité, mais aussi avec netteté."* Pierre, the leader, was described as a magnificent specimen of manhood. He had been a well-known Rugby international before the war.

The third morning found the boat still far from land, and François still hopefully nursing the recalcitrant motor. When all the moisture was wiped off the terminals and electric system he would shelter it from flying spray with his coat while someone swung the starting-handle. Everything in the boat was wet, and it was back-breaking work to get the motor turning against its high compression. It would at last start with a most encouraging roar, but invariably the damp would creep into the carefully dried terminals, and after a mile or so it would splutter and stop. Nevertheless the boat was gradually drawing nearer to the English coast in spite of its drift, but the land was still hidden in the mists to the northward, and another day and night were to pass before the five men could say their voyage was ended. The morning of the fourth day broke gray and stormy with the sea still rough. The night had been spent drifting to a sea anchor streamed out from the bows. Baling had to be kept up all night, the men taking it in turns while the others rested. Lack of sleep began to tell on everyone, and their eyes smarted and ached with salt from the spray which beat on their faces throughout the voyage.[1] They tasted salt, breathed salt, and were crusted

[1] In nautical language a voyage is a journey out and home, a return trip. The crossing of the Channel would be described as a passage. Any trip between two ports is a passage.

with salt. There was no relief, no escape from the all-pervading salt and the all-pervading water. The chicken had long since been eaten, likewise the sardines. Some of the excellent Bordeaux wine remained, and this was drunk sparingly to make it last as long as possible.

The fourth morning brought no sight of land, but the visibility was poor and the English coast was nearer than they knew. All day they crouched in the boat, buffeted by the seas which drove them round every point of the compass, but always the main drift was in the right direction. There were signs of the proximity of land, driftwood, seaweed, and sea-birds, but the coast continued coyly to hide in the mists to the north. They expected to make the coast of Cornwall or Devon, but they knew that the shore was rocky and dangerous and a sharp look-out was kept. The day dragged by, and night came without any sight of the land. Still the men knew that the land was near, so near perhaps they might run into it in the dark. It must have been about two in the morning when a number of small steamers were seen in the gloom. They were steaming in formation known as *en échelon*, and each carried a small gun on the fo'c'sle. François recognized them as minesweepers, but was uncertain of their nationality. What if they were German? They dared not think of it. Soon their fears were put to rest by the sight of British sailors and an English voice hailing them. Though they did not know it till later, they were picked up close to the coast opposite the very point they had chosen on the map as their landing-place. They had been in the Channel 105 hours in an open boat, drifting, most of the time in bad weather, without dry clothes and without sleep. But this was all a memory now. The bluff British sailors slapped them on the back and talked to them in bad French and gave them hot food and drink. While their clothes were drying they went to bed, but too excited to sleep. They wondered if the Germans had discovered their absence and hoped that the man who sold them the boat had not got into trouble for doing so.

The minesweepers came into port at dawn, and Pierre, François, Jean, René, and Claude were given railway warrants to take them to London. Arriving in the metropolis, they lost no time in going to General de Gaulle's headquarters. Here they were questioned by the French Intelligence officers about conditions in France, and then they were sent to join units of the Free French Forces. Pierre, Jean, and René joined the French Navy and donned the picturesque matelot's rig with the red pom-pom on the cap. François and Claude evinced a desire to go into the tank corps—"Corps des Chars d'Assaut."

CHAPTER XI

Escape from Norway

ON MONDAY, April 8, 1940, Norway was a neutral country at peace with its neighbors. On Tuesday, April 9, she was at war. Overnight she had been invaded by the German Army and Navy, and willy-nilly was instantly embroiled in war. The Norsemen, a peace-loving people, had endured much, had swallowed lots of threats to remain at peace. All their efforts availed them nothing, for in the early hours of April 9, when most of their people were asleep in their beds, the principal ports—Oslo, Bergen, Trondheim, and Narvik—were simultaneously invaded. Harbors, air ports, railway stations, and land forts were attacked by sailors, soldiers, airplanes, and parachute troops. Utterly unprepared, the friendly, trusting Norwegians were bewildered by the suddenness of the attack, and the capital, Oslo, was occupied almost without fighting. Norway was too weak for any effective defense against the Nazi legions. The invader was helped by spies and sympathizers within the country, who were led by the Norwegian deputy Quisling, whose name forever afterwards was associated with those who would collaborate with an enemy.

Though the Norwegians were anxious to preserve the peace almost at any price, once they were attacked they fought back with the vigor and determination of a brave race, but even with the help of Britain and France they could not hold back the Nazi flood which overwhelmed their land in a short few weeks.

The Nazis had laid their plans cunningly. German merchant ships, with their holds full of hidden shock troops, waited in Norwegian harbors for the zero hour of attack. Some of these ships were disguised as neutral vessels, carrying neutral flags. At sea Nazi warships waited for the moment to steam into the key ports of Oslo, Bergen, and Narvik. There was no warning, no formality of an ultimatum. To have sent an ultimatum would have given the victim a brief respite to prepare his defense, and total war had swept away the convention of a formal declaration. At Narvik two Norwegian armed patrol ships, tied up alongside the dock, were ordered to surrender, and when they refused they were torpedoed and sunk. Within twelve hours of the start of the invasion the country was paralyzed, as nearly all the key points were either destroyed or in enemy hands. Five out of Norway's six airfields were taken within an hour, and the small Norwegian air force was all but wiped out.

Most neutral eyewitnesses agreed that Norway was conquered through its Fifth Column, its Trojan Horse. The Trojan Horse idea was exploited in a modern way by the enemy when they sent peaceful-looking merchantmen full of armed troops into Norwegian ports. At the zero hour the hatches opened, and out poured soldiers armed to the teeth, against whom the unarmed townsmen had no chance whatever. Help came from Britain and France across four hundred miles of sea, but in insufficient numbers as to both men and arms to more than delay the inevitable surrender. Even the largest ships can carry only a few battalions, and these were a trickle compared with the legions Germany could pour in across the narrows that divided the southern tip of Norway from Denmark which was occupied simultaneously with the invasion of Norway. The Royal Navy played a greater part in that war than either the Army or the Air Force, and consequently paid a heavy price in ships and men. The 22,000-ton aircraft-carrier *Glorious* was lost by enemy action off the Norwegian coast; also the cruiser *Curlew*, and the destroyers *Glowworm, Hardy, Hunter, Gurkha, Acastra, Ardent,* and *Afridi,* and the sloop *Bittern.* It had always been the policy of the Royal Navy to take risks, and the Norwegian campaign was no exception. But if their naval losses were great the enemy losses were, on the whole, greater, with ten destroyers and at least four cruisers sent to the bottom.

A glance at the map of Northern Europe will show that the southern end of Norway lies in latitude 58°, which is on a line running north of the Isle of Skye. The nearest port to this country is Bergen, about 310 miles from Aberdeen. Narvik, in the far north, is over a thousand miles from Aberdeen. It is farther north than Iceland, and is ice-bound for most of the year. The coast of Norway is deeply indented with hundreds of inlets and bays—the familiar fiords—from which the mountains rise steeply from the sea. These fiords are natural harbors for Norwegian fishermen, and during the war were perfect hide-outs for the many Norwegians who were planning to escape by sea. A secret patriot radio urged the young men to revolt, or, if that were impossible, to get away to Britain and enlist in the Norwegian forces overseas. Of the hundreds who tried to escape most were caught at the outset, but some were luckier, and here is the story of a group of these modern Vikings who finally got away after narrowly escaping capture in the first attempt.

The penalty for attempting to escape from Norway was death. The Germans posted in Norwegian towns notices stating that any young man caught trying to escape from the country would be shot immediately wherever he was found. This sort of thing encouraged extreme taciturnity

An upturned ship's lifeboat, supporting four exhausted survivors of a torpedoed merchantman, is brought alongside a British warship. *British Combine Photos*.

The sinking of H.M.S. *Ark Royal. British Combine Photos.*

in the naturally taciturn Norwegians planning to escape. They had to use the greatest caution, not even daring to tell their families of their intentions, lest some remark, innocently made, might arouse the suspicion of the ubiquitous Gestapo. Young men planning to escape and anxious to recruit others for their scheme would not approach the subject openly, but drop a hint with some such remark as that they would like to travel or go on a fishing trip. The subject was too dangerous to speak of openly, for spies were everywhere and everyone was suspicious. But if a person was interested in such a scheme he would secretly get in touch with the man who wanted to go on a fishing trip, and so the thing would start.

At a certain coastal town five young men got together and planned to take a fisherman's motor-boat and steal away one dark night. They had saved up enough money to buy the boat and sufficient gasoline to take it across the North Sea, but, since it would be unsafe openly to approach the owner of the craft and offer to buy it, they decided to take it without asking and post the money to him in an envelope so that he would get it when they were well out at sea. The gasoline was bought from a man who was able to get German supplies which he sold to the boys at black market prices—*i.e.*, four shillings a gallon. They obtained in this way forty-five gallons, sufficient to take them to Iceland if they should by any chance miss Scotland. For food they had eighteen loaves of bread, some tinned meat, fishballs, and condensed milk.

Dressed as fishermen, the five young men, the oldest of whom was twenty years of age, went down to the edge of the fiord where the boat was tied up and waited till dark before setting out. While they were waiting a fishing-smack came alongside, and the fishermen, noticing the cans of petrol on board, tried to find out if the boys were planning an escape to England. When the boys cautiously denied any such intention the fishermen laughed and tossed into the motor-boat a rolled-up paper which proved to be a large chart of the North Sea. As the fishermen left they laughed again and wished the boys luck in their venture. After dark they put out to sea, but during the night, while they were still in sight of land, the motor broke down, and though they worked on it all night it refused to start, and, after holding a council of war, it was decided to hoist the sail and turn back, as discovery by Nazi air or sea patrols was certain with daylight. To avoid the risk of being caught at sea with so much fuel on board they dumped the cans of precious spirit into the sea.

In spite of this setback, the boys were not deterred from their intention, and once back at their homes again they began making other plans. Meanwhile three of them returned to high school as if nothing had happened, to continue their studies until the summer vacation, when they agreed to join their companions in another attempt. The twenty-year-old leader, Roald, had been busy getting in touch by secret channels with other bold fellows anxious to get away and join the Norwegian forces abroad, and when the time came to make the attempt there were eleven in the band. Their rendezvous and hiding-place for accumulated food and petrol was a ravine high up above the fiord, and here they met to make their plans. A large motor-boat had been secured, and gasoline for the engine was stolen nightly, a tin or two at a time, from a German airdrome, and hidden in the woods. Roald managed to obtain several bottles of brandy from a relative who had at first pleaded with him not to go for fear the Nazis should carry out reprisals on the families of those who got away; but this relative's patriotism proved stronger than his fears, and he wished the venture success.

Unfortunately, the Nazis found the boat and arrested four of the youths who were on board at the time, preparing it for sea. The rest were warned by friends when they were on the way down to the boat, and they had to escape to the mountains as the Nazis had forced from the captured boys the names of the others, and they dared not return to their homes, which were already occupied by the Nazi police. Seven of the boys were still free, and as they had all the stores cached in the secret hiding-place they decided to continue their plans for escape. Roald told them that he had a friend living on a small island just off the shore who had a couple of boats and whom he knew to be a patriotic Norseman. Leaving his six companions in the hiding-place, he descended to the fiord and found a fisherman willing to row him out to the island. On the island Roald found his friend not only ready to let him have a boat, but to go with him to England as he had for a long time planned to do. The friend and boat-owner provided a compass and charts, together with his saved-up food rations, and the pair took the boat back to the fiord, where the six hiding in the ravine joined them. The first thing the escapers did was to overhaul the boat thoroughly and make sure that there were no serious leaks before they put out to sea.

Roald, as captain, decided to steer an elusive course at first, for although it was not a direct course for Scotland, it would lessen the risk of discovery by enemy patrols. Starting out after dark, they skirted the coast for several hours, and just at dawn passed through a German minefield. About midday the motor showed signs of being overheated, and Roald discovered that the intake for the water-cooling system was clogged, so it was decided to risk putting into a small fishing port where repairs could be carried out. At first the local people refused to help them for fear of Nazi vengeance, but after dark some of them returned to the dock, and under cover of a tarpaulin to hide the lantern they set to work with a will and cleared the cooling system within an hour. By midnight the boat was ready, and with the good wishes of the local people the boys set out again under a starry sky. Three hours later they ran into a storm, and for the next few hours they had an anxious time of it in keeping the motor going and avoiding capsize. The water-casks were lashed down, and the food was wrapped in tarpaulin, but even so it was partly spoiled by sea-water, though at the time this did not matter as all but Roald, the only sailor in the boat, were seasick.

The storm continued all night and throughout the next day, and everything in the boat was soaking wet, except the precious sparking-plug terminals, which were kept dry by constant attention to the tarpaulin hood which covered the top of the engine. The heavy seas, in slowing down the boat's speed, seriously upset the calculated gasoline allowance, which was being used up at such a rate it threatened to give out before the journey was more than half completed. Roald changed the course to a southerly one as the wind and sea were driving the boat so far north there was a risk of missing the land, which he hoped to sight the next day—if the gasoline held out so far. The great danger was in missing it and being driven out into the North Atlantic, where shipping was so infrequent they might never be found. Some of the younger ones, unused to boats, were unhappy at the way theirs rolled and pitched, fearing that it would fill and sink, but with the stoicism of their Viking ancestors they said nothing and despite seasickness did their full share at the pumps. Another night came, and by now everyone was wet and cold, but comforted in the knowledge that the Germans were less likely to be out on patrol in such weather than if it were fine. The rough seas and high wind were friends in disguise, and of the two dangers this was preferable to the other.

At daybreak the seas were still running high, and the wind was as strong as ever, but the sky had cleared, and Roald told the others that they should sight land that afternoon. Everyone had a little breakfast, eaten cold, and managed to keep it down.

There was no means of making a hot drink, but a ration of brandy proved a good substitute in an emergency. The seas were running so high that it was impossible to see far except when the boat rose to the top of a wave. At the risk of being tipped overboard the boys frequently stood up to look for land when the boat was lifted high on the crest of one of the big rollers, but as the day wore on and the expected land did not appear Roald secretly wondered if the storm had carried them so far north they had missed the land and were drifting in the Atlantic. The day passed and the third night came, but still there was no sign of the land. Fortunately the wind and sea were moderating, and the boys were able to get some sleep in turns. In the morning, with no land yet in sight, Roald decided to change the course to due west, believing that this would bring them either to the Shetland or the Danish Faeroe Islands.

During the morning an airplane was sighted flying straight towards the boat, and the boys had a few anxious moments until the plane was close enough for them to see that it had British markings. They cheered it as it swooped low over the boat twice and then flew off to the west as though showing them the way, but the boys did not realize this at the time and made no change in the course. In the middle of the afternoon, however, birds flew over the boat, and kelp floated past. Everyone was now on the alert watching for the first sight of land, which they believed would be one of the Shetland Isles. An hour after seeing the first birds one of the sharp-eyed youngsters sighted a headland with a wireless mast on its summit. The end of the journey was in sight, and to celebrate this event another bottle of brandy was opened and drunk. As the boat neared land a fishing-boat was seen coming out to meet it. When the fishermen were within hailing distance they called out in a Norse language, and the boys knew that the island must be one of the Faeroes.

The harbor entrance was narrow and dangerous, and the Norwegian boat had to wait for a patrol launch to come out and lead the way through the channel. In the port the young escapers were loudly cheered, and were made much of by the local people, who crowded round them plying them with a hundred questions, and pressing on them food, cigarettes, and dry clothing. The young Norwegians were deeply touched by such a welcome, which contrasted so forcibly with the hunted life they had been leading in their own homeland. But in spite of the wonderful reception the boys were not yet free, and for the first two or three days they were virtual prisoners in an hotel in the town while their stories were checked and their possessions thoroughly examined.

Once the necessary precautions were finished with and the integrity of the new arrivals established nothing was too good for them, and as soon as possible they were taken across to the mainland (Scotland), where they were turned over to the Norwegian consul, who saw to it that they got their wish to enlist in the Norwegian forces—Army, Navy, and Air Force. They were taken to London, where they were fêted once more before settling down to the long and arduous training to fit them for doing their part in the battles that lay ahead.

Most of the Norwegian youths who left the land they loved, and in leaving risked their lives, did so because they were impelled by a strong sense of duty, the duty to fight for their country. Many left their homes while still at a tender age without even telling their parents of their plans, lest the knowledge should bring upon their families terrible reprisals. If their mothers and fathers knew nothing they could tell nothing. If they knew nothing they could not be implicated as conspirators. The greatest caution had to be exercised at all times, and in this these youths showed a discretion and wisdom far beyond their years. Their ages were from fifteen to twenty-one years, and sometimes they were joined by girls and young women whose sense of patriotism and desire to serve were stronger than their love of home.

In October 1941 a small Norwegian motor fishing-smack reached a British port. It was crowded with no less than thirty-eight people, including three girls, one of whom was only sixteen. The oldest man was the skipper, aged thirty, who was formerly an officer in the Norwegian merchant service. They had been at sea over three days and had a rough time during the passage as the boat was so crowded and the weather so bad that it had been impossible to get any sleep. The only one to understand the engine was so seasick he forgot to oil it, with the result that it stopped, and was started again only with the greatest difficulty. Meanwhile the boat drifted helplessly back towards the Norwegian coast. Some of those on board begged to be taken back, but the young skipper bluntly refused, pointing out that to return now would mean certain disaster, whereas if they kept on there was a good chance of reaching England. To return and attempt a landing in the dark would mean being wrecked on the rock-bound coast and to land in the daylight certain capture by Nazi patrols. So they repaired the motor and continued the voyage. The skipper was a man of few words and also a good sailor, and, in spite of their miseries, when they reached a British harbor they were glad and voted that after all it had been a pretty good trip, and they had no regrets. In England the men lost no time in joining their Norwegian compatriots in the forces, and the three women became nurses.

The most popular branch of the service among the young Norwegians was the Flying Corps, and hundreds of them were sent to Canada to train in the Royal Norwegian Air Force, which had set up a training station near Toronto. Their youth, physical fitness, and magnificent *sang froid* made them excellent pilots. They had been trained to hate war, to believe that war was stupid, and to love peace, just as the Nazi youth had been trained to glorify war. It almost seemed as though five hundred years of peace had made the descendants of the hardy Norsemen soft. But after recovering from their bewilderment at the invasion of their land they showed that they had lost nothing of the old Viking spirit, as the repeated escapes at the risk of execution proved conclusively enough. The only deterrent was the fear of reprisals against their own families and friends, but for the most part those left behind to face the Nazi police willingly took the risk in order that their sons and brothers and sweethearts should do what seemed right. Norway had been conquered, but to these young men Norwegians were still in the war, and not to try to escape was equivalent to treason.

In August 1941 two Norwegian youths living in an inland town got word that the Nazis were about to make it illegal for anyone to leave the town without a pass from the military governor. They decided therefore to get out before the new rule came into force, and, although they had had no sea experience, planned to secure a boat and sail to England. With what little money they had saved up they left home and traveled to a small port on the west coast, after giving it out to their parents and friends that they were going on a fishing holiday. To give the appearance of truth to this little deception they took fishing-rods and baskets and dressed the part of river fishermen—that is, in heavy woolen clothing, hobnailed boots, and oilskins. In a hired boat they leisurely sailed down the fiord and along the coast apparently fishing, but in reality looking out for a suitable craft in which to make the escape. They needed a boat strongly built and able to stand a sea voyage. At this time their plans were a trifle nebulous and depended largely on the opportunity that sooner or later they felt would present itself. With the optimism of youth, they had no doubt whatever that something would turn up.

While at a little hamlet on the coast they got into talk with three men who admitted that they were anxious to escape from Norway. Two of these men had been recently released from a Nazi concentration camp and were out on parole—that is, they had to report to the police every day, so that if they were to escape their absence would be noticed within twenty-four hours. With a certain recklessness unusual in Norway at that time, when a careless word might bring disaster, the strangers told the boys of their plans, which were mainly concerned with securing a boat from a man living on one of the cluster of islands a few miles off the coast. Many other would-be escapers had secured boats from islanders along that rugged coast, and the boys, eager to take the first chance offering freedom, arranged to be on a certain night at the rendezvous, where a boat would be waiting. After waiting for two nights at the appointed place without any sign of the boat the boys decided it would be unwise to linger in that place for fear of arousing suspicion, and so began looking round for other means of getting away. They dared not return home now since their absence must have been noticed, and this added a further incentive to getting away quickly. The three men arranged to help them if a plan could be agreed upon, and meanwhile the boys went to stay with a fisherman on one of the islands, where they kept up the pretense of being on a fishing holiday. After a few days on the island they received a message from their three friends, who were staying on another island, that a fisherman, the owner of a big boat, wanted to go to England and would take a number of people if they would buy his boat and contribute each his share of food stores. The boys eagerly accepted the chance, and meanwhile were instructed to wait and continue to act the part of amateur fishermen until they received word that all was ready.

A fortnight later a message came telling them to take a boat alone out to a rocky cove where they would find the others waiting. They followed instructions, and on their arrival at the rendezvous were astonished to find a crowd of about thirty young people, including several girls, waiting. Everybody seemed to have brought a friend, and though the boat was a roomy, broad-beamed craft twenty-eight feet long it was scarcely large enough to carry some thirty people, half a dozen of whom were girls, across five hundred miles of open sea. The only way to stow so many people on board was to get them to lie down in the bottom of the boat in close-packed rows, and to make the lying a little less hard straw was first put down. Then the leaders decided it was impossible to take so many people, and so the girls must remain behind, but on hearing this they cried so bitterly that the men gave in, and, smiling through their tears, they stepped aboard.

The smack was, of course, undecked, and to give some protection from the weather a tarpaulin was stretched over the after half, but those crouched in the bottom amidships got very wet as soon as they put to sea. A small and ancient motor provided the power, and it took the heavily laden boat across the stormy North Sea safely without once breaking down. The three days at sea were rough and stormy, and all but the fishermen among the party were ill and suffering from exposure, but they were glad that the weather was so bad since it made it much more difficult for Nazi patrols to spot the boat. The fishermen were magnificent sailors, and had it not been for their courage and skilful handling of the boat it would have foundered in a gale which blew with hurricane force at times. Once when a Nazi plane passed over most of the people lay still under the canvas while a few pretended to be hauling in lines like trawlermen, and the plane flew right over them apparently satisfied of their innocent purpose. The very rough seas never gave the occupants of the boat a moment's respite from the pitching and dizzy rising and falling, and the strain began to tell on the craft's ancient timbers, so that when on the third day the party reached a little Scottish port the boat sank within half an hour after they had landed.

During the worst of the gale, when the little boat was being tossed about like a piece of driftwood, a German torpedo-boat sighted them, but for some mysterious reason made no attempt to interfere. The fishermen said it was because it looked as if the boat was doomed any way in such a storm. The log of that voyage was a record of misery and suffering compressed into three nightmare days. On arrival at the Scottish port most of the people were too weak to walk and had to be carried ashore; but under the tender care of the kindly Scots they quickly recovered from their ordeal. After a few days' rest, during which time the police had checked their stories, they were sent to London to join various Norwegian units. The girls became nurses and cooks; the men soldiers, sailors, and airmen. The boat, as we have said, sank in dock shortly after the refugees had left it. The overloading and the pounding in rough seas had been too much for the old craft, but it had held together just long enough to bring the passengers safely across. Had it foundered a few hours sooner the party of young patriots would have been lost, and Norway's cause would have been the poorer for it.

CHAPTER XII

Castaways

Of all the trials and tests of human fortitude and courage surely none is more calculated to bring out the best and worst qualities in men than the physical and mental stress of spending a long period in an open boat, ill and starving and without hope.

The author, in searching through the shipping records and the photographs at the Ministry of Information, came across a number of photographs captured from the Germans—pictures of castaways in boats and on rafts taken by U-boat commanders. One particularly tragic photo is of a half-naked man on a small raft, alone and apparently without food or water. On the back of the photo it is merely said that he was sighted by the U-boat crew, who came close enough to the castaway to take his photograph and then left him to his fate. There is another photo of some men in the water. Their ship had gone down, and they are kept afloat by their life-jackets, but since they could not live long in the icy water their doom was certain. There is still another, taken from the deck of a British escort vessel, of an unconscious Chinese seaman lying limp on a ship's raft.

This fellow was one of the more fortunate castaways. There have been cases of men surviving after their boat has capsized, men who have clung like limpets to the keel of their craft in a rough sea for many days before being found. A ship's lifeboat is a heavy craft and impossible to right by men swimming in the sea as there is nothing on the smooth, rounded surface to get hold of. For this reason an improved type of ship's lifeboat was put in some ships during the second year of the war. Among the improvements were outside bilge keels with slots along their length for handgrips for just such an emergency. Incidentally, the improved type of ship's boat was fitted with a bilge-pump, wireless transmitting set, a 10-h.p. motor, a red sail (for visibility), ample food, including anti-thirst chocolate, pemmican, and water stores; medicine chest, navigating instruments, blankets, and 'Channel swimmers' oil' for protecting exposed parts of the body against the sea.

Rafts, which are part of the equipment of all ships, are a poor substitute for lifeboats, since they offer no shelter whatever, nor are they capable of being navigated like a boat. Their great advantage is that they are unsinkable, non-capsizable, and easily launched. As a temporary refuge they have saved thousands of lives, but as a refuge for a prolonged period they leave much to be desired.

Late in the summer of 1941 a British freighter was torpedoed in the South Atlantic between Brazil and Africa. The crew was a mixed one of seventy-four Europeans and Mohammedans. Seventeen men, six Europeans and eleven Lascars, got away on four small rafts, which were lashed together for greater security. There was almost no food or water, and although the steamer had gone down in a part of the Atlantic where, owing to the war, ships were seldom seen, the castaways did not abandon hope. The white men figured that they might be a month adrift before being picked up, but this guess was proved to be wrong as they were rescued some days before the month was up. The burning rays of the tropic sun were their worst enemy, and to protect their heads they made caps of cloth, which was obtained by cutting off their trousers at the knee. Rare rain-squalls brought them water, and a shark caught on a hook baited with a flying-fish provided them with food for two days. There were some ship's biscuits in a sealed tin on one of the rafts, and these were mashed up with the shark-flesh and boiled in the tin to make a sort of shark stew. As it was impossible to sail or row the four small floating platforms, the castaways were unable to set a course for the nearest land, and were resigned to drifting at the will of the ocean currents. In this way they drifted northward over a hundred miles, and were sighted by a Spanish freighter bound for St. Vincent, where they were taken. All were alive, and all recovered from their ordeal.

How rafts saved the lives of 230 men was told in an official communiqué early in March 1942. Although the survivors were not long at sea, the fact that so many men were saved by rafts gives the episode an unusual interest. A British merchant ship carrying over two hundred officers and men of the R.A.F. and the Royal Australian Air Force across the Java Sea was torpedoed by a Japanese submarine near the coast of Java early in February. The ship's complement consisted of thirty-five men, and there was only one lifeboat big enough to hold more than half a dozen men. As the ship did not sink for over an hour the crew had time to instruct the aircraftmen how to make rafts by lashing planks together, and in this way about sixty tiny rafts were constructed and floated overboard. The ship carried five floats, and these, together with the one lifeboat, accommodated a few dozen men, the rest having to rely on the flotilla of small rafts. This odd-looking fleet spent the night at sea, and by morning most of the survivors were suffering from the cold and wet, for the rafts were so small they floated awash, and the men were thus forced to sit in water for the twenty-odd hours they were adrift. About the middle of the next day they were picked up by a vessel of the Australian Navy. All were alive, but they were so weak from exposure that they had to be treated in hospital before returning to their units.

To be cast away on a raft is not an uncommon experience, but to be cast away on the keel of an upturned boat is an experience that has not fallen to the lot of many men. Yet, during the U-boat war on Allied shipping, two authentic cases of sailors surviving after spending days on the keels of their upturned boats are on record. And strange as it may seem, in each case three men survived the ordeal. For to be cast away on the keel of a capsized boat in the North Atlantic in midwinter is surely an ordeal which only the strongest could endure and survive. It would seem humanly impossible, without food or drink or shelter from the biting winds, to cling to such a dancing perch for long, yet the subjects of the following narrative managed to survive *five days* on the keel of their upturned boat in the Atlantic, while the sea did its utmost to tear them from their refuge.

Their ship, a British freighter, was part of an Atlantic convoy when she was attacked by a U-boat during a howling gale. The weather had been stormy for several days, and the seas were running so high that a U-boat attack was not expected. The rise and fall of the huge waves would prevent a torpedo from maintaining its predetermined depth and cause it to 'porpoise'—*i.e.*, to leap clear of the sea—as it sped towards its target. The convoy was well out in the Atlantic and beginning to feel reasonably safe from attack when the first warning of a U-boat's presence in the vicinity was the dull boom of the torpedo exploding against the ship's bilge as she rolled in the opposite direction from which the attack came. In spite of the suddenness of the attack there was no confusion on board, and

A flotilla of motor gun boats passing a minesweeper. These heavily armed M.G.B.'s serve as the spearhead of attack on convoys off the enemy coast. *British Official Photograph.*

An Allied convoy fights through to Russia. *British Official Photograph.*

every man who was able calmly went to the boat stations.

The ship was taking water rapidly and already beginning to settle, with a steep list which made it impossible to lower the boats on one side. On the other side, the bosun, a South Shields man named William Magrs, superintended the launching of a boat into which twenty-five men had scrambled. The manila falls creaked with the great weight, and he watched the lowering anxiously, until the boat had touched the water. This was the most delicate moment of all, for the scend of the sea threatened to smash the craft against the steel side of the ship before it could be pulled clear. The oars were already shipped and the men in the bow and stern were waiting, ready to cast off the moment the fall blocks were unhooked. The boat was launched without capsizing, and the crew had just begun to pull away when two more unseen torpedoes hit the stricken ship. The blast turned the boat over, spilling the crew into the sea.

When the fountain of water, erupted by the explosions, had fallen back into the sea the lifeboat appeared floating bottom upwards, and around it the heads of swimming men. Their ship was sinking fast, and the boat was their only refuge. It was a clinker-built, wooden boat about thirty feet long. As it rolled in the steep seas, from time to time its top strake would show above the water, and as this plank was thicker than the others it formed a ledge by which an active man might secure a hold to hoist himself up on to the keel, which ran like a narrow ridge the full length of the boat. The bosun, a powerfully built man, contrived, after several attempts, to get a knee over the top strake and claw his way over the rounded surface by clutching the reversed overlap of the planking until he reached the keel. From here he helped others out of the water until eight men lay sprawled across the keel.

Unfortunately, a little later a big wave swept over the craft, and when it had receded three of the eight had disappeared. With their loss went the only chance of righting the boat, for it would prove a far too heavy task for the remaining five men. The capsized boat had drifted away from the sinking ship and the convoy had disappeared over the horizon. The prospect was grim enough, but the men were not downhearted. There was nothing on the boat to sustain life: neither food, nor water, nor shelter. Nor had they any rope with which to lash themselves to the narrow perch. On either side of the three-inch-thick keel the garboard strake, the plank nearest the keel, was for three-quarters of its length an almost horizontal plank, but the next plank to it sloped noticeably, and the rest of the planking dropped steeply away at an angle of forty-five degrees, so that the space on which the five men could lie was a strip less than a foot wide on either side of the keel, which stuck up like the backbone of a starving horse. Its one advantage was that it afforded a hand-and-knee grip against the pitching and rolling of the upturned boat. How welcome would have been those bilge keels which were later recommended as standard fitments to all ships' boats!

The first night the gale raged with unabated fury, as though trying to tear the five human limpets from the upturned shell. The bosun remained a tower of strength, cheering and encouraging the others. He pointed out that the boat would be more conspicuous in its present posture, showing its white bottom to passing ships or patrolling airplanes, and therefore there was an advantage in being on an upturned boat. We must pass over the subsequent days the survivors were adrift before the boat was sighted. At the end of the second day one man died, and a few hours before help arrived another man died. The bosun, William Magrs, had sustained the spirits of the others throughout the ordeal, and had even, after great labor, succeeded in hacking a hole in the planking with a sheath knife, to try and get at stores inside the boat. Unfortunately these had been washed away, and his labor was wasted. Everyone kept a look-out, and as the boat would ride high on the crest of a wave they scanned the empty ocean for sight of a distant ship. A ship would perhaps show up before dark, or tomorrow at the latest. Such thoughts sustained them, and the effort of watching gave them something to do.

That afternoon the look-out of a British destroyer out on patrol noticed something unusual appearing and disappearing on the sea a couple of miles away. Through the glasses it seemed to be an upturned boat, but it was still too far away for him to be quite certain. The destroyer was headed towards the floating object, and on a nearer approach it was unmistakably identified as a white-painted ship's lifeboat floating bottom up, and on it was a dark lump which a few minutes later separated into three men who lay sprawled across the boat's keel. It seemed impossible that they could hang on to such a narrow perch, and the warship was brought alongside the capsized boat with great care not to jar it and spill the men into the sea. But when a line was thrown across the boat they made no effort to change their prone position. It afterwards turned out that they were so enfeebled from their experience that they dared not immediately release their hold to grasp the line for fear of slipping off the keel. However, the bosun presently summoned strength enough to grasp a circular lifebuoy which was heaved to him fast to another line. Some of the destroyer's ratings got down on to the boat and passed lines round the men, and by this means they were helped aboard. When these tough and hardy sailors were helped on board a momentary reaction overcame them, but they quickly recovered. They had been five days on the capsized boat, and at the beginning there were eight of them. The three survivors were Magrs, the bosun, and two able seamen, Ernest Wilson and John Perridge, both of Hull.

A few weeks later the *London Gazette* included in the latest list of awards for gallantry at sea the name of Boatswain William J. Magrs, of South Shields, who had been awarded the British Empire Medal.

By one of those curious coincidences that are stranger than fiction a similar adventure befell three British seamen who were marooned on an upturned boat in the Atlantic after their ship was sunk by a U-boat. The lifeboats, properly stocked with food and water, were safely launched in a rough sea, and in one boat were four men whose subsequent ordeal bore a certain resemblance to the experience of William Magrs and his two companions. The four men were two able seamen, James Stokes and John Cook; Second Mate John Noble, and an unnamed negro seaman. From the outset the poorly clad men suffered severely from the bitter cold. They had no protection against the icy rain which beat down on them day after day without respite. A few hours after their ship had gone down they sighted a steamer some miles away, and with only three oars (the fourth was lost overboard) they pulled through the steep seas towards the vessel—to discover that she was an abandoned tanker in a sinking condition. In spite of this, they made an effort to board her in the hope of making a fire to dry their clothes and get a hot meal, but the seas were too rough to enable them to come alongside and the attempt had to be abandoned. For the next ten days the four men fought to keep their boat afloat in the mountainous seas. That gale blew with unabated fury, bringing squalls of cold rain, which froze on the gunwales and thwarts, weighing the craft down dangerously. On the eleventh day an extra big sea rolled the boat over, spilling men and gear into the water. They had seen it coming, towering over them like a green cliff, but were too weak to bring the boat's head round in time. Seaman Stokes came up beneath the craft and, realizing where he was, dived under the gunwale and came to the surface. Noble, the second mate, and Seaman Cook were already on the keel, and they hauled him up alongside them. The Negro had disappeared.

Clinging to the keel, shivering in their wet clothes, and dazed by their icy immersion, for a time they were silent; then someone suggested that they hold hands and drown together. In despair they even threw their life-jackets away, but, though all hope was abandoned, they continued to lie on their bellies, clinging to the keel with frozen fingers. They were in this posture when their ears heard the unmistakable blast of a ship's siren, and, looking up, they saw as though in a dream a British destroyer quite close. At the sight of the ship the three men became hysterical and began singing and laughing. The destroyer maneuvered with great care alongside the boat, and the men were hoisted aboard in slings. In the sick-bay they were wrapped in hot blankets and their limbs massaged, and by the next day they had completely recovered from their terrible experience.

Only those who have felt starvation, who have suffered, sat in wet clothes exposed to an icy wind, denied rest or sleep, can begin to understand what these men endured.

CHAPTER XIII

Convoy Actions

THE SAFETY of a convoy largely depends on the strength of its escort, though weakly protected convoys sometimes got through without any casualties whatsoever, especially after the U-boats began hunting in packs, which meant that they were operating in another area and so missed finding the lucky convoy. The demands on the limited resources of the Royal Navy made it impossible to provide as many escort ships as desired—sufficient, let us say, to form an unbroken screen round the convoyed merchantmen. In the third year of the war, after Japan had joined in the conflict, the Navy was escorting convoys across the Atlantic, through the Mediterranean, round the Cape of Good Hope to the Indian Ocean, and to North Russia via the North Cape of Norway and the Arctic Ocean.

These long sea-routes stretched the Navy's resources beyond the limits prudence demanded, for if the balance of sea-power was to be maintained the main strength of the Navy had to be kept in home waters and in the Mediterranean. The backbone of the Home and Mediterranean fleets was made up of the big ships, battle-cruisers, battleships, and aircraft-carriers. The capital ships could not be spared for convoy work, and this was left mainly to the smaller units of the Navy—destroyers and corvettes. By January 1942 the Navy lost five capital ships and three aircraft-carriers—a heavy blow which left no reserves to spare for Britain's growing commitments. After the American losses at Pearl Harbor and the British losses off Malaya, Britain suffered a naval eclipse in the Far East, and for the first time for four hundred years found herself unable to defend all her possessions.

Meanwhile Russia needed all the war supplies that could be sent her, and the only sea-route was via the Arctic Ocean round the northern end of Norway to Murmansk, a journey of over two thousand miles, most of which skirted the enemy-occupied coast of Norway. In the harbors of Bergen, Trondheim, Tromsö, and Narvik, German warships waited, ready to dash out and attack British convoys carrying supplies to Russia. Nazi reconnaissance planes, flying far out to sea, reported the presence of ships to naval units lurking in the fiords, so that it was impossible to send a convoy to Russia undetected. Hence all convoys from Britain to Murmansk ran a serious risk, especially after the discovery that the giant battleship *Tirpitz*, sister-ship to *Bismarck*, was in Trondheim harbor. Late in March an unsuccessful attempt was made to destroy the largest convoy that had ever been sent to Russia, and in the running battle which followed the enemy employed airplanes, surface craft, and U-boats. The convoy, an exceptionally valuable one, carrying tanks, guns, shells, planes, and other supplies, mainly from United States factories, was escorted by destroyers and cruisers, as an attack from enemy bases in Norway was regarded as probable.

On Sunday morning, March 29, 1942, the convoy, flanked by its escorts, was pushing through the gray seas in a heavy snowstorm north-west of Tromsö when it was sighted by a German patrol plane, which radioed to its base the presence and position of the convoy. From Tromsö and Trondheim enemy destroyers set out to intercept the British ships, and with them a squadron of Junkers 88 dive-bombers, which, however, were driven off by a fierce anti-aircraft barrage and Fleet Air Arm fighters. Some time later they returned and renewed the attack, but were again driven off. The thick, driving snow, lowering visibility to zero, was favorable for the convoy, but the enemy warships hung on to its flanks and kept up a running fight which lasted all day. One of the Navy's newest ships, the 8000-ton cruiser *Trinidad* (Captain L. S. Saunders, R.N.), and the destroyer *Eclipse* (Lieutenant-Commander E. Mack, D.S.C., R.N.) were hit and suffered some casualties, but were able to continue under their own steam. The enemy lost one destroyer, and two others were seriously damaged, one being on fire when last seen. Three U-boats were damaged by depth-charges, but it was not possible to determine if any of them were destroyed. The enemy claimed to have sunk a 10,000-ton American ship and two smaller transports, and even if this was correct the greater part of the convoy reached its destination, although it was pursued through the Barents Sea, and the last attack was made at the entrance to Kola Bay, which leads to the harbor of Murmansk. The safe arrival of the greater part of the convoy was entirely due to the fine conduct of the officers and men of the escorting warships, who fought with the utmost coolness and determination in protecting the transports. Losses were expected, and the smallness of the loss was a tribute to the resourcefulness, seamanship, and fighting spirit of the Navy's personnel.

There were thirty-two killed or fatally wounded in the cruiser *Trinidad* and the destroyer *Eclipse* during the Barents Sea action. Six officers and fifteen ratings and nine Royal Marines—all musicians in *Trinidad*—were killed, and one rating died later of wounds.

Maintaining the convoys to Russia became more and more dangerous as the war went on, especially through the

Arctic summer, when there is nearly twenty-four hours of daylight every day for months, making it impossible for any convoy to get through to Murmansk undiscovered. Ceaseless reconnaissance patrols of Nazi planes flying from Norwegian bases covered every square mile of those northern waters—the Atlantic and the Barents Sea. The airplane, with its bombs and torpedoes, constituted a greater menace than the enemy battleships, for the enemy did not care to risk his most valuable ships in attacking convoys. *Bismarck* was lost through sending her out to raid the Atlantic supply routes. Nevertheless, Admiral Sir John Tovey, Commander-in-Chief of the Home Fleet, was faced with one of the most difficult jobs in the war—the protection of the Russian convoys against enemy opposition through the summer months of 1942, probably the crucial year of the Second World War. The middle third of the route, when the convoys were within range of enemy dive-bombers sallying out of Norwegian ports, but outside the range of Russian air protection, was the most dangerous. When the convoys reached the Barents Sea, Russian fighter planes met them and drove off the Stuka dive-bombers from Finnish airfields. Air support then was the answer to air attack. The invention of the internal-combustion engine had altered the form of warfare beyond men's wildest imagining. A fragile torpedo-carrying airplane costing $20,000 could destroy a battleship costing $25,000,000. The answer to the convoy problem was aircraft—aircraft for scouting, for spotting, for bombing, for fighting, and for torpedo attacks.

During the war the British people suffered many severe blows in a series of naval and military disasters. The liner *Athenia* was torpedoed and sunk within only a few hours of the declaration of war. Then followed *Royal Oak, Courageous, Glorious, Hood, Prince of Wales, Repulse*, and *Barham*, and some of the nation's finest merchant ships. The tonnage lost in the Battle of the Atlantic was a grave threat to Britain's life-line. The enemy was building U-boats in vast numbers to starve Britain, and using this weapon with callous ferocity. The people of Britain, watching their food rations shrinking and wondering when it all would end, were greatly cheered when the year of 1942 opened with the best New Year's gift of all—the news of a successful beating off of a five-day attack on a convoy in the Atlantic. The attack was an exceptionally determined one in which U-boats and Focke-Wulf bombers took part.

The convoy, a medium-sized one of thirty-odd merchant ships, was escorted by corvettes and destroyers, including the ex-American destroyer *Stanley*, H.M. sloop *Stork*, and H.M.S. *Audacity*. The latter was a converted merchant-man of 5500 tons, captured from the enemy in March 1940, and formerly the *Hanover*. H.M.S. *Stanley*, one of the fifty American destroyers transferred to Britain under the agreement of 1940, was formerly the U.S.S. *Bailey*. She was built at the Fore River Yards, Quincy, Massachusetts, in 1919, and had a displacement of 1190 tons, an armament of four 4-inch and two A.A. guns, and the exceptional number of twelve torpedo-tubes. She was commanded by Lieutenant-Commander David Byam Shaw, R.N. H.M.S. *Stork* (Commander F. S. Walker, R.N.) was an 1190-ton sloop armed with six 4-inch guns. *Audacity* was commanded by Commander D. W. MacKendrick, R.N.

On the morning of December 17 a plane escorting the convoy spotted a U-boat traveling on the surface some miles away and at once signaled the position to the escorting warships, one of which raced to the spot, but not before the U-boat had dived. This submarine turned out to be U131 (740 tons). The escort attacked and dropped depth-charges, which opened some of her hull plates, leaving her commander no alternative but to come to the surface.

The moment her long snout poked out of the water, and before the crew had come on deck, the escort ships closed on her at high speed and opened fire. The shells could be seen hitting the hull as the crew swarmed out of the conning-tower and dived into the sea. Less than a minute later the U131 went down with her conning-tower hatches open and the sea pouring through a dozen holes in her hull. The water was dotted with the heads of swimming men. The destroyers launched boats and succeeded in saving the entire crew of the U-boat, forty-eight all told. A keen look-out was kept for any signs of other U-boats, for it was known that they had been recently hunting in packs, but nothing more of the enemy was seen that day and the convoy continued its voyage undisturbed after the brief but exciting diversion in the morning. The whole thing was over before noon. The prisoners explained that the depth-charges had caught their boat before they could get away, and had put out all the lights. They were astonished at the speed with which the British attacked. Had they known that the escort was so alert they would not have surfaced so close to the convoy.

Throughout the afternoon the convoy steamed through a calm sea with perfect visibility, conditions under which it would be extremely difficult for a U-boat to approach undetected. During the afternoon two large aircraft, which were identified as Focke-Wulf long-range bombers, approached, but they were met with such a terrific barrage of A.A. fire from the ships that they never came near enough to drop their bombs. Naval aircraft from H.M.S. *Audacity* flew off and engaged the enemy, who then withdrew and was not seen again that day. These naval planes kept a constant patrol for miles round the convoy, watching for the dark shadows of U-boats below the surface, but nothing at all suspicious was seen and night came with the convoy intact. At dusk the airplanes returned to the *Audacity,* and the watch on board the ships was doubled, as night was the favorite time for U-boat attacks, especially at dusk and just before dawn.

The next morning (December 18) broke fine with a blue sky and a fairly calm sea. Hundreds of pairs of eyes were scanning the ocean for the tell-tale track of a torpedo or a periscope raised above the surface for a fleeting moment. Only by such incessant vigils could a convoy steam through submarine-infested waters with a reasonable degree of security. A momentary lapse might mean the loss of a ship and her crew. The escorting warships rushed back and forth on the flanks of the convoy, a mile or so to either side, their look-outs on the bridge covering every foot of sea with their binoculars, while at the stern seamen stood ready at a signal to release depth-charges. Fast ships with speed enough to get well away before the charge exploded simply rolled them over the stern, but slower ships lobbed the 300-pound cylinders well clear of the ship by a special thrower first introduced in 1917 by Thornycroft's, who produced three thousand of them for the Admiralty during the World War of 1914–18. The depth-charge is the submarine commander's greatest worry. To escape its terrible destructive effect he must dive deep, a risky alternative since the sea-pressure on the shell of a submarine in a deep dive is likely to give it such a squeeze that the joints in the plating are forced open. Depth-charges brought about the loss of more submarines of all the belligerents than any other anti-submarine device.

As the convoy proceeded on its way on the morning after the encounter with U131 a keen look-out was kept, for further attacks were expected from the sea or the air—perhaps both. There was a tense feeling of expectancy, and the gunners at their stations wished nothing better than to have a chance to fight it out with a U-boat. But the submarine is shy of guns, for it has no armor to withstand even the smallest shells, and so prefers whenever possible to attack unseen. The crews of the convoy suspected that they were being stalked by the enemy somewhere under the sea. The escort ships were nervously rushing about, throwing up curling white bow waves as they tore through the sea. There was trouble pending, but from what direction no one could tell. Suddenly a great fountain of water was seen to rise from the sea half a mile away, followed a second later by the muffled boom of an explosion. The destroyer *Stanley* had dropped a depth-charge, and this was followed almost immediately by several more. She signaled that she had sighted a U-boat which had at once made a crash-dive. Explosions followed one another in regular succession as the escorts circled over the spot dropping their depth-charges where the U-boat had dived. The explosions continued, and the sea in the area was churned up into foaming rings of white water. One escort dropped charges a quarter of a mile away, evidently on a private hunt of its own. All eyes of the convoy were now excitedly watching the spot that had been so thoroughly treated with depth-charges, but nothing immediately happened. The turmoil died down, but the escorts continued to watch the spot hopefully.

Then suddenly the long black snout of a U-boat shot out of the sea, followed by the conning-tower. It appeared suddenly as though in a desperate hurry to come to the surface. The depth-charges had again done the trick. The terrible pressure waves set up under the sea by the explosion had partially flooded the control-room, jammed the steering-gear, and started fires. She was the 500-ton U434, carrying a crew of forty-four officers and men. Water poured into the boat, and she sank almost immediately after coming to the surface. An officer on one of the escort vessels happened to have a small ciné-camera on board and just managed to take a few feet of film of the doomed U-boat. This film was afterwards shown on the news-reels in Britain and clearly showed the smoke pouring out of the conning-tower a few seconds before she went down. Considering that she was so badly damaged and sank so quickly, it was remarkable that only two of the crew of forty-four lost their lives. The survivors all jumped overboard, and as the sea was fairly calm the British ships had no difficulty in picking them all up. Within twenty-four hours two U-boats had been sunk and ninety prisoners taken, so far without loss to the convoy or escort. The rest of the day passed without further incident. Thousands of dead fish lay on the surface, thrown up by the depth-charges, and possibly other and larger 'fish,' fish made of steel and carrying torpedoes, had been sent to the bottom leaving no trace to prove their destruction.

At dusk the usual look-out was doubled, for there was no doubt now that the convoy was being shadowed by a pack of U-boats. Nevertheless, the night passed without any sign of the enemy, and dawn of December the 19th broke fine and clear. A cold breeze rippled the surface of the sea, and the officers on duty in the escorts, wearing warm duffle coats, peered round ever on the alert for the 'feather' of foam that marks the position of a periscope. Ahead the ex-American destroyer *Stanley* kept watch, unaware that she herself was being shadowed by a U-boat.

Keeping well outside the lines of the convoy, the U574, a new 500-ton boat, commanded by Oberleutnant zur See Gegnelbach, raised its periscope for a brief moment, while the lieutenant took a look round. His eyes lit up with excitement when he saw crossing the eyepiece of the periscope the unmistakable silhouette of the ex-American destroyer with its flush deck, four funnels, and its characteristic bridge structure. It would give the lieutenant great pleasure to sink one of these destroyers which had been sent to Britain to war against Germany. The U574 approached a little closer, and the periscope was raised again for another quick look. Turning the periscope round the full circle of the horizon, the lieutenant saw ships everywhere, a richly laden convoy waiting for his torpedoes. But first the destroyer must be sunk. Once she was got rid of, the convoy would be easy prey. One more peep through the periscope, a quick calculation for range and inclination, and the order to fire was given. Down periscope and wait for the explosion. A minute later came the distant boom that told him his torpedoes had found their mark. It was good shooting and must have split the thin steel side of the destroyer wide open. But there was no time to take another look, for his hydrophones picked up the sound of escort ships rushing towards his position. He gave the order to dive, and the needle of the big depth-gauge began to move round the dial.

On the surface all was commotion. The handsome destroyer had taken on a dangerous list and was rapidly sinking. Men could be seen getting a boat over. The convoy was ordered to proceed on a zig-zag course. *Audacity* and *Stork* rushed about dropping depth-charges, making those waters highly unhealthy for any U-boat in the vicinity. Scores of depth-charges were dropped, and a pattern of giant fountains covered the sea, which boiled from the series of submarine explosions. The escort, out to revenge the loss of the destroyer, were determined to get its attacker. It would be much more satisfactory to bring it to the surface, but two had already been accounted for that way, and such luck could hardly hold for a third kill. But that is precisely what happened. The U574 was badly damaged by the terrible concussion of those scores of depth-charges. Both her main motors were wrecked; the electric system shorted and started fires which filled the boat's interior with noxious fumes. Water spurted in through numerous burst seams and valve seatings, and the boat was in grave danger of sinking beyond the depth she was built to withstand. Ober-leutnant Gegnelbach, a brave and resolute man, wished to remain below and chance it, but his officers, who had no wish to commit suicide, demanded that the boat be taken to the surface. The depth-gauge showed that it was still sinking, and soon it would be too late and everyone on board would be drowned like rats. A heated altercation followed, and Gegnelbach was obliged to take the U-boat to the surface, risking the British war vessels.

As the U574 broke surface the nearest ship to her was H.M.S. *Stork*, which instantly turned to ram before the enemy could bring his gun to bear. With submarines it was unsafe to parley, and the law of self-preservation left no room for sentiment. The U-boat's crew, however, made no attempt to fire their deck-gun, and those who got out of the conning-tower in time jumped into the sea when they saw the sharp bows of *Stork* rushing towards them. A moment later the forefoot of the sloop ripped through the hull of the U-boat, and she sank like a stone in a few seconds, taking down with her the brave commander and one other officer, as well as twenty-five ratings. Four officers and twelve men were picked up and made prisoner. The sixteen new prisoners made a total of 106 men from three U-boats. In three days the U131, U434, and U574 had been destroyed for certain. Each of these submarines had been in commission for approximately six months, and during that time they had sunk one merchant ship and the de-stroyer *Stanley*. All three had been patrolling in the North Atlantic before they were ordered south. The U131 had made only two operational cruises. The first U-boat had been sunk by gunfire, the second by depth-charges, and the third by ramming. Although no more prisoners were taken, it was probable that other U-boats had been accounted for. Ramming has since the beginning of history been a classic mode of attack in naval warfare, and some men-of-war are still fitted with heavily armored, horn-shaped bows designed expressly for ramming.

On the day that U574 was sunk three Focke-Wulf heavy bombers appeared and made several attempts to attack the convoy, but naval aircraft flown from H.M.S. *Audacity* went up and engaged them. In the aerial dog-fight which followed one of the bombers was badly damaged, and the other two were shot down and crashed in the sea. So far the British forces had lost one old destroyer for the destruction of three U-boats, but the tide of successes had reached its peak, and on the day after the torpedoing of H.M.S. *Stanley* the Navy suffered its second loss. On December 20 the converted enemy merchantman H.M.S. *Audacity* was hit by a torpedo and within a short time sank. Commander D. W. MacKendrick, her skipper, was later reported missing and presumed lost. He was a qualified air pilot and had flown naval planes from the aircraft-carriers *Argus*, *Courageous*, and *Glorious*. Lieutenant-Commander David Byam Shaw, who was in command of H.M.S. *Stanley*, and a relative of the famous British artist Byam Shaw, was also reported missing and presumed killed.

The next day, December 21, the remainder of the U-boat wolf-pack continued to shadow the convoy, but were relentlessly hunted and heavily depth-bombed. No more were forced to the surface, although it was felt certain that at least one was sunk, for a great patch of oil spread over the sea and a cloud of air bubbles came up. The personnel of the convoy had put up a valiant fight for five days against the unseen foe, but they were immensely relieved when a squadron of American-built Liberator planes of the Coastal Command appeared and joined the convoy. The loss of *Audacity* had deprived the ships of the air support so vital in detecting the presence of under-water craft. The arrival of the Liberators almost certainly saved the convoy from further losses, and in an all-day hunt during which the sea was thoroughly bombed, the convoy was finally freed from the menace. It had lost two merchant ships and the two escorts, a loss approximately 10 per cent of the total number of ships, which, considering the duration and persistence of the attacks, was comparatively small. The sinkings had not been accomplished by the enemy without a proportionately greater loss to himself, as it is obvious that two merchant ships and a pair of old escort vessels were not worth the cost of three modern submarines whose potential destructive capacity is practically unlimited. The Germans claimed that nine merchantmen totaling 37,000 tons were sunk, an exaggeration of something like 600 per cent.

In recognition of his part in the action the D.S.O. was awarded to Commander F. S. Walker, of H.M.S. *Stork*, which rammed and sank the U574. Commander Walker, who had joined the Navy in 1909, had specialized in anti-submarine warfare, and for many years was Fleet Anti-submarine Officer with the Atlantic and Mediterranean fleets. The Commodore of the convoy was Vice-Admiral Raymond Fitzmaurice, D.S.O., who had performed valua-able service as commodore of convoys during the war. He had won the D.S.O. during the First World War for his part in the famous operation in the Rufiji River when he blocked the river to prevent the escape of the cruiser *Königsberg*.

The five-day attack on the convoy was notable chiefly

for the loss of the three U-boats, an event that had only once been duplicated during the war, and is rarer than a golfer holing out in one stroke. The personnel of all ships concerned fully merited the Commodore's congratulatory signal, "well done." And every man from the humblest cabin-boy to the highest executive officer deserved that praise, for nothing less than a selfless devotion to duty, calmness in danger, refusal to be stampeded, discipline, and perfect team work had saved the convoy from total destruction, for the enemy had carefully planned what was to be an exceptional effort to prevent the richly laden ships reaching port.

Down in the Mediterranean three months later a spectacular attack was made by Italian warships and aircraft on a British convoy bound for the beleaguered island of Malta. The convoy was such a valuable one that it was decided to protect it with cruisers as well as destroyers. The convoy was assembled at Alexandria and put to sea on Friday, March 20, escorted by one 6-inch-gun cruiser, two 5¼-inch-gun anti-aircraft cruisers, and a number of destroyers. Note that the biggest gun mounted in any of these ships was of 6-inch caliber, and note also that should the cruiser meet an Italian battleship her guns would not be powerful enough to so much as dent the heavy armor of the latter. The voyage from Alexandria to Malta, over a thousand miles away, gave the enemy ample opportunity to discover the convoy's presence and bring out an overwhelming attacking force. The ships of the convoy carried vital munitions and food to the besieged island, and the enemy would spare no effort to prevent it reaching its destination. For months the Axis air fleets had been making determined attempts to reduce the island's docks and airfields by persistent bombing, and it was essential that at all costs the convoy must be got through.

The convoy (commanded by Rear-Admiral Philip N. Vian, who had several times distinguished himself in the war, particularly during the Norway actions) encountered very heavy seas at the outset of the voyage. Although this made it difficult and dangerous to keep stations, the rough seas, low visibility, and wind of almost hurricane force discouraged enemy reconnaissance, and so on the whole were welcomed. All day on Friday and Saturday the convoy plunged through the tremendous seas without sight of enemy planes, and the crews dared to allow themselves to hope that they might sneak into Valetta undetected. But just before dark on Saturday evening about half a dozen big Junkers troop-carrying planes escorted by Messerschmitt fighters were sighted flying high in a northerly direction, evidently coming from Libya. The ships' A.A. guns were raised to their extreme elevation and trained on the planes, but they were flying too high, and to fire on them would have been a waste of ammunition. Every man in the convoy realized that this was the end of their good luck, for those planes would certainly report the presence of the ships, and within a few hours at the most they would be attacked.

Malta was still a long way off and the enemy would have ample time to intercept with his main battle fleet if he so desired, in which case the convoy would indeed be fortunate if half the ships escaped destruction. In anticipation of the coming battle all defensive measures were thoroughly rehearsed during the night and when dawn broke the light squadron of cruisers and destroyers were ready for whatever might come. The vessels were by this time in the widest part of the Mediterranean and not far from the scene of the Matapan battle. For the first two hours of daylight the convoy proceeded on its course, to all appearances alone on the ocean. About half-past nine the far-away drone of airplane engines was heard, and soon the drone became a distant roar, and high in the winter sky minute specks were seen flying in formation like wild geese. As the bombers drew near they split up into separate units to dive down on the convoy. At a low level they could be seen releasing torpedoes which glinted in the morning light as they fell into the sea. The planes dipped and climbed, filling the air full of the sound of roaring engines, and at once hell broke loose from the warship's guns, adding to the pandemonium of noise. The heaving seas were criss-crossed with the white wakes of torpedoes, but for a while the ships skilfully dodged them. The first attackers were driven off without the loss of a ship, but soon another wave of planes appeared. These were forced by their intensity and accuracy of the convoy's A.A. fire, to drop their torpedoes from such a high level that accuracy of aim was made impossible. Other planes were compelled to release their torpedoes while still so far away from the outer fringe of the convoy that the missiles never reached their target.

After this attack was driven off there was a lull for the rest of the morning, but it was only the peace before the storm, for about midday another wave of bombers came out of the north-west and, flying at several thousand feet to avoid the devastating screen of multiple pom-pom fire, tried to wipe out the convoy with sheer weight of bombs, but were driven off without any loss to either side. Within twenty minutes another wave came, torpedo-carrying planes again, to try to penetrate the A.A. screen by low-level attack, but they too were driven off.

After this all hands were served with a snack meal, for more attacks were expected at any moment. During the lull everyone speculated on what the enemy would do next. Would he be content with depending on air attacks, or would he send his navy? Two hours later they had their answer, for above the northern horizon appeared a long bank of smoke, and within half an hour the sinister dark shapes of four suspicious-looking warships appeared on the rim of the sea, and through the glasses they were identified as Italian cruisers. A few minutes later there appeared through the smoke more ships—destroyers for miles along the northern horizon, and towering above them, like a great black island, was an enormous battleship. This ship alone could have dealt with the British squadron. It looked as though the whole Italian fleet was out. The Admiral signaled the convoyed transports to alter course and steer south with all speed while the escort engaged the enemy. The Admiral of the British squadron thus hoped to delay the superior forces of the enemy for at least the rest of the day, until darkness covered the fleeing transports. So the two opposing forces steamed towards each other: on one side one 6-inch-gun cruiser, two anti-aircraft cruisers, and some destroyers: on the other side one 15-inch-gun 35,000,-ton battleship of the *Littorio* class; two 8-inch-gun cruisers of the *Trento* class; four 6-inch-gun cruisers of the *Condottieri* class, and an uncounted number of destroyers. Before such a formidable armada the small squadron of Admiral Vian would have been justified in declining battle; but—well, Englishmen are said to be mad, and here they were demonstrating their traditional madness by taking on an adversary capable of blowing them out of the sea. To make doubly sure of destroying the British naval force, whose reputation for fighting was not denied even by their enemies, the Italians had brought squadrons of dive-bombers with them. Admiral Vian had therefore to contend not only with a fleet many times his strength but with an air armada also.

But if the Briton takes mad chances there is usually method in the madness, and Admiral Vian had decided to model his tactics somewhat after those employed by the three British cruisers at the Battle of the Plate when the battleship *Graf Spee* was outmaneuvered. Admiral Vian's small force was, of course, easily outranged by the enemy's guns, and the only chance of getting in close enough to use the 6-inch guns was by advancing under cover of a smoke-screen. This simple maneuver was successful: the British advancing in dense clouds of black smoke confused the enemy, who had to fire more or less blindly with his heavy guns, without, however, causing any casualties. As soon as Vian's forces had closed the range so that their lighter guns could reach the target they altered course and fired a broad-side. This unexpected maneuver confused the enemy, but it uncovered the British force, and the foe, quickly finding the range, began dropping 15-inch shells close enough to be dangerous. Admiral Vian was thus driven to depend on a hit-and-run game to avoid disaster, and his cruisers began zigzagging and dashing in to fire a salvo and then out again, keeping this up for nearly two hours, until, to the great astonishment of the British, the enemy withdrew into the dense screen of smoke which hung over the ocean like a heavy curtain. Possibly he did not wish to expose his forces to a torpedo attack from the British destroyers, which had been milling around all the time waiting for just such an opportunity. It had always been his policy to guard his ships, especially capital ships, and the British bluff had worked at least for the time being. Realizing that he could not hope to defeat such a powerful force, and profiting by the short respite, Admiral Vian signaled his ships to rejoin the convoy, which was still in sight on the horizon and be-ing attacked by waves of dive-bombers and torpedo-carry-ing planes. But the Italians saw his intention and came through the smoke-screen firing heavy salvos at the British forces, obliging them to resume the former tactics of playing hide-and-seek in the smoke and firing a salvo whenever they had a chance. Overhead Axis planes repeatedly attacked the British ships, some of their bombs exploding perilously close.

Vian's main object was to fight a delaying action, engaging the enemy long enough for the convoy to escape under cover of night, and the Italians, understanding this, but unable to shake off the British forces, tried to smash the convoy with 15-inch salvos from the battleship. If the delaying action could only be kept up a little longer the convoy would be safe, for the afternoon had nearly gone, and in another hour it would be getting dark. The enemy was fully alive to this and made one final determined effort to sink the transports. He was in the position of a giant harassed by a lot of pygmies. He could have dealt with some of them, but not all of them at one time. Now he decided to ignore for the moment the British squadron and finish off the convoy, but as soon as he began chasing it Admiral Vian's forces rushed in to attack him again, forcing him to turn on the audacious ships that dared to dash in and fire their ridiculous guns at him. While the convoy was trying to escape on another course which was signaled from the flagship Vian's forces laid a dense smoke-screen for another game of hide-and-seek. Incensed at this impertinence, the Italian fleet came dashing through the smoke to put an end to the nuisance, and approached to within point-blank range of the British forces. At this range his 15-inch shells could have blasted a cruiser apart, but so great was the confusion that his heavy salvos all missed, though the concussion rocked the British ships, and some of his secondary armament scored hits, causing some casualties.

The situation had suddenly taken a very serious turn, and Admiral Vian, who found it was becoming increasingly difficult to avoid the heavy salvos, ordered his destroyers to go in and make a torpedo attack. In the running battle the enemy had managed to edge within close range of the convoy, which he had begun shelling, and the destroyers had to be risked in a desperate effort to save the convoy. Immediately one of them was hit by a shell, but the rest dashed in and loosed off their torpedoes. The destroyers did valiant work dashing under the very muzzles of the enemy's big guns, firing their torpedoes and racing back into the smoke. The noise and confusion were indescribable, and after a short, sharp action the enemy was seen retiring in the growing dusk, leaving the somewhat bruised but triumphant British forces to return to the convoy, which was overtaken after dark. The result of the action was one cruiser and three destroyers damaged but none seriously. The casualties among the personnel were not heavy, considering the violence of the action. The enemy battleship had been hit by one torpedo and set ablaze by gunfire. One cruiser appeared seriously damaged, but all got away, and no sinkings were claimed by the British. On Monday, March 23, the convoy was attacked from the air by torpedo-carrying planes and bombers. One merchant ship was sunk and a destroyer damaged, but it was able to reach port under its own steam. On Tuesday the enemy made a final effort to smash the convoy by air attacks, but all failed and no further damage was done.

That Admiral Vian's forces had escaped from what seemed certain destruction can only be explained by a combination of luck, dash, and the fighting spirit. Certainly it was not due to lack of courage on the part of the foe; to suggest such would be to lessen the British success. And this philosophy might apply to all the narratives of gallantry related in this book. To mock at an enemy, to suggest he is lacking in courage, is to belittle the valor of one's own people. The truth is, of course, that most men are potential heroes if the need arises, but there are degrees of courage, and the courage demanded of sailors, whether their role is passive or belligerent, is of the highest quality. Without the stimulus of a fanfare of trumpets or the applause of the crowd, without hope of earthly reward, they give their lives in the course of duty while the landsman at home is striking for higher pay and grumbling at the hardness of his lot. As this is written while the war still rages, it is salutary to think upon these things and give all honor to the band of devoted men who go down to the sea in ships.

Index

www.ingramcontent.com/pod-product-compliance
Lightning Source LLC
Chambersburg PA
CBHW071402150726
48000CB00001B/125